MW00846137

ning with

TensorFlow 1.x

Second generation machine learning with Google's brainchild
- TensorFlow 1.x

Quan Hua
Shams Ul Azeem
Saif Ahmed

BIRMINGHAM - MUMBAI

Machine Learning with TensorFlow 1.x

First published: November 2017

Production reference: 1171117

Published by Packt Publishing Ltd.
Livery Place
35 Livery Street
Birmingham
B3 2PB, UK.

ISBN 978-1-78646-296-1

www.packtpub.com

Credits

Authors
Quan Hua
Shams Ul Azeem
Saif Ahmed

Reviewer
Nathan Lintz

Commissioning Editor
Kunal Parikh

Acquisition Editor
Tushar Gupta

Content Development Editor
Siddhi Chavan

Technical Editor
Mehul Singh

Copy Editor
Zainab Bootwala

Project Coordinator
Prajakta Naik

Proofreader
Safis Editing

Indexer
Rekha Nair

Graphics
Jason Monteiro

Production Coordinator
Deepika Naik

About the Authors

Quan Hua is a Computer Vision and Machine Learning Engineer at BodiData, a data platform for body measurements, where he focuses on developing computer vision and machine learning applications for a handheld technology capable of acquiring a body avatar while a person is fully clothed. He earned a bachelor of science degree from the University of Science, Vietnam, specializing in Computer Vision. He has been working in the field of computer vision and machine learning for about 3 years at start-ups.

Quan has been writing for Packt since 2015 for a Computer Vision book, *OpenCV 3 Blueprints*.

> *I wish to thank everyone who has encouraged me on the way while writing this book.*
>
> *I want to express my sincere gratitude to my co-authors, editors, and reviewers for their advice and assistance.*
>
> *I would like to thank the members of my family and my wife, Kim Ngoc, who supported and encouraged me in spite of all the time it took me away from them. They all kept me going, and this book would not have been possible without them.*
>
> *I would also like to thank my teachers who gave me knowledge of Computer Vision and Machine Learning.*

Shams Ul Azeem is an undergraduate in electrical engineering from NUST Islamabad, Pakistan. He has a great interest in the computer science field, and he started his journey with Android development. Now, he's pursuing his career in Machine Learning, particularly in deep learning, by doing medical-related freelancing projects with different companies.
He was also a member of the RISE lab, NUST, and he has a publication credit at the IEEE International Conference, ROBIO as a co-author of *Designing of motions for humanoid goalkeeper robots*.

Saif Ahmed is an accomplished quantitative analyst and data scientist with 15 years of industry experience. His career started in management consulting at Accenture and lead him to quantitative and senior management roles at Goldman Sachs and AIG Investments. Most recently, he co-founded and runs a start-up focused on applying Deep Learning to automating medical imaging. He obtained his bachelor's degree in computer science from Cornell University and is currently pursuing a graduate degree in data science at U.C. Berkeley.

About the Reviewer

Nathan Lintz is a Machine Learning researcher, focusing on text classification. When he began with Machine Learning, he primarily used Theano but quickly switched to TensorFlow when it was released. TensorFlow has greatly reduced the time it takes to build Machine Learning systems thanks to its intuitive and powerful neural network utilities.

I want to thank my family and professors for all the help they have given me. Without them, I would have never been able to pursue my passion for software engineering and Machine Learning.

www.PacktPub.com

For support files and downloads related to your book, please visit www.PacktPub.com.

Did you know that Packt offers eBook versions of every book published, with PDF and ePub files available? You can upgrade to the eBook version at www.PacktPub.com and as a print book customer, you are entitled to a discount on the eBook copy. Get in touch with us at service@packtpub.com for more details.

At www.PacktPub.com, you can also read a collection of free technical articles, sign up for a range of free newsletters and receive exclusive discounts and offers on Packt books and eBooks.

https://www.packtpub.com/mapt

Get the most in-demand software skills with Mapt. Mapt gives you full access to all Packt books and video courses, as well as industry-leading tools to help you plan your personal development and advance your career.

Why subscribe?

- Fully searchable across every book published by Packt
- Copy and paste, print, and bookmark content
- On demand and accessible via a web browser</li>

Customer Feedback

Thanks for purchasing this Packt book. At Packt, quality is at the heart of our editorial process. To help us improve, please leave us an honest review on this book's Amazon page at https://www.amazon.com/dp/1787123421. If you'd like to join our team of regular reviewers, you can email us at customerreviews@packtpub.com. We award our regular reviewers with free eBooks and videos in exchange for their valuable feedback. Help us be relentless in improving our products!

Table of Contents

Preface

Machine Learning has revolutionized the modern world. Many machine learning algorithms, especially deep learning, have been used worldwide, ranging from mobile devices to cloud-based services. TensorFlow is one of the leading open source software libraries and helps you build, train, and deploy your Machine Learning system for a variety of applications. This practical book is designed to bring you the best of TensorFlow and help you build real-world Machine Learning systems.

By the end of this book, you will have a deep understanding of TensorFlow and be able to apply Machine Learning techniques to your application.

What this book covers

Chapter 1, *Getting Started with TensorFlow*, shows how to install Tensorflow and get started on Ubuntu, macOS, and Windows.

Chapter 2, *Your First Classifier*, guides you through your first journey with a handwriting recognizer.

Chapter 3, *The TensorFlow Toolbox*, gives you an overview of the tools that Tensorflow provides to work more effectively and easily.

Chapter 4, *Cats and Dogs*, teaches you how to build an image classifier using Convolutional Neural Networks in TensorFlow.

Chapter 5, *Sequence to Sequence Models—Parlez-vous Français?*, discusses how to build an English to French translator using sequence-to-sequence models.

Chapter 6, *Finding Meaning*, explores the ways to find the meaning in the text by using sentiment analysis, entity extraction, keyword extraction, and word-relation extraction.

Chapter 7, *Making Money with Machine Learning*, dives into an area with copious amounts of data: the financial world. You will learn how to work with the time series data to solve the financial problems.

Chapter 8, *The Doctor Will See You Now*, investigates ways to tackle an *enterprise-grade* problem—medical diagnosis—using deep neural networks.

Chapter 9, *Cruise Control - Automation*, teaches you how to create a production system, ranging from training to serving a model. The system can also receive user feedbacks and automatically train itself every day.

Chapter 10, *Go Live and Go Big*, guides you through the world of Amazon Web Services and shows you how to take advantage of a multiple GPUs system on Amazon servers.

Chapter 11, *Going Further - 21 Problems*, introduces 21 real-life problems that you can use in deep learning—TensorFlow to solve after reading this book.

Appendix, *Advanced Installation*, discusses GPUs and focuses on a step-by-step CUDA setup and a GPU-based TensorFlow installation.

What you need for this book

For software, the whole book is based on TensorFlow. You can use either Linux, Windows, or macOS.

For hardware, you will need a computer or laptop that runs Ubuntu, macOS, or Windows. As authors, we encourage you to have an NVIDIA graphics card if you want to work with deep neural networks, especially when you want to work with large-scale datasets.

Who this book is for

This book is ideal for you if you aspire to build Machine Learning systems that are smart and practical enough for real-world applications. You should be comfortable with Machine Learning concepts, Python programming, IDEs, and the command line. This book will be useful to people who program professionally as part of their job, or those who are working as scientists and engineers and need to learn about Machine Learning and TensorFlow in support of their work.

Conventions

In this book, you will find a number of text styles that distinguish between different kinds of information. Here are some examples of these styles and an explanation of their meaning.

Code words in text, database table names, folder names, filenames, file extensions, pathnames, dummy URLs, user input, and Twitter handles are shown as follows: "We can include other contexts through the use of the `include` directive."

A block of code is set as follows:

```
batch_size = 128
num_steps = 10000
learning_rate = 0.3
data_showing_step = 500
```

When we wish to draw your attention to a particular part of a code block, the relevant lines or items are set in bold:

```
Layer 1 CONV (32, 28, 28, 4)
Layer 2 CONV (32, 14, 14, 4)
Layer 3 CONV (32, 7, 7, 4)
```

Any command-line input or output is written as follows:

```
sudo apt-get install python-pip python-dev
```

New terms and **important words** are shown in bold.

 Warnings or important notes appear like this.

 Tips and tricks appear like this.

Reader feedback

Feedback from our readers is always welcome. Let us know what you think about this book—what you liked or disliked. Reader feedback is important for us as it helps us develop titles that you will really get the most out of.

To send us general feedback, simply e-mail feedback@packtpub.com, and mention the book's title on the subject of your message.

If there is a topic that you have expertise in and you are interested in either writing or contributing to a book, see our author guide at www.packtpub.com/authors.

Customer support

Now that you are the proud owner of a Packt book, we have a number of things to help you to get the most from your purchase.

Downloading the example code

You can download the example code files for this book from your account at http://www.packtpub.com. If you purchased this book elsewhere, you can visit http://www.packtpub.com/support and register to have the files e-mailed directly to you.

You can download the code files by following these steps:

1. Log in or register to our website using your e-mail address and password.
2. Hover the mouse pointer on the **SUPPORT** tab at the top.
3. Click on **Code Downloads & Errata**.
4. Enter the name of the book in the **Search** box.
5. Select the book for which you're looking to download the code files.
6. Choose from the drop-down menu where you purchased this book from.
7. Click on **Code Download**.

Once the file is downloaded, please make sure that you unzip or extract the folder using the latest version of:

- WinRAR / 7-Zip for Windows
- Zipeg / iZip / UnRarX for Mac
- 7-Zip / PeaZip for Linux

The code bundle for the book is also hosted on GitHub at https://github.com/PacktPublishing/Machine-Learning-with-TensorFlow-1.x. We also have other code bundles from our rich catalog of books and videos available at https://github.com/PacktPublishing/. Check them out!

Downloading the color images of this book

We also provide you with a PDF file that has color images of the screenshots/diagrams used in this book. The color images will help you better understand the changes in the output. You can download this file from `https://www.packtpub.com/sites/default/files/downloads/MachineLearningwithTensorFlow1.x_ColorImages.pdf`.

Errata

Although we have taken every care to ensure the accuracy of our content, mistakes do happen. If you find a mistake in one of our books—maybe a mistake in the text or the code—we would be grateful if you could report this to us. By doing so, you can save other readers from frustration and help us improve subsequent versions of this book. If you find any errata, please report them by visiting `http://www.packtpub.com/submit-errata`, selecting your book, clicking on the **Errata Submission Form** link, and entering the details of your errata. Once your errata are verified, your submission will be accepted and the errata will be uploaded to our website or added to any list of existing errata under the Errata section of that title.

To view the previously submitted errata, go to `https://www.packtpub.com/books/content/support` and enter the name of the book in the search field. The required information will appear under the **Errata** section.

Piracy

Piracy of copyrighted material on the Internet is an ongoing problem across all media. At Packt, we take the protection of our copyright and licenses very seriously. If you come across any illegal copies of our works in any form on the Internet, please provide us with the location address or website name immediately so that we can pursue a remedy.

Please contact us at `copyright@packtpub.com` with a link to the suspected pirated material.

We appreciate your help in protecting our authors and our ability to bring you valuable content.

Questions

If you have a problem with any aspect of this book, you can contact us at `questions@packtpub.com`, and we will do our best to address the problem.

1
Getting Started with TensorFlow

The proliferation of large public datasets, inexpensive GPUs, and open-minded developer culture has revolutionized machine learning efforts in recent years. Training data, the lifeblood of machine learning, has become widely available and easily consumable in recent years. Computing power has made the required horsepower available to small businesses and even individuals. The current decade is incredibly exciting for data scientists.

Some of the top platforms used in the industry include Caffe, Theano, and Torch. While the underlying platforms are actively developed and openly shared, usage is limited largely to machine learning practitioners due to difficult installations, non-obvious configurations, and difficulty with productionizing solutions.

Late 2015 and 2016 brought additional platforms into the landscape—**TensorFlow** from Google, **CNTK** from Microsoft, and **Veles** from Samsung, among other options. Google's TensorFlow is the most exciting for several reasons.

TensorFlow has one of the easiest installations of any platform, bringing machine learning capabilities squarely into the realm of casual tinkerers and novice programmers. Meanwhile, high-performance features, such as—multiGPU support, make the platform exciting for experienced data scientists and industrial use as well. TensorFlow also provides a reimagined process and multiple user-friendly utilities, such as **TensorBoard,** to manage machine learning efforts. Finally, the platform has significant backing and community support from the world's largest machine learning powerhouse--Google. All this is before even considering the compelling underlying technical advantages, which we'll dive into later.

In this chapter, we will cover the following topics:

- macOS X
- Microsoft Windows and Linux, both the core software and all the dependencies
- VM setup to enable Windows installation

Current use

Although TensorFlow has been public for just two years, numerous community efforts have already successfully ported over existing machine learning projects. Some examples include handwriting recognition, language translation, animal classification, medical image triage, and sentiment analysis. The wide applicability of machine learning to so many industries and problems always intrigues people. With TensorFlow, these problems are not only feasible but easily achievable. In fact, we will tackle and solve each of the preceding problems within the course of this book!

Installing TensorFlow

TensorFlow conveniently offers several types of installation and operates on multiple operating systems. The basic installation is CPU-only, while more advanced installations unleash serious horsepower by pushing calculations onto the graphics card, or even to multiple graphics cards. We recommend starting with a basic CPU installation at first. More complex GPU and CUDA installations will be discussed in `Appendix`, *Advanced Installation*.

Even with just a basic CPU installation, TensorFlow offers multiple options, which are as follows:

- A basic Python `pip` installation
- A segregated Python installation via Virtualenv
- A fully segregated container-based installation via Docker

We recommend a Python installation via Virtualenv, but our examples will use a basic Python `pip` installation to help you focus on the crux of our task, that is, getting TensorFlow up and running. Again, more advanced installation types will be covered in `Appendix`, *Advanced Installation*.

TensorFlow can fully work on Linux and macOS with both Python 2.7 and 3.5. On Windows, we can only use TensorFlow with Python 3.5.x or 3.6.x. It can also be easily used on Windows by running a **Linux virtual machine** (**VM**). With an Ubuntu virtual machine, we can use TensorFlow with Python 2.7. However, we can't use TensorFlow with GPU support in a virtual machine. As of TensorFlow 1.2, TensorFlow doesn't provide GPU support on macOS. Therefore, if you want to use macOS with GPU-enabled TensorFlow, you will have to compile from sources, which is out of the scope of this chapter. Otherwise, you can still use TensorFlow 1.0 or 1.1, which provides GPU support out of the box on macOS. Linux and Windows users can use TensorFlow with both CPU and GPU support.

Ubuntu installation

Ubuntu is one of the best Linux distributions for working with Tensorflow. We highly recommend that you use an Ubuntu machine, especially if you want to work with GPU. We will do most of our work on the Ubuntu terminal. We will begin with installing `python-pip` and `python-dev` via the following command:

```
sudo apt-get install python-pip python-dev
```

A successful installation will appear as follows:

```
ubuntu@ubuntu-PC:~$ sudo apt-get install python-pip python-dev
Reading package lists... Done
Building dependency tree
Reading state information... Done
python-dev is already the newest version (2.7.11-1).
python-pip is already the newest version (8.1.1-2ubuntu0.4).
0 upgraded, 0 newly installed, 0 to remove and 222 not upgraded.
ubuntu@ubuntu-PC:~$
```

If you find missing packages, you can correct them via the following command:

```
sudo apt-get update --fix-missing
```

Then, you can continue the `python` and `pip` installation.

We are now ready to install TensorFlow. We will do a CPU-only installation, and if you wish to do an advanced GPU-enabled installation, we will cover that in `Appendix`, *Advanced Installation*.

The CPU installation is initiated via the following command:

```
sudo pip install tensorflow
```

A successful installation will appear as follows:

```
    100% |                              | 890kB 924kB/s
Collecting werkzeug>=0.11.10 (from tensorflow-tensorboard<0.2.0,>=0.1.0->tensor
    Downloading Werkzeug-0.12.2-py2.py3-none-any.whl (312kB)
    100% |                              | 317kB 965kB/s
Collecting setuptools (from protobuf>=3.3.0->tensorflow)
    Downloading setuptools-36.5.0-py2.py3-none-any.whl (478kB)
    100% |                              | 481kB 852kB/s
Installing collected packages: six, funcsigs, pbr, mock, numpy, backports.weakr
5lib, bleach, markdown, setuptools, protobuf, werkzeug, tensorflow-tensorboard,
    Found existing installation: six 1.10.0
      Not uninstalling six at /usr/lib/python2.7/dist-packages, outside environme
    Found existing installation: wheel 0.29.0
      Not uninstalling wheel at /usr/lib/python2.7/dist-packages, outside environ
    Running setup.py install for html5lib ... done
    Running setup.py install for markdown ... done
    Found existing installation: setuptools 20.7.0
      Not uninstalling setuptools at /usr/lib/python2.7/dist-packages, outside en
Successfully installed backports.weakref-1.0.post1 bleach-1.5.0 funcsigs-1.0.2
999 markdown-2.6.9 mock-2.0.0 numpy-1.13.1 pbr-3.1.1 protobuf-3.4.0 setuptools-
.0 tensorflow-1.3.0 tensorflow-tensorboard-0.1.6 werkzeug-0.12.2 wheel-0.30.0
You are using pip version 8.1.1, however version 9.0.1 is available.
You should consider upgrading via the 'pip install --upgrade pip' command.
ubuntu@ubuntu-PC:~$
```

macOS installation

If you use Python, you will probably already have the Python package installer, `pip`. However, if not, you can easily install it using the `easy_install pip` command. You'll note that we actually executed `sudo easy_install pip`—the `sudo` prefix was required because the installation requires administrative rights.

We will make the fair assumption that you already have the basic package installer, `easy_install`, available; if not, you can install it from `https://pypi.python.org/pypi/setuptools`. A successful installation will appear as shown in the following screenshot:

```
                        saif — -bash — 80×24
Last login: Thu Feb 18 12:52:14 on ttys001
~ @ alpha-al-ghaib (saif) ::  sudo easy_install pip
Password:
Searching for pip
Best match: pip 8.0.2
Adding pip 8.0.2 to easy-install.pth file
Installing pip script to /Users/saif/anaconda/bin
Installing pip2.7 script to /Users/saif/anaconda/bin
Installing pip2 script to /Users/saif/anaconda/bin

Using /Users/saif/anaconda/lib/python2.7/site-packages
Processing dependencies for pip
Finished processing dependencies for pip
```

Next, we will install the `six` package:

```
sudo easy_install --upgrade six
```

A successful installation will appear as shown in the following screenshot:

```
                        saif — -bash — 80×24
~ @ alpha-al-ghaib (saif) ::  sudo easy_install --upgrade six
Password:
Searching for six
Reading https://pypi.python.org/simple/six/
Best match: six 1.10.0
Processing six-1.10.0-py2.7.egg
six 1.10.0 is already the active version in easy-install.pth

Using /Users/saif/anaconda/lib/python2.7/site-packages/six-1.10.0-py2.7.egg
Processing dependencies for six
Finished processing dependencies for six
```

Surprisingly, those are the only two prerequisites for TensorFlow, and we can now install the core platform. We will use the `pip` package installer mentioned earlier and install TensorFlow directly from Google's site. The most recent version at the time of writing this book is v1.3, but you should change this to the latest version you wish to use:

```
sudo pip install tensorflow
```

The `pip` installer will automatically gather all the other required dependencies. You will see each individual download and installation until the software is fully installed.

A successful installation will appear as shown in the following screenshot:

```
Requirement already satisfied: funcsigs>=1; python_version < "3.3" in /usr/local/lib/python2.7/site-packages (from mock>=2.0.0->tensorflow)
Requirement already satisfied: pbr>=0.11 in /usr/local/lib/python2.7/site-packages (from mock>=2.0.0->tensorflow)
Collecting html5lib==0.9999999 (from tensorflow-tensorboard<0.2.0,>=0.1.0->tensorflow)
  Downloading html5lib-0.9999999.tar.gz (889kB)
    100% |████████████████████████████████| 890kB 1.2MB/s
Collecting werkzeug>=0.11.10 (from tensorflow-tensorboard<0.2.0,>=0.1.0->tensorflow)
  Downloading Werkzeug-0.12.2-py2.py3-none-any.whl (312kB)
    100% |████████████████████████████████| 317kB 2.2MB/s
Collecting markdown>=2.6.8 (from tensorflow-tensorboard<0.2.0,>=0.1.0->tensorflow)
  Downloading Markdown-2.6.9.tar.gz (271kB)
    100% |████████████████████████████████| 276kB 3.0MB/s
Collecting bleach==1.5.0 (from tensorflow-tensorboard<0.2.0,>=0.1.0->tensorflow)
  Downloading bleach-1.5.0-py2.py3-none-any.whl
Installing collected packages: backports.weakref, protobuf, html5lib, werkzeug, markdown, bleach, tensorflow-tensorboard, tensorflow
  Found existing installation: html5lib 0.999999999
    Uninstalling html5lib-0.999999999:
      Successfully uninstalled html5lib-0.999999999
  Running setup.py install for html5lib ... done
  Running setup.py install for markdown ... done
  Found existing installation: bleach 2.0.0
    Uninstalling bleach-2.0.0:
      Successfully uninstalled bleach-2.0.0
Successfully installed backports.weakref-1.0.post1 bleach-1.5.0 html5lib-0.9999999 markdown-2.6.9 protobuf-3.4.0 tensorflow-1.3.0 tensorflow-tensorboard-0.1.7 werkzeug-0.12.2
 → ~ 
```

That's it! If you were able to get to this point, you can start to train and run your first model. Skip to `Chapter 2`, *Your First Classifier*, to train your first model.

macOS X users wishing to completely segregate their installation can use a VM instead, as described in the Windows installation.

Windows installation

As we mentioned earlier, TensorFlow with Python 2.7 does not function natively on Windows. In this section, we will guide you through installing TensorFlow with Python 3.5 and set up a VM with Linux if you want to use TensorFlow with Python 2.7.

First, we need to install Python 3.5.x or 3.6.x 64-bit from the following links:

```
https://www.python.org/downloads/release/python-352/
```

```
https://www.python.org/downloads/release/python-362/
```

Make sure that you download the 64-bit version of Python where the name of the installation has `amd64`, such as `python-3.6.2-amd64.exe`. The Python 3.6.2 installation looks like this:

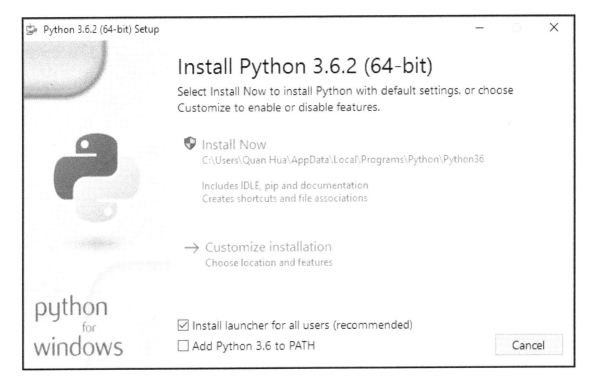

We will select **Add Python 3.6 to PATH** and click **Install Now**. The installation process will complete with the following screen:

We will click the **Disable path length limit** and then click **Close** to finish the Python installation. Now, let's open the **Windows PowerShell** application under the Windows menu. We will install the CPU-only version of Tensorflow with the following command:

```
pip3 install tensorflow
```

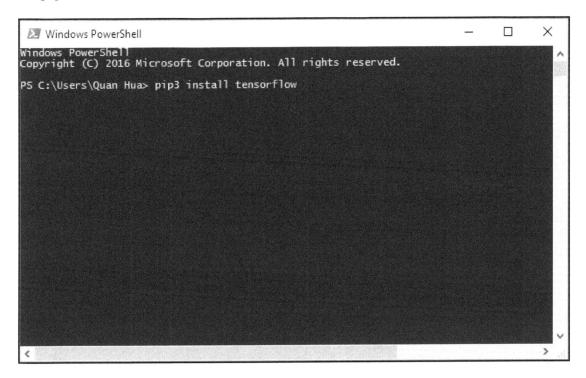

The result of the installation will look like this:

```
Windows PowerShell                                          —    □    ×
    100% |                                  | 2.2MB 640kB/s
Collecting numpy>=1.11.0 (from tensorflow)
  Downloading numpy-1.13.1-cp36-none-win_amd64.whl (7.8MB)
    100% |                                  | 7.8MB 209kB/s
Collecting wheel>=0.26 (from tensorflow)
  Downloading wheel-0.30.0-py2.py3-none-any.whl (49kB)
    100% |                                  | 51kB 2.3MB/s
Collecting protobuf>=3.3.0 (from tensorflow)
  Downloading protobuf-3.4.0-py2.py3-none-any.whl (375kB)
    100% |                                  | 378kB 586kB/s
Collecting six>=1.10.0 (from tensorflow)
  Downloading six-1.11.0-py2.py3-none-any.whl
Collecting bleach==1.5.0 (from tensorflow-tensorboard<0.2.0,>=0.1.0->tensorflow)
  Downloading bleach-1.5.0-py2.py3-none-any.whl
Collecting html5lib==0.9999999 (from tensorflow-tensorboard<0.2.0,>=0.1.0->tensorflow)
  Downloading html5lib-0.9999999.tar.gz (889kB)
    100% |                                  | 890kB 880kB/s
Collecting werkzeug>=0.11.10 (from tensorflow-tensorboard<0.2.0,>=0.1.0->tensorflow)
  Downloading Werkzeug-0.12.2-py2.py3-none-any.whl (312kB)
    100% |                                  | 317kB 969kB/s
Collecting markdown>=2.6.8 (from tensorflow-tensorboard<0.2.0,>=0.1.0->tensorflow)
  Downloading Markdown-2.6.9.tar.gz (271kB)
    100% |                                  | 276kB 1.5MB/s
Requirement already satisfied: setuptools in c:\users\quan hua\appdata\local\programs\pytho
(from protobuf>=3.3.0->tensorflow)
Installing collected packages: six, protobuf, numpy, html5lib, bleach, wheel, werkzeug, mar
, tensorflow
  Running setup.py install for html5lib ... done
  Running setup.py install for markdown ... done
Successfully installed bleach-1.5.0 html5lib-0.9999999 markdown-2.6.9 numpy-1.13.1 protobuf
1.3.0 tensorflow-tensorboard-0.1.6 werkzeug-0.12.2 wheel-0.30.0
PS C:\Users\Quan Hua>
```

Congratulations, you can now use TensorFlow on Windows with Python 3.5.x or 3.6.x support. In the next section, we will show you how to set up a VM to use TensorFlow with Python 2.7. However, you can skip to the *Test installation* section of `Chapter 2`, *Your First Classifier*, if you don't need Python 2.7.

Now, we will show you how to set up a VM with Linux to use TensorFlow with Python 2.7. We recommend the free VirtualBox system available at `https://www.virtualbox.org/wiki/Downloads`. The latest stable version at the time of writing is v5.0.14, available at the following URL:

`http://download.virtualbox.org/virtualbox/5.1.28/VirtualBox-5.1.28-117968-Win.exe`

A successful installation will allow you to run the **Oracle VM VirtualBox Manager** dashboard, which looks like this:

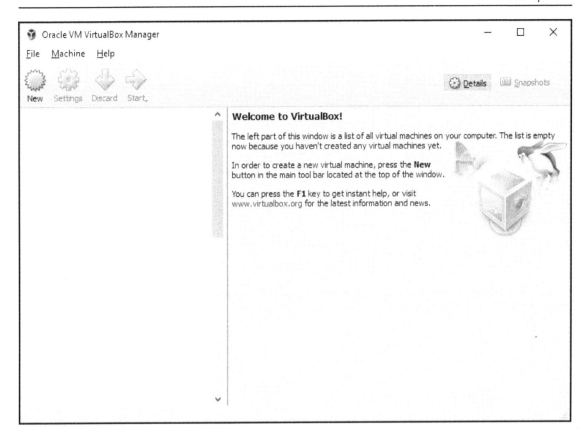

Virtual machine setup

Linux comes in numerous flavors, but as the TensorFlow documentation mostly mentions Ubuntu, we'll be working with Ubuntu Linux. You are welcome to use any flavor of Linux, but you should be aware that there are subtle differences across flavors and versions of each flavor. Most differences are benign, but some may trip up the installation or even usage of TensorFlow.

Even after choosing Ubuntu, there are many versions and configurations; you can see some at http://cdimage.ubuntu.com/ubuntu-gnome/releases/14.04/release/.

We will install the most popular version, which is Ubuntu 14.04.4 LTS (make sure to download a version appropriate for your computer). Versions marked x86 are designed to run on 32-bit machines, while those marked with some variation of 64 are designed to run on 64-bit machines. Most modern machines are 64-bit, so if you are unsure, go with the latter.

Installations happen via an ISO file, which is, essentially, a file equivalent of an installation CD. The ISO for Ubuntu 14.04.4 LTS is `ubuntu-gnome-14.04-desktop-amd64.iso`.

Once you have downloaded the installation ISO, we will set up a VM and use the ISO file to install Ubuntu Linux on the VM.

Setting up the VM on **Oracle VM VirtualBox Manager** is relatively simple, but pay close attention as the default options are not sufficient for TensorFlow. You will go through the following seven screens, and at the end, it will prompt you for the installation file, which was just downloaded.

We will first set up the type of operating system and configure the **random access memory** (**RAM**) allocated to the VM:

1. Note that we selected a 64-bit installation as that is the image we're using; you can choose to use a 32-bit image if you need:

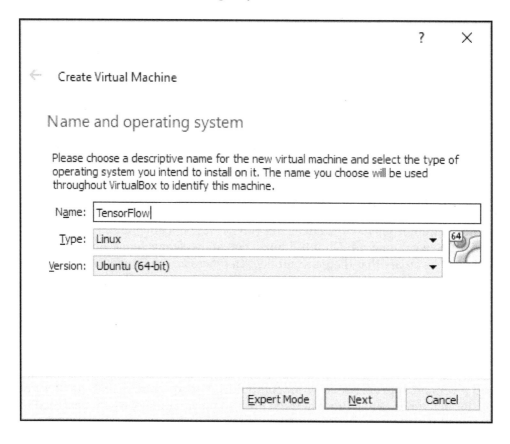

2. How much RAM you allocate depends on how much your machine has. In the following screenshot, we will allocate half our RAM(8 GB) to our VM. Remember that this is consumed only while we are running the VM, so we can be liberal with our allocations. We can allocate at least 4 GB:

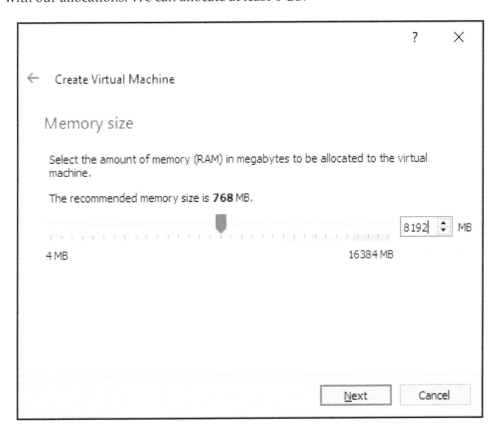

3. Our VM will need a hard disk. We'll create a **Virtual Hard Disk** (**VHD**), as shown in the following screenshot:

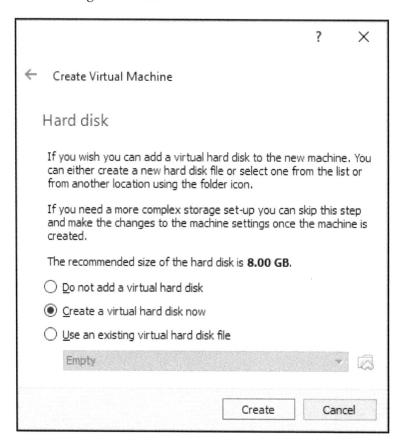

4. Then, we will choose the type of hard drive for the VM, that is, **VDI (VirtualBox Disk Image)**, as shown in the following screenshot:

5. Next, we will choose how much space to allocate for the VHD. This is important to understand as we will soon work with extremely large datasets:

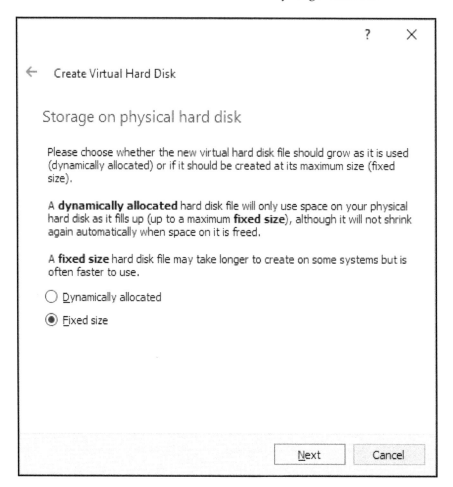

6. We will allocate 12 GB because TensorFlow and typical TensorFlow applications have an array of dependencies, such as `NumPy`, `SciPy`, and `Pandas`. Our exercises will also be downloading large datasets, which are to be used for training:

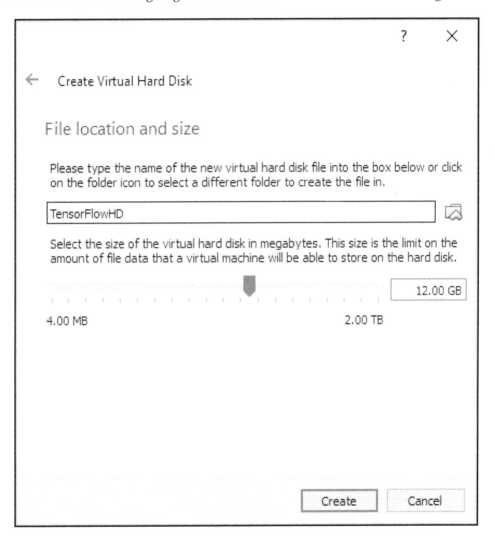

7. After setting up the VM, it will appear on the left side VM listing. Select it and click on **Start**. This is the equivalent of booting up the machine:

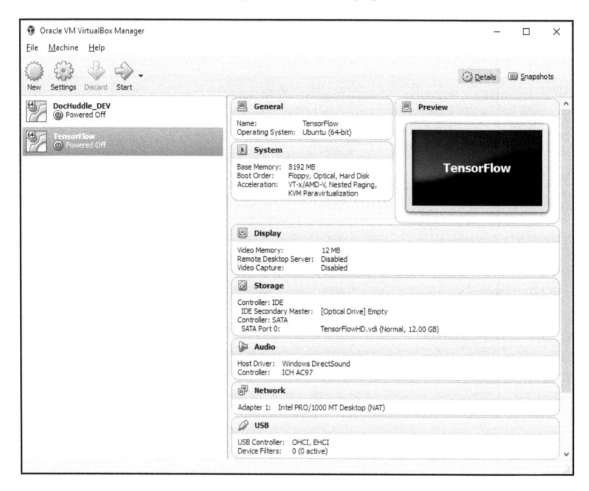

8. As the machine boots for the first time, provide it the installation CD (in our case, the Ubuntu ISO we downloaded earlier):

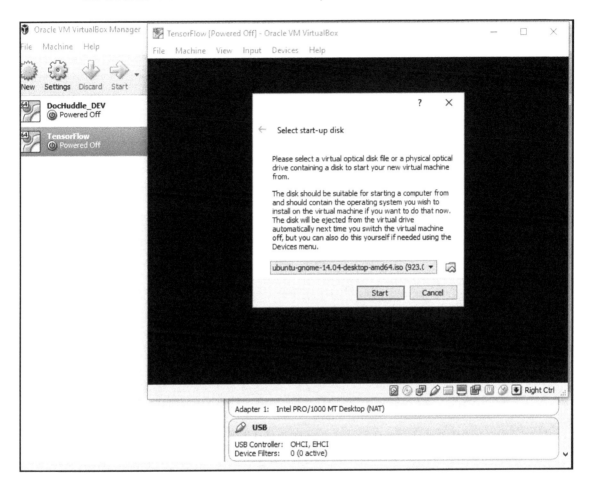

Follow the installation instructions and you'll have a full Ubuntu Linux installation ready to use! After that, you can follow the Ubuntu installation at the beginning of this chapter.

Testing the installation

In this section, we will use TensorFlow to compute a simple math operation. First, open your terminal on Linux/macOS or Windows PowerShell in Windows.

Now, we need to run `python` to use TensorFlow with the following command:

```
python
```

Enter the following program in the Python shell:

```
import tensorflow as tf
a = tf.constant(1.0)
b = tf.constant(2.0)
c = a + b
sess = tf.Session()
print(sess.run(c))
```

The result will look like the following screen where `3.0` is printed at the end:

Summary

In this chapter, we covered TensorFlow installation on the three major operating systems, so all readers should be up and running with the platform. Windows users faced an extra challenge, as TensorFlow on Windows only supports Python 3.5.x or Python 3.6.x 64-bit version. However, even Windows users should now be up and running. Congratulations, now the fun begins!

You now have TensorFlow installed. The immediate next step is to test the installation with a sample built-in training effort. Next, we will write our first classifier from scratch—a handwriting recognizer.

In the upcoming chapters, we will review TensorFlow tools and use them on our projects. We will also review the major deep learning concepts, using each in the context of a project. You will have a chance to try projects in multiple industries, ranging from finance to medicine to language.

2
Your First Classifier

With TensorFlow now installed, we need to kick the tires. We will do so by writing our first classifier and then training and testing it from start to finish!

Our first classifier will be a handwriting recognizer. One of the most common datasets to train is the **MNIST** handwritten digits dataset. We'll be using a similar dataset called notMNIST, which features the first ten letters of the English alphabet.

The key parts

There are three key parts to most machine learning classifiers, which are as follows:

- The training pipeline
- The neural network setup and training outputs
- The usage pipeline

The training pipeline obtains data, stages it, cleanses it, homogenizes it, and puts it in a format acceptable to the neural network. Do not be surprised if the training pipeline takes 80% to 85% of your effort initially—this is the reality of most machine learning work. Generally, the more realistic the training data, the more time spent on the training pipeline. In enterprise settings, the training pipeline might be an ongoing effort being enhanced perpetually. This is especially true as datasets get larger.

The second part, the neural network setup, and training, can be quick for routine problems and can be a research-grade effort for harder problems. You may find yourself making small changes to the network setup, over and over, until you finally achieve the desired classifier accuracy. The training is the most computationally expensive part, so it takes time before you can evaluate the result of each incremental modification.

Once the initial setup is complete and the network is trained to a sufficient level of accuracy, we can just use it over and over. In `Chapter 10`, *Go Live and Go Big*, we'll explore more advanced topics, such as continuous learning, where even usage can feed back into further training the classifier.

Obtaining training data

Machine learning requires training data—often a lot of training data. One of the great things about machine learning is the availability of standard training datasets. These are often used to benchmark node models and configurations and provide a consistent yardstick to gauge performance against previous progress. Many of the datasets are also used in annual global competitions.

This chapter uses training data, which is kindly provided by Yaroslav Bulatov, a machine learning researcher.

Downloading training data

You should start by downloading the training data from the following links:

- `http://yaroslavvb.com/upload/notMNIST/notMNIST_small.tar.gz`
- `http://yaroslavvb.com/upload/notMNIST/notMNIST_large.tar.gz`

We will download this programmatically, but we should start with a manual download just to peek at the data and structure of the archive. This will be important when we write the pipeline, as we'll need to understand the structure so we can manipulate the data.

The small set is ideal for peeking. You can do this via the following command line, or just use a browser to download the file with an unarchiver to extract the files (I suggest getting familiarized with the command line as all of this needs to be automated):

```
cd ~/workdir
wget http://yaroslavvb.com/upload/notMNIST/notMNIST_small.tar.gz
tar xvf notMNIST_small.tar.gz
```

The preceding command line will reveal a container folder called `notMNIST_small` with ten subfolders underneath, one for each letter of the alphabet `a` through `j`. Under each lettered folder, there are thousands of 28x28 pixel images of the letter. Additionally, an interesting thing to note is the filename of each letter image, (`QnJhbmRpbmcgSXJvbi50dGY=`), suggesting a random string that does not contain information of use.

Understanding classes

The classifier we're writing seeks to assign unknown images to a class. Classes can be of the following types:

- Feline versus canine
- Two versus seven
- Tumor versus normal
- Smiling versus frowning

In our case, we are considering each letter a class for a total of 10 classes. The training set will reveal 10 subfolders with thousands of images underneath each subfolder. The name of the subfolder is important as it is the label for each of the images. These details will be used by the pipeline to prepare data for TensorFlow.

Automating the training data setup

Ideally, we will want the entire process automated. This way, we can easily run the process end to end on any computer we use without having to carry around ancillary assets. This will be important later, as we will often develop on one computer (our development machine) and deploy on a different machine (our production server).

I have already written the code for this chapter, as well as all the other chapters; it is available at https://github.com/mlwithtf/MLwithTF. Our approach will be to rewrite it together while understanding it. Some straightforward parts, such as this, may be skipped. I recommend forking the repository and cloning a local copy for your projects:

```
cd ~/workdir
git clone https://github.com/mlwithtf/MLwithTF
cd chapter_02
```

The code for this specific section is available at— https://github.com/mlwithtf/mlwithtf/blob/master/chapter_02/download.py.

Preparing the dataset is an important part of the training process. Before we go deeper into the code, we will run `download.py` to automatically download and prepare the dataset:

```
python download.py
```

The result will look like this:

```
/notMNIST_small/J
Started loading images from: /home/ubuntu/github/mlwithtf/datasets/notMNIST/test
/notMNIST_small/J
Finished loading data from: /home/ubuntu/github/mlwithtf/datasets/notMNIST/test/
notMNIST_small/J
        Started pickling: J
Finished pickling: J
Finished loading testing data
Started pickling final dataset
Merging train, valid data
Merging test data
('Training set', (200000, 28, 28), (200000,))
('Validation set', (10000, 28, 28), (10000,))
('Test set', (10000, 28, 28), (10000,))
('Compressed pickle size:', 690800514)
Finished pickling final dataset
Finished preparing notMNIST dataset
After reformat:
('Training set', (200000, 784), (200000, 10))
('Validation set', (10000, 784), (10000, 10))
('Test set', (10000, 784), (10000, 10))
(work2) ubuntu@ubuntu-PC:~/github/mlwithtf/chapter_02$
```

Now, we will take a look at several functions that are used in `download.py`. You can find the code in this file:

`https://github.com/mlwithtf/mlwithtf/blob/master/data_utils.py`

The following `downloadFile` function will automatically download the file and validate it against an expected file size:

```python
from __future__ import print_function
import os
from six.moves.urllib.request import urlretrieve
import datetime
def downloadFile(fileURL, expected_size):
    timeStampedDir=datetime.datetime.now()
      .strftime("%Y.%m.%d_%I.%M.%S")
    os.makedirs(timeStampedDir)
    fileNameLocal = timeStampedDir + "/" +
    fileURL.split('/')[-1]
    print ('Attempting to download ' + fileURL)
    print ('File will be stored in ' + fileNameLocal)
    filename, _ = urlretrieve(fileURL, fileNameLocal)
    statinfo = os.stat(filename)
```

```
    if statinfo.st_size == expected_size:
        print('Found and verified', filename)
    else:
        raise Exception('Could not get ' + filename)
    return filename
```

The function can be called as follows:

```
tst_set =
downloadFile('http://yaroslavvb.com/upload/notMNIST/notMNIST_small
.tar.gz', 8458043)
```

The code to extract the contents is as follows (note that the additional import is required):

```
import os, sys, tarfile
from os.path import basename

def extractFile(filename):
    timeStampedDir=datetime.datetime.now()
     .strftime("%Y.%m.%d_%I.%M.%S")
    tar = tarfile.open(filename)
    sys.stdout.flush()
    tar.extractall(timeStampedDir)
    tar.close()
    return timeStampedDir + "/" + os.listdir(timeStampedDir)[0]
```

We call the `download` and extract methods in sequence as follows:

```
tst_src='http://yaroslavvb.com/upload/notMNIST/notMNIST_small.tar.
gz'
tst_set = downloadFile(tst_src, 8458043)
print ('Test set stored in: ' + tst_set)
tst_files = extractFile(tst_set)
print ('Test file set stored in: ' + tst_files)
```

Additional setup

The next part will focus on image processing and manipulation. This requires some extra
libraries you may not have. At this point, it may make sense to just install all the typical
packages required in scientific computing, which can be done as follows:

```
sudo apt-get install python-numpy python-scipy python-matplotlib
ipython ipython-notebook python-pandas python-sympy python-nose
```

Additionally, install the image processing library, some external matrix mathematics libraries, and underlying requirements, which can be done as follows:

```
sudo pip install ndimage
sudo apt-get install libatlas3-base-dev gcc gfortran g++
```

Converting images to matrices

Much of machine learning is just operations on matrices. We will start that process next by converting our images into a series of matrices—essentially, a 3D matrix as wide as the number of images we have.

Almost all matrix operations that we will perform in this chapter, and the entire book, use NumPy—the most popular scientific computing package in the Python landscape. NumPy is available at http://www.numpy.org/. You should install it before running the next series of operations.

The following code opens images and creates the matrices of data (note the three extra imports now required):

```
import numpy as np
from IPython.display import display, Image
from scipy import ndimage

image_size = 28  # Pixel width and height.
pixel_depth = 255.0  # Number of levels per pixel.
def loadClass(folder):
 image_files = os.listdir(folder)
 dataset = np.ndarray(shape=(len(image_files),
 image_size,
  image_size), dtype=np.float32)
 image_index = 0
 print(folder)
 for image in os.listdir(folder):
   image_file = os.path.join(folder, image)
   try:
     image_data =
     (ndimage.imread(image_file).astype(float) -
                 pixel_depth / 2) / pixel_depth
     if image_data.shape != (image_size, image_size):
       raise Exception('Unexpected image shape: %s' %
     str(image_data.shape))
     dataset[image_index, :, :] = image_data
     image_index += 1
   except IOError as e: l
```

```
print('Could not read:', image_file, ':', e, '-
it\'s ok,
  skipping.')
return dataset[0:image_index, :, :]
```

We have our extracted files from the previous section. Now, we can simply run this procedure on all our extracted images, as follows:

```
classFolders = [os.path.join(tst_files, d) for d in
os.listdir(tst_files) if os.path.isdir(os.path.join(tst_files,
d))]
print (classFolders)
for cf in classFolders:
    print ("\n\nExaming class folder " + cf)
    dataset=loadClass(cf)
    print (dataset.shape)
```

The procedure essentially loads letters into a matrix that looks something like this:

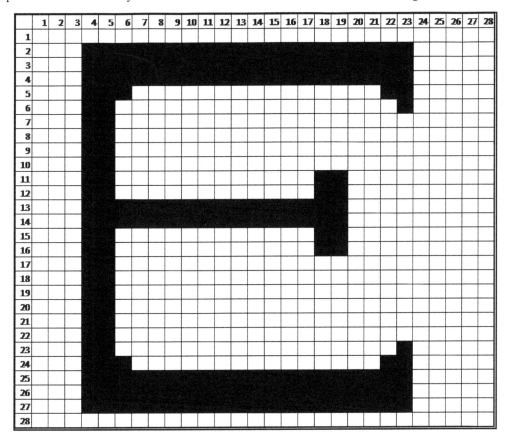

However, a peek into the matrix reveals more subtlety. Go ahead and take a look by printing an arbitrary layer on the stack (for example, `np.set_printoptions(precision=2); print (dataset[47])`. You will find a matrix not of bits, but of floating point numbers:

```
  0.19  0.01 -0.14 -0.5 ]
[-0.5  -0.5  -0.5  -0.5  -0.5  -0.5  -0.48 -0.48 -0.43 -0.35 -0.5  -0.49
 -0.49 -0.5  -0.42 -0.49  0.2   0.05  0.46  0.5   0.5   0.5   0.49  0.4
  0.15 -0.29 -0.12 -0.5 ]
[-0.5  -0.5  -0.5  -0.45 -0.42 -0.46 -0.05 -0.21 -0.35 -0.44 -0.5  -0.5
 -0.45 -0.48 -0.49 -0.36  0.12  0.25  0.5   0.5   0.5   0.5   0.48  0.36
  0.28 -0.08 -0.48 -0.5 ]
[-0.49 -0.5  -0.5  -0.48 -0.15  0.02  0.45  0.47  0.39  0.21 -0.07 -0.06
 -0.22 -0.43 -0.38  0.24  0.24  0.48  0.5   0.5   0.5   0.5   0.5   0.43
  0.1  -0.39 -0.47 -0.43]
[-0.48 -0.44 -0.36 -0.02  0.34  0.45  0.45  0.5   0.5   0.5   0.43  0.29
  0.03 -0.08  0.15  0.48  0.5   0.5   0.5   0.5   0.5   0.48  0.5   0.06
  0.03 -0.27 -0.33 -0.46]
[-0.43 -0.5  -0.2   0.48  0.45  0.45  0.49  0.5   0.49  0.48  0.47  0.5
  0.46  0.49  0.5   0.5   0.49  0.5   0.5   0.49  0.5   0.32  0.42  0.06
 -0.1  -0.3  -0.46 -0.5 ]
[-0.5  -0.41 -0.43 -0.21 -0.23  0.13  0.46  0.48  0.5   0.5   0.5   0.49
  0.5   0.48  0.47  0.49  0.5   0.48  0.48  0.5   0.32  0.2   0.35 -0.37
 -0.44 -0.33 -0.5  -0.49]
[-0.5  -0.5  -0.5  -0.39 -0.36 -0.1   0.16  0.14  0.44  0.42  0.47  0.48
  0.5   0.5   0.5   0.48  0.46  0.5   0.5   0.41  0.07  0.04 -0.17 -0.45
 -0.47 -0.5  -0.5  -0.5 ]
[-0.5  -0.5  -0.49 -0.45 -0.47 -0.43 -0.37 -0.35 -0.17 -0.02  0.17  0.23
  0.01  0.02  0.15  0.3   0.18  0.01 -0.06 -0.14 -0.15 -0.41 -0.44 -0.5
 -0.5  -0.49 -0.5  -0.5 ]
[-0.5  -0.5  -0.5  -0.5  -0.5  -0.5  -0.5  -0.5  -0.5  -0.5  -0.5  -0.45
 -0.42 -0.37 -0.26 -0.23 -0.32 -0.48 -0.5  -0.47 -0.37 -0.49 -0.5  -0.5
 -0.5  -0.5  -0.5  -0.5 ]]

[anaconda] S:\ _WORKSPACE\PyCharm\book>
```

The images first get loaded into a matrix of values **0** to **255**:

	1	2	3	4	5	6	7	8	9	10	11	12	13	14	15	16	17	18	19	20	21	22	23	24	25	26	27	28
1																												
2				255	255	255	255	255	255	255	255	255	255	255	255	255	255	255	255	255	255	255	255					
3				255	255	255	255	255	255	255	255	255	255	255	255	255	255	255	255	255	255	255	255					
4				255	255	255	255	255	255	255	255	255	255	255	255	255	255	255	255	255	255	255	255					
5				255	255	253																251	253					
6				255	255																		251					
7				255	255																							
8				255	255																							
9				255	255																							
10				255	255																							
11				255	255													251	253									
12				255	255													255	255									
13				255	255	255	255	255	255	255	255	255	255	255	255	255	255	255	255									
14				255	255	255	255	255	255	255	255	255	255	255	255	255	255	255	255									
15				255	255													255	255									
16				255	255													251	253									
17				255	255																							
18				255	255																							
19				255	255																							
20				255	255																							
21				255	255																							
22				255	255																							
23				255	255																		251					
24				255	255	253																251	253					
25				255	255	255	255	255	255	255	255	255	255	255	255	255	255	255	255	255	255	255	255					
26				255	255	255	255	255	255	255	255	255	255	255	255	255	255	255	255	255	255	255	255					
27				255	255	255	255	255	255	255	255	255	255	255	255	255	255	255	255	255	255	255	255					
28																												

These get scaled down to numbers between **-0.5** and **0.5,** we will revisit the reasons why later. We will end up with a stack of images that looks like this:

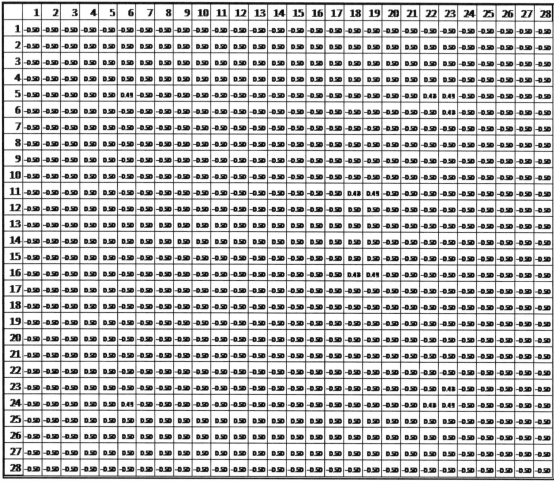

These are all greyscale images, so we will deal with just one layer. We'll deal with color images in future chapters; in those cases, each photo will have a matrix of height three and a separate matrix for red, green, and blue.

Logical stopping points

Downloading our training file took a long time. Even extracting all the images took a while. To avoid repeating all this, we will try to do all the work just once and then create **pickle files**—archives of the Python data structures.

The following procedure runs through each class in our training and test set and creates a separate `pickle` file for each. In future runs, we'll just begin from here:

```
def makePickle(imgSrcPath):
    data_folders = [os.path.join(tst_files, d) for d in
     os.listdir(tst_files) if os.path.isdir(os.path.join(tst_files,
     d))]
    dataset_names = []
    for folder in data_folders:
        set_filename = folder + '.pickle'
        dataset_names.append(set_filename)
        print('Pickling %s.' % set_filename)
        dataset = loadClass(folder)
        try:
            with open(set_filename, 'wb') as f:
                pickle.dump(dataset, f, pickle.HIGHEST_PROTOCOL)
        except Exception as e:
            print('Unable to save data to', set_filename, ':', e)
    return dataset_names
```

The `Pickle` files are essentially persistable and reconstitutable dumps of dictionaries.

The machine learning briefcase

We just created nice, clean, `pickle` files with preprocessed images to train and test our classifier. However, we've ended up with 20 `pickle` files. There are two problems with this. First, we have too many files to keep track of easily. Secondly, we've only completed part of our pipeline, where we've processed our image sets but have not prepared a TensorFlow consumable file.

Now we will need to create our three major sets—the training set, the validation set, and the test set. The training set will be used to nudge our classifier, while the validation set will be used to gauge progress on each iteration. The test set will be kept secret until the end of the training, at which point, it will be used to test how well we've trained the model.

The code to do all this is long, so we'll leave you to review the Git repository. Pay close attention to the following three functions:

```python
def randomize(dataset, labels):
    permutation = np.random.permutation(labels.shape[0])
    shuffled_dataset = dataset[permutation, :, :]
    shuffled_labels = labels[permutation]
    return shuffled_dataset, shuffled_labels

def make_arrays(nb_rows, img_size):
    if nb_rows:
        dataset = np.ndarray((nb_rows, img_size, img_size),
dtype=np.float32)
        labels = np.ndarray(nb_rows, dtype=np.int32)
    else:
        dataset, labels = None, None
    return dataset, labels

def merge_datasets(pickle_files, train_size, valid_size=0):
 num_classes = len(pickle_files)
 valid_dataset, valid_labels = make_arrays(valid_size,
 image_size)
 train_dataset, train_labels = make_arrays(train_size,
 image_size)
 vsize_per_class = valid_size // num_classes
 tsize_per_class = train_size // num_classes

 start_v, start_t = 0, 0
 end_v, end_t = vsize_per_class, tsize_per_class
 end_l = vsize_per_class+tsize_per_class
 for label, pickle_file in enumerate(pickle_files):
   try:
     with open(pickle_file, 'rb') as f:
       letter_set = pickle.load(f)
       np.random.shuffle(letter_set)
       if valid_dataset is not None:
         valid_letter = letter_set[:vsize_per_class, :, :]
         valid_dataset[start_v:end_v, :, :] = valid_letter
         valid_labels[start_v:end_v] = label
         start_v += vsize_per_class
         end_v += vsize_per_class

       train_letter = letter_set[vsize_per_class:end_l, :, :]
       train_dataset[start_t:end_t, :, :] = train_letter
       train_labels[start_t:end_t] = label
       start_t += tsize_per_class
       end_t += tsize_per_class
   except Exception as e:
```

```
print('Unable to process data from', pickle_file, ':', e)
raise

return valid_dataset, valid_labels, train_dataset, train_labels
```

These three complete our pipeline methods. But, we will still need to use the pipeline. To do so, we will first define our training, validation, and test sizes. You can change this, but you should keep it less than the full size available, of course:

```
train_size = 200000
valid_size = 10000
test_size = 10000
```

These sizes will then be used to construct merged (that is, combining all our classes) datasets. We will pass in the list of `pickle` files to source our data from and get back a vector of labels and a matrix stack of images. We will finish by shuffling our datasets, as follows:

```
valid_dataset, valid_labels, train_dataset, train_labels =
 merge_datasets(
   picklenamesTrn, train_size, valid_size)
_, _, test_dataset, test_labels = merge_datasets(picklenamesTst,
 test_size)
train_dataset, train_labels = randomize(train_dataset,
 train_labels)
test_dataset, test_labels = randomize(test_dataset, test_labels)
valid_dataset, valid_labels = randomize(valid_dataset,
 valid_labels)
```

We can peek into our newly-merged datasets as follows:

```
print('Training:', train_dataset.shape, train_labels.shape)
print('Validation:', valid_dataset.shape, valid_labels.shape)
print('Testing:', test_dataset.shape, test_labels.shape)
```

Whew! That was a lot of work we do not want to repeat in the future. Luckily, we won't have to, because we'll re-pickle our three new datasets into a single, giant, `pickle` file. Going forward, all learning will skip the preceding steps and work straight off the giant `pickle`:

```
pickle_file = 'notMNIST.pickle'

try:
  f = open(pickle_file, 'wb')
  save = {
     'datTrn': train_dataset,
   'labTrn': train_labels,
```

```
        'datVal': valid_dataset,
        'labVal': valid_labels,
        'datTst': test_dataset,
        'labTst': test_labels,
        }
    pickle.dump(save, f, pickle.HIGHEST_PROTOCOL)
    f.close()
except Exception as e:
    print('Unable to save data to', pickle_file, ':', e)
    raise

statinfo = os.stat(pickle_file)
print('Compressed pickle size:', statinfo.st_size)
```

The ideal way to feed the matrices into TensorFlow is actually as a one-dimensional array; so, we'll reformat our 28x28 matrices into strings of 784 decimals. For that, we'll use the following `reformat` method:

```
def reformat(dataset, labels):
    dataset = dataset.reshape((-1, image_size *
      image_size)).astype(np.float32)
    labels = (np.arange(num_labels) ==
      labels[:,None]).astype(np.float32)
    return dataset, labels
```

Our images now look like this, with a row for every image in the training, validation, and test sets:

	1	2	3	4	5	6	7	...	780	781	782	783	784
1	-0.50	-0.50	-0.50	-0.50	-0.50	-0.50	-0.50	...	-0.50	-0.50	-0.50	-0.50	-0.50
2	-0.50	-0.50	-0.49	-0.50	-0.50	-0.50	0.50	...	0.50	0.50	0.50	0.50	0.50
3	-0.50	-0.50	-0.49	-0.50	-0.50	-0.50	0.50	...	0.50	0.50	0.50	0.50	0.50
...	...	...	...	...	...	...	...	...	...	...	...	...	...
200000	-0.50	-0.50	-0.40	-0.50	-0.50	-0.50	0.50	...	0.50	0.50	0.50	0.50	0.50
200001	-0.50	-0.50	-0.40	-0.50	-0.50	-0.50	0.50	...	0.50	0.50	0.50	0.50	0.50
200002	-0.50	-0.50	-0.40	-0.50	-0.50	-0.50	0.50	...	0.50	0.50	0.50	0.50	0.50
200003	-0.50	-0.50	-0.39	-0.50	-0.50	-0.50	-0.50	...	-0.50	-0.50	-0.50	-0.50	-0.50

Finally, to open up and work with the contents of the `pickle` file, we will simply read the variable names chosen earlier and pick off the data like a hashmap:

```
with open(pickle_file, 'rb') as f:
  pkl = pickle.load(f)
  train_dataset, train_labels = reformat(pkl['datTrn'],
   pkl['labTrn'])
  valid_dataset, valid_labels = reformat(pkl['datVal'],
   pkl['labVal'])
  test_dataset, test_labels = reformat(pkl['datTst'],
   pkl['labTst'])
```

Training day

Now, we arrive at the fun part—the neural network. The complete code to train this model is available at the following link:
`https://github.com/mlwithtf/mlwithtf/blob/master/chapter_02/training.py`

To train the model, we'll import several more modules:

```
import sys, os
import tensorflow as tf
import numpy as np
sys.path.append(os.path.realpath('..'))
import data_utils
import logmanager
```

Then, we will define a few parameters for the training process:

```
batch_size = 128
num_steps = 10000
learning_rate = 0.3
data_showing_step = 500
```

After that, we will use the `data_utils` package to load the dataset that was downloaded in the previous section:

```
dataset, image_size, num_of_classes, num_of_channels =
data_utils.prepare_not_mnist_dataset(root_dir="..")
dataset = data_utils.reformat(dataset, image_size,
num_of_channels,
 num_of_classes)
print('Training set', dataset.train_dataset.shape,
dataset.train_labels.shape)
print('Validation set', dataset.valid_dataset.shape,
dataset.valid_labels.shape)
```

```
print('Test set', dataset.test_dataset.shape,
dataset.test_labels.shape)
```

We'll start off with a fully-connected network. For now, just trust the network setup (we'll jump into the theory of setup a bit later). We will represent the neural network as a graph, called graph in the following code:

```
graph = tf.Graph()
with graph.as_default():
# Input data. For the training data, we use a placeholder that
will
be fed
# at run time with a training minibatch.
tf_train_dataset = tf.placeholder(tf.float32,
shape=(batch_size, image_size * image_size * num_of_channels))
tf_train_labels = tf.placeholder(tf.float32, shape=(batch_size,
num_of_classes))
tf_valid_dataset = tf.constant(dataset.valid_dataset)
tf_test_dataset = tf.constant(dataset.test_dataset)
# Variables.
weights = {
'fc1': tf.Variable(tf.truncated_normal([image_size * image_size *
num_of_channels, num_of_classes])),
'fc2': tf.Variable(tf.truncated_normal([num_of_classes,
num_of_classes]))
}
biases = {
'fc1': tf.Variable(tf.zeros([num_of_classes])),
'fc2': tf.Variable(tf.zeros([num_of_classes]))
}
# Training computation.
logits = nn_model(tf_train_dataset, weights, biases)
loss = tf.reduce_mean(
tf.nn.softmax_cross_entropy_with_logits(logits=logits,
labels=tf_train_labels))
# Optimizer.
optimizer =
tf.train.GradientDescentOptimizer(learning_rate).minimize(loss)
# Predictions for the training, validation, and test data.
train_prediction = tf.nn.softmax(logits)
valid_prediction = tf.nn.softmax(nn_model(tf_valid_dataset,
weights, biases))
test_prediction = tf.nn.softmax(nn_model(tf_test_dataset, weights,
biases))
The most important line here is the nn_model where the neural
network is defined:
def nn_model(data, weights, biases):
layer_fc1 = tf.matmul(data, weights['fc1']) + biases['fc1']
```

```
relu_layer = tf.nn.relu(layer_fc1)
return tf.matmul(relu_layer, weights['fc2']) + biases['fc2']
```

The `loss` function that is used to train the model is also an important factor in this process:

```
loss = tf.reduce_mean(
tf.nn.softmax_cross_entropy_with_logits(logits=logits,
labels=tf_train_labels))
# Optimizer.
optimizer =
tf.train.GradientDescentOptimizer(learning_rate).minimize(loss)
```

This is the optimizer being used (Stochastic Gradient Descent) along with the `learning_rate` (0.3) and the function we're trying to minimize (softmax with cross-entropy).

The real action, and the most time-consuming part, lies in the next and final segment—the training loop:

```
with tf.Session(graph=graph) as session:
    session.run(tf.global_variables_initializer())
    print("Initialized")
    for step in range(num_steps + 1):
        sys.stdout.write('Training on batch %d of %d\r' % (step + 1, num_steps))
        sys.stdout.flush()
        # Pick an offset within the training data, which has been randomized.
        # Note: we could use better randomization across epochs.
        offset = (step * batch_size) % (dataset.train_labels.shape[0] - batch_size)
        # Generate a minibatch.
        batch_data = dataset.train_dataset[offset:(offset + batch_size), :]
        batch_labels = dataset.train_labels[offset:(offset + batch_size), :]
        # Prepare a dictionary telling the session where to feed the minibatch.
        # The key of the dictionary is the placeholder node of the graph to be fed,
        # and the value is the numpy array to feed to it.
        feed_dict = {tf_train_dataset: batch_data, tf_train_labels: batch_labels}
        _, l, predictions = session.run([optimizer, loss, train_prediction], feed_dict=feed_dict)
        if step % data_showing_step == 0:
            acc_minibatch = accuracy(predictions, batch_labels)
            acc_val = accuracy(valid_prediction.eval(), dataset.valid_labels)
            logmanager.logger.info('# %03d  Acc Train: %03.2f%%  Acc Val: %03.2f%% Loss %f' % (
                step, acc_minibatch, acc_val, l))
    logmanager.logger.info("Test accuracy: %.1f%%" % accuracy(test_prediction.eval(), dataset.test_labels))
```

We can run this training process using the following command in the `chapter_02` directory:

```
python training.py
```

Running the procedure produces the following output:

```
Initialized
2017-09-29 03:33:28,900 - MLwithTF - INFO - # 000   Acc Train: 11.72%  Acc Val: 18.66% Loss 33.751575
2017-09-29 03:33:29,295 - MLwithTF - INFO - # 500   Acc Train: 68.75%  Acc Val: 69.35% Loss 1.133016
2017-09-29 03:33:29,683 - MLwithTF - INFO - # 1000  Acc Train: 66.41%  Acc Val: 68.23% Loss 0.997880
2017-09-29 03:33:30,101 - MLwithTF - INFO - # 1500  Acc Train: 77.34%  Acc Val: 75.75% Loss 0.744131
2017-09-29 03:33:30,491 - MLwithTF - INFO - # 2000  Acc Train: 69.53%  Acc Val: 76.69% Loss 1.102222
2017-09-29 03:33:30,897 - MLwithTF - INFO - # 2500  Acc Train: 69.53%  Acc Val: 77.12% Loss 0.942900
2017-09-29 03:33:31,290 - MLwithTF - INFO - # 3000  Acc Train: 80.47%  Acc Val: 77.96% Loss 0.652119
2017-09-29 03:33:31,689 - MLwithTF - INFO - # 3500  Acc Train: 77.34%  Acc Val: 78.18% Loss 0.738713
2017-09-29 03:33:32,088 - MLwithTF - INFO - # 4000  Acc Train: 75.78%  Acc Val: 75.89% Loss 0.811817
2017-09-29 03:33:32,486 - MLwithTF - INFO - # 4500  Acc Train: 76.56%  Acc Val: 71.15% Loss 0.767980
2017-09-29 03:33:32,890 - MLwithTF - INFO - # 5000  Acc Train: 78.91%  Acc Val: 79.68% Loss 0.725805
2017-09-29 03:33:33,291 - MLwithTF - INFO - # 5500  Acc Train: 78.91%  Acc Val: 79.76% Loss 0.720853
2017-09-29 03:33:33,688 - MLwithTF - INFO - # 6000  Acc Train: 81.25%  Acc Val: 79.60% Loss 0.630755
2017-09-29 03:33:34,094 - MLwithTF - INFO - # 6500  Acc Train: 81.25%  Acc Val: 79.94% Loss 0.717576
2017-09-29 03:33:34,483 - MLwithTF - INFO - # 7000  Acc Train: 82.03%  Acc Val: 79.53% Loss 0.730982
2017-09-29 03:33:34,870 - MLwithTF - INFO - # 7500  Acc Train: 82.81%  Acc Val: 80.48% Loss 0.606189
2017-09-29 03:33:35,257 - MLwithTF - INFO - # 8000  Acc Train: 78.91%  Acc Val: 79.64% Loss 0.683653
2017-09-29 03:33:35,647 - MLwithTF - INFO - # 8500  Acc Train: 82.81%  Acc Val: 80.42% Loss 0.643934
2017-09-29 03:33:36,023 - MLwithTF - INFO - # 9000  Acc Train: 83.59%  Acc Val: 80.34% Loss 0.608325
2017-09-29 03:33:36,420 - MLwithTF - INFO - # 9500  Acc Train: 82.81%  Acc Val: 80.38% Loss 0.595343
2017-09-29 03:33:36,820 - MLwithTF - INFO - # 10000  Acc Train: 74.22%  Acc Val: 80.62% Loss 0.943106
2017-09-29 03:33:36,840 - MLwithTF - INFO - Test accuracy: 87.4%
(work2) ubuntu@ubuntu-PC:~/github/mlwithtf/chapter_02$
```

We are running through hundreds of cycles and printing indicative results once every 500 cycles. Of course, you are welcome to modify any of these settings. The important part is to appreciate the cycle:

- We will cycle through the process many times.
- Each time, we will create a mini batch of photos, which is a carve-out of the full image set.
- Each step runs the TensorFlow session and produces a loss and a set of predictions. Each step additionally makes a prediction on the validation set.
- At the end of the iterative cycle, we will make a final prediction on our test set, which is a secret up until now.
- For each prediction made, we will observe our progress in the form of prediction accuracy.

We did not discuss the accuracy method earlier. This method simply compares the predicted labels against known labels to calculate a percentage score:

```
def accuracy(predictions, labels):
    return (100.0 * np.sum(np.argmax(predictions, 1) ==
    np.argmax(labels, 1))
            / predictions.shape[0])
```

Just running the preceding classifier will yield accuracy in the general range of 85%. This is remarkable because we have just begun! There are much more tweaks that we can continue to make.

Saving the model for ongoing use

To save variables from the TensorFlow session for future use, you can use the `Saver()` function, which is as follows:

```
saver = tf.train.Saver()
```

Later, you can retrieve the state of the model and avoid tedious retraining by restoring the following checkpoint:

```
ckpt = tf.train.get_checkpoint_state(FLAGS.checkpoint_dir)
if ckpt and ckpt.model_checkpoint_path:
saver.restore(sess, ckpt.model_checkpoint_path)
```

Why hide the test set?

Notice how we did not use the test set until the last step. Why not? This is a pretty important detail to ensure that the test remains a good one. As we iterate through the training set and nudge our classifier one way or another, we can sometimes *wrap the classifier* around the images or overtrain. This happens when you learn the training set rather than learn the features inside each of the classes.

When we overtrain, our accuracy on the iterative rounds of the training set will look promising, but that is all false hope. Having a never-before-seen test set should introduce reality back into the process. Great accuracy on the training set followed by poor results on the test set suggests overfitting.

This is why we've kept a separate test set. It helps indicate the real accuracy of our classifier. This is also why you should never shuffle your dataset or intermingle the dataset with the test set.

Using the classifier

We will demonstrate the usage of the classifier with `notMNIST_small.tar.gz`, which becomes the test set. For ongoing use of the classifier, you can source your own images and run them through a similar pipeline to test, not train.

You can create some 28x28 images yourself and place them into the test set for evaluation. You will be pleasantly surprised!

The practical issue with field usage is the heterogeneity of images in the wild. You may need to find images, crop them, downscale them, or perform a dozen other transformations. This all falls into the usage pipeline, which we discussed earlier.

Another technique to cover larger images, such as finding a letter on a page-sized image, is to slide a small window across the large image and feed every subsection of the image through the classifier.

We'll be taking our models into production in future chapters but, as a preview, one common setup is to move the trained model into a server on the cloud. The façade of the system might be a smartphone app that takes photos and sends them off for classification behind the scenes. In this case, we will wrap our entire program with a web service to accept incoming classification requests and programmatically respond to them. There are dozens of popular setups and we will explore several of them in `Chapter 9`, *Cruise Control - Automation*.

Deep diving into the network

Notice how we achieved 86% accuracy. This is a great result for two hours of work, but we can do much better. Much of the future potential is in changing the neural network. Our preceding application used a **fully-connected** setup, where each node on a layer is connected to each node on the previous layer and looks like this:

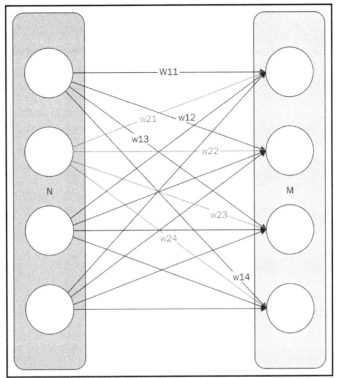

As you will learn with more complex network setups in coming chapters, this setup is fast but not ideal. The biggest issue is the large number of parameters, which can cause overfitting of the model on the training data.

Skills learned

You should have learned these skills in the chapter:

- Preparing training and test data
- Creating a training set consumable by TensorFlow
- Setting up a basic neural network graph
- Training the TensorFlow classifier
- Validating the classifier
- Piping in real-world data

Summary

Superb progress! We just built a handwriting classifier that would have been world class a decade ago. Also, we built an entire pipeline around the process to fully automate the training setup and execution. This means that our program can be migrated to almost any server and continue to function almost turn-key.

3
The TensorFlow Toolbox

Most machine learning platforms are focused toward scientists and practitioners in academic or industrial settings. Accordingly, while quite powerful, they are often rough around the edges and have few user-experience features.

Quite a bit of effort goes into peeking at the model at various stages and viewing and aggregating performance across models and runs. Even viewing the neural network can involve far more effort than expected.

While this was acceptable when neural networks were simple and only a few layers deep, today's networks are far deeper. In 2015, Microsoft won the annual **ImageNet** competition using a deep network with 152 layers. Visualizing such networks can be difficult, and peeking at weights and biases can be overwhelming.

Practitioners started using home-built visualizers and bootstrapped tools to analyze their networks and run performance. TensorFlow changed this by releasing TensorBoard directly alongside their overall platform release. TensorBoard runs out of the box with no additional installations or setup.

Users just need to instrument their code according to what they wish to capture. It features plotting of events, learning rate, and loss over time; histograms, for weights and biases; and images. The Graph Explorer allows interactive reviews of the neural network.

In this chapter, we will focus on several areas, which are as follows:

- We will start with the instrumentation required to feed TensorBoard using four common models and datasets as examples, highlighting the required changes.
- We will then review the data captured and ways to interpret it.
- Finally, we will review common graphs as visualized by Graph Explorer. This will help you visualize common neural network setups, which will be introduced in later chapters and projects. It will also be a visual introduction to common networks.

A quick preview

Without even having TensorFlow installed, you can play with a reference implementation of TensorBoard. You can get started here:

```
https://www.tensorflow.org/tensorboard/index.html#graphs.
```

You can follow along with the code here:

```
https://github.com/tensorflow/tensorflow/blob/master/tensorflow/model
s/image/cifar10/cifar10_train.py.
```

The example uses the **CIFAR-10** image set. The CIFAR-10 dataset consists of 60,000 images in 10 classes compiled by Alex Krizhevsky, Vinod Nair, and Geoffrey Hinton. The dataset has become one of several standard learning tools and benchmarks for machine learning efforts.

Let's start with the Graph Explorer. We can immediately see a convolutional network being used. This is not surprising as we're trying to classify images here:

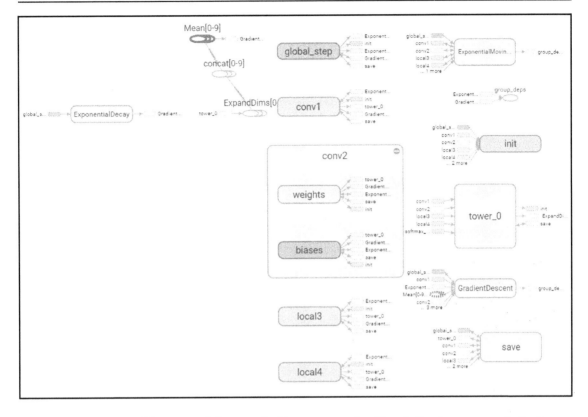

This is just one possible view of the graph. You can try the Graph Explorer as well. It allows deep dives into individual components.

Our next stop on the quick preview is the **EVENTS** tab. This tab shows scalar data over time. The different statistics are grouped into individual tabs on the right-hand side. The following screenshot shows a number of popular scalar statistics, such as loss, learning rate, cross entropy, and sparsity across multiple parts of the network:

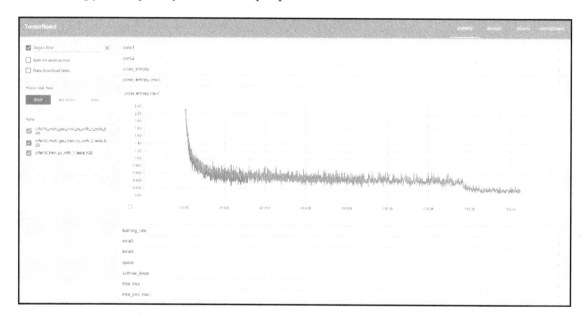

The **HISTOGRAMS** tab is a close cousin as it shows tensor data over time. Despite the name, as of TensorFlow v0.7, it does not actually display histograms. Rather, it shows summaries of tensor data using percentiles.

The summary view is shown in the following figure. Just like with the **EVENTS** tab, the data is grouped into tabs on the right-hand side. Different runs can be toggled on and off and runs can be shown overlaid, allowing interesting comparisons.

It features three runs, which we can see on the left side, and we'll look at just the `softmax` function and associated parameters.

For now, don't worry too much about what these mean, we're just looking at what we can achieve for our own classifiers:

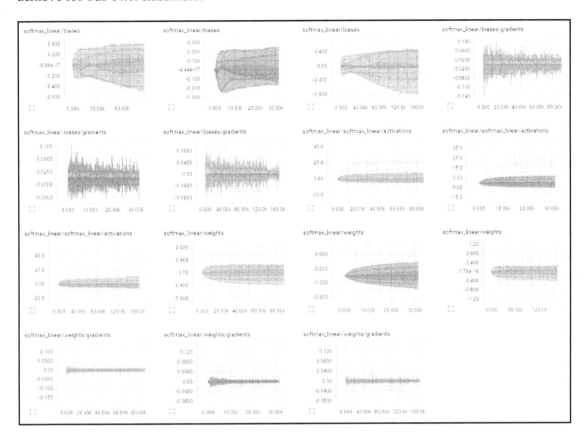

However, the summary view does not do justice to the utility of the **HISTOGRAMS** tab. Instead, we will zoom into a single graph to observe what is going on. This is shown in the following figure:

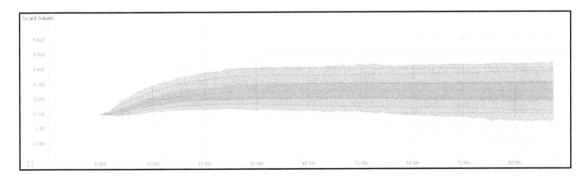

Notice that each histogram chart shows a time series of nine lines. The top is the maximum, in middle the median, and the bottom the minimum. The three lines directly above and below the median are 1½ standard deviation, 1 standard deviation, and ½ standard deviation marks.

Obviously, this does represent multimodal distributions as it is not a histogram. However, it does provide a quick gist of what would otherwise be a mountain of data to shift through.

A couple of things to note are how data can be collected and segregated by runs, how different data streams can be collected, how we can enlarge the views, and how we can zoom into each of the graphs.

Enough of graphics, let's jump into the code so we can run this for ourselves!

Installing TensorBoard

TensorFlow comes prepackaged with TensorBoard, so it will already be installed. It runs as a locally served web application accessible via the browser at `http://0.0.0.0:6006`. Conveniently, there is no server-side code or configurations required.

Depending on where your paths are, you may be able to run it directly, as follows:

```
tensorboard --logdir=/tmp/tensorlogs
```

If your paths are not correct, you may need to prefix the application accordingly, as shown in the following command line:

```
tf_install_dir/ tensorflow/tensorboard --
logdir=/tmp/tensorlogs
```

On Linux, you can run it in the background and just let it keep running, as follows:

```
nohup tensorboard --logdir=/tmp/tensorlogs &
```

Some thought should be put into the directory structure though. The **Runs** list on the left side of the dashboard is driven by subdirectories in the `logdir` location. The following image shows two runs--`MNIST_Run1` and `MNIST_Run2`. Having an organized `runs` folder will allow plotting successive runs side by side to see differences:

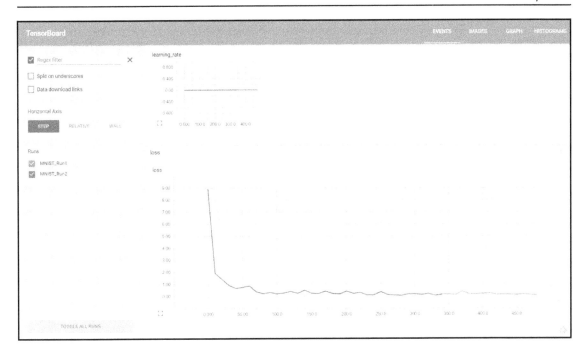

When initializing `writer`, you will pass in the directory for the log as the first parameter, as follows:

```
writer = tf.summary.FileWriter("/tmp/tensorlogs",
sess.graph)
```

Consider saving a base location and appending run-specific subdirectories for each run. This will help organize outputs without expending more thought on it. We'll discuss more about this later.

Incorporating hooks into our code

The best way to get started with TensorBoard is by taking existing working examples and instrument them with the code required for TensorBoard. We will do this for several common training scripts.

Handwritten digits

Let's start with the typical Hello World of machine learning with images--the MNIST handwritten numeral classification exercise.

The MNIST database being used has 60,000 images for training and another 10,000 for testing. It was originally collected by Chris Burges and Corinna Cortes and enhanced by Yann LeCun. You can find out more about the dataset on Yann LeCun's website (http://yann.lecun.com/exdb/mnist/).

TensorFlow conveniently comes with a test script demonstrating a convolutional neural network using the MSNIST handwritten, available at https://github.com/tensorflow/models/blob/master/tutorials/image/mnist/convolutional.py.

Let's modify this script to allow TensorBoard usage. If you wish to peek ahead, download a golden copy or see deltas; our full set of changes is available on the book's GitHub repository (https://github.com/mlwithtf/mlwithtf).

For now, we recommend following along and making changes incrementally to understand the process.

Early on in the main class, we will define holders for convn_weights, convn_biases, and other parameters. Directly afterward, we will write the following code to add them to the histogram:

```
tf.summary.histogram('conv1_weights', conv1_weights)
tf.summary.histogram('conv1_biases', conv1_biases)
tf.summary.histogram('conv2_weights', conv2_weights)
tf.summary.histogram('conv2_biases', conv2_biases)
tf.summary.histogram('fc1_weights', fc1_weights)
tf.summary.histogram('fc1_biases', fc1_biases)
tf.summary.histogram('fc2_weights', fc2_weights)
tf.summary.histogram('fc2_biases', fc2_biases)
```

The preceding lines capture the values for the **HISTOGRAMS** tab. Notice that the captured values form subsections on the **HISTOGRAMS** tab, which is shown in the following screenshot:

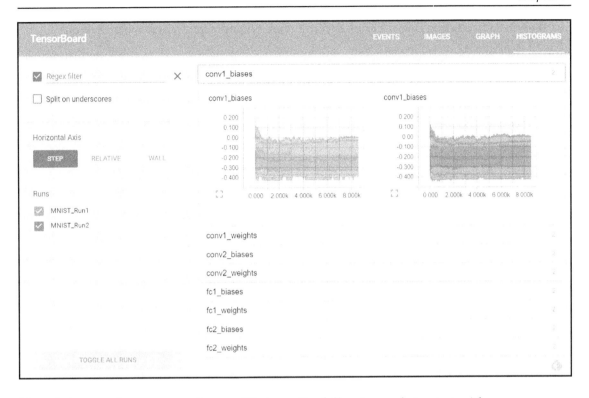

Next, let's record some `loss` figures. We have the following code to start with:

```
loss += 5e-4 * regularizers
```

We will add a `scalar` summary for the `loss` figures after the preceding line:

```
tf.summary.scalar("loss", loss)
```

Similarly, we will start with the standard code calculating the `learning_rate`:

```
learning_rate = tf.train.exponential_decay(
    0.01,  # Base learning rate.
    batch * BATCH_SIZE,  # Current index into the
    dataset.
    train_size,  # Decay step.
    0.95,  # Decay rate.
    staircase=True)
```

We will add a `scalar` summary for the `learning_rate` figures, which is as follows:

```
tf.summary.scalar("learning_rate", learning_rate)
```

Just these two preceding lines help us capture these to important scalar metrics in our **EVENTS** tab:

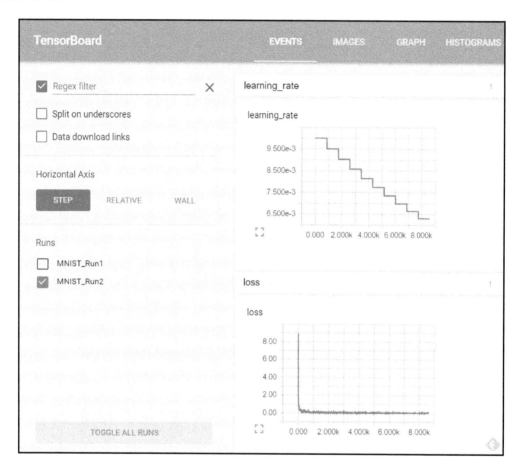

Finally, let's instruct our script to save the graph setup. Let's find the section of the script which creates the `session`:

```
# Create a local session to run the training.
start_time = time.time()
with tf.Session() as sess:
```

Just after defining the `sess` handle, we will capture the graph as follows:

```
writer = tf.summary.FileWriter("/tmp/tensorlogs",
sess.graph)
merged = tf.summary.merge_all()
```

We will need to add our `merged` object when running the session. We originally had the following code:

```
l, lr, predictions = sess.run([loss, learning_rate,
train_prediction], feed_dict=feed_dict)
```

We will add our `merged` object when running the session as such:

```
# Run the graph and fetch some of the nodes.
sum_string, l, lr, predictions = sess.run([merged,
loss,
learning_rate, train_prediction],
feed_dict=feed_dict)
```

Finally, we will need to write summaries at specified steps, much like we typically output validation set accuracy periodically. So, we do add one more line after the `sum_string` is computed:

```
writer.add_summary(sum_string, step)
```

That is all! We have just captured our loss and learning rates, key intermediate parameters on our neural network, and the structure of the graph. We have already examined the **EVENTS** and **HISTOGRAMS** tab, now let's look at the **GRAPH** tab:

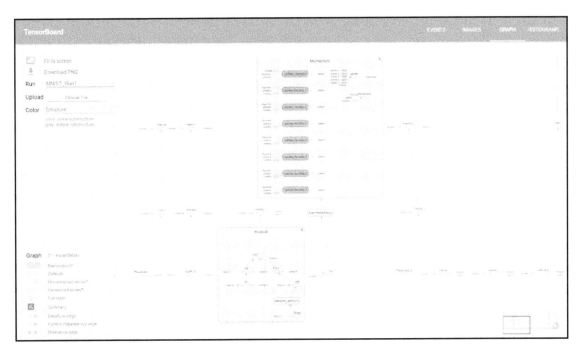

AlexNet

Anyone involved in deep learning with images should become familiar with AlexNet. The network was introduced in the landmark paper, *ImageNet Classification with Deep Convolutional Neural Networks*, by Alex Krizhevsky, Ilya Sutskever, and Geoffrey E. Hinton. The paper can be viewed at `http://www.cs.toronto.edu/~fritz/absps/imagenet.pdf`.

This network architecture achieved then-record accuracy on the annual ImageNet competition. The architecture is described in their paper, as shown in the following image. We will be using this network architecture in later chapters, but for now, let's browse through the network using TensorBoard:

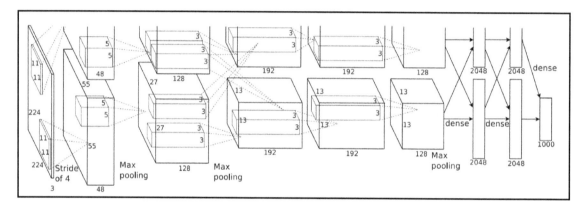

We will not review line-by-line changes to the existing AlexNet code, but the reader can easily see changes by noting differences between the original model code provided by Google and the revised code that we have included with the book's code repository.

The original AlexNet TensorFlow implementation from Google is available at:

`https://github.com/tensorflow/models/blob/master/tutorials/image/alexnet/alexnet_benchmark.py`.

The revised AlexNet TensorFlow implementation with TensorBoard instrumentation can be found at:

`https://github.com/mlwithtf/mlwithtf/blob/master/chapter_03/alexnet_benchmark.py`.

The changes introduced are very similar to those done for our MNIST example.

First, find the location of this code:

```
sess = tf.Session(config=config)
sess.run(init)
```

Then, replace it with the following code:

```
sess = tf.Session(config=config)
writer = tf.summary.FileWriter("/tmp/alexnet_logs",
sess.graph)
sess.run(init)
```

Finally, you can run the Python file `alexnet_benchmark.py` and TensorBoard command to visualize the graph:

```
python alexnet_benchmark.py
tensorboard --logdir /tmp/alexnet_logs
```

Our focus for this section is just the graph. The following figure shows a section of the Graph Explorer. We have deep dived into convolutional layer 3 of 5 and we are looking at weights and biases for this layer.

Clicking on the weights node on the graph is interesting because we see details such as the shape:
`{"shape":{"dim":[{"size":3},{"size":3},{"size":192},{"size":384}]}}`. We can match many of these details right back to the original paper and the previously referenced diagram! We can also trace details back to the network setup in the code:

```
with tf.name_scope('conv3') as scope:
  kernel = tf.Variable(tf.truncated_normal([3, 3, 192, 384],
                            dtype=tf.float32,
                            stddev=1e-1), name='weights')
  conv = tf.nn.conv2d(pool2, kernel, [1, 1, 1, 1],
   padding='SAME')
  biases = tf.Variable(tf.constant(0.0, shape=[384],
   dtype=tf.float32),
                       trainable=True, name='biases')
  bias = tf.nn.bias_add(conv, biases)
  conv3 = tf.nn.relu(bias, name=scope)
  parameters += [kernel, biases]
```

The details in the Graph Explorer and code are equivalent, but the flow of data is very easily visualized using TensorBoard. It is also easy to collapse repetitive sections and expand sections of interest:

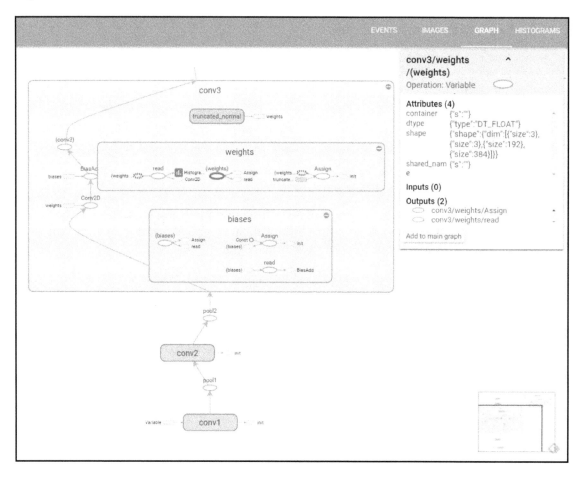

The graph is the most interesting part of this section, but of course, you can also run our revised script and review the training performance, as well as a host of other data we're capturing. You can even capture additional data. Give it a try!

Automating runs

When trying to train a classifier, we will often end up with multiple variables for which we don't know a good setting. Viewing values used by solutions for similar problems is a good starting point. However, we are often left with an array of possible values that we need to test. To make things more complicated, we often have several such parameters, resulting in numerous combinations that we may need to test.

For such situations, we suggest keeping the parameters of interest as values that can be passed into the trainer. Then, a `wrapper` script can pass in various combinations of the parameters, along with a unique output log subdirectory that is possibly tagged with a descriptive name.

This will allow an easy comparison of results and intermediate values across multiple tests. The following figure shows four runs' losses plotted together. We can easily see the underperforming and overperforming pairs:

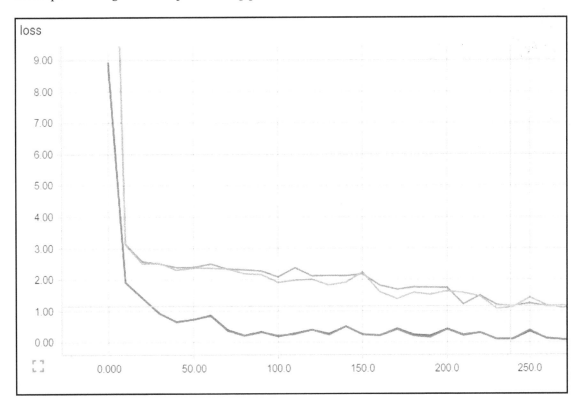

Summary

In this chapter, we covered the major areas of TensorBoard--**EVENTS**, **HISTOGRAMS**, and viewing **GRAPH**. We modified popular models to see the exact changes required before TensorBoard could be up and running. This should have demonstrated the fairly minimal effort required to get started with TensorBoard.

Finally, we focused on various popular models by viewing their network design. We did this by instrumenting the code with TensorBoard hooks and using the TensorBoard Graph Explorer to deep dive into the network setups.

The reader should now be able to use TensorBoard more effectively, gauge training performance, and plan runs and modify training scripts.

Next, we're going to jump into convolutional networks. We'll use parts of our prior work so we can hit the ground running. But, we'll focus on more advanced neural network setups to achieve better accuracy. The focus on training accuracy reflects the focus of most practitioner's efforts, so it is the time we face the challenge.

4
Cats and Dogs

Back in `Chapter 2`, *Your First Classifier*, we constructed a simple neural network for our character recognition effort. We ended the chapter with commendable mid-80% accuracy. Good start, but we can do much better!

In this chapter, we will retrofit our earlier classifier with far more powerful network architecture. Then, we'll delve into a much more difficult problem—handling color images from the CIFAR-10 dataset. The images will be much more difficult (cats, dogs, airplanes, and so on), so we'll bring more powerful tools to the table—specifically, a convolutional neural network. Let's begin.

Revisiting notMNIST

Let's start our effort incrementally by trying the technical changes on the `notMNIST` dataset we used in `Chapter 2`, *Your First Classifier*. You can write the code as you go through the chapter, or work on the book's repository at:

`https://github.com/mlwithtf/mlwithtf/blob/master/chapter_02/training.py.`

We will begin with the following imports:

```
import sys, os
import tensorflow as tf
sys.path.append(os.path.realpath('../..'))
from data_utils import *
from logmanager import *
import math
```

There are not many substantial changes here. The real horsepower is already imported with the `tensorflow` package. You'll notice that we reuse our `data_utils` work from before. However, we'll need some changes there.

The only difference from before is the `math` package, which we will use for ancillary `math` functions, such as `ceiling`.

Program configurations

Now, let's look at our old program configurations, which are as follows:

```
batch_size = 128
num_steps = 10000
learning_rate = 0.3
data_showing_step = 500
```

We will need more configurations this time. Here is what we will use now:

```
batch_size = 32
num_steps = 30000
learning_rate = 0.1
data_showing_step = 500
model_saving_step = 2000
log_location = '/tmp/alex_nn_log'

SEED = 11215

patch_size = 5
depth_inc = 4
num_hidden_inc = 32
dropout_prob = 0.8
conv_layers = 3
stddev = 0.1
```

The first four configurations are familiar:

- We will still train for a certain number of steps (`num_steps`), just as we did earlier. But, you'll notice the number of steps has gone up. They will get even higher because our datasets will be more complex and require more training.
- We will revisit subtleties around the learning rate (`learning_rate`) later, but to start with, you are already familiar with it.
- We will review results intermediately every five hundred steps, which is trivially controlled by the `data_showing_step` variable.

- Finally, `log_location` controls where our TensorBoard logs are dumped. We are quite familiar with this from `Chapter 3`, *The TensorFlow Toolbox*. We will use it again in this chapter but without explanations this time.

The next configuration—the **random seed** (`SEED`) variable - can be helpful. This can be left unset and TensorFlow will randomize numbers on each run. However, having a `seed` variable set, and constant across runs, will allow consistency from run to run as we debug our system. If you do use it, which you should do to start off, you can set it to any number you wish: your birthday, anniversary date, first phone number, or lucky number. I use the ZIP code for my beloved neighborhood. Enjoy the small things.

Finally, we will encounter seven new variables—`batch_size`, `patch_size`, `depth_inc`, `num_hidden_inc`, `conv_layers`, `stddev`, and `dropout_prob`. These are at the heart of how our newer, more advanced **Convolutional neural networks** (**CNNs**) works and will be introduced in context as we explore the network we're using.

Understanding convolutional networks

CNNs are more advanced neural networks specialized for machine learning with images. Unlike the hidden layers we used before, CNNs have some layers that are not fully connected. These convolutional layers have depth in addition to just width and height. The general principle is that an image is analyzed patch by patch. We can visualize the 7x7 patch in the image as follows:

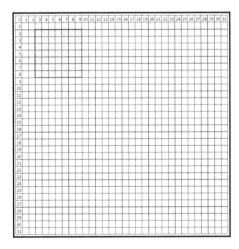

This reflects a 32x32 greyscale image, with a 7x7 patch. Example of sliding the patch from left to right is given as follows:

If this were a color image, we'd be sliding our patch simultaneously over three identical layers.

You probably noticed that we slid the patch over by one pixel. That is a configuration as well; we could have slid more, perhaps by two or even three pixels each time. This is the stride configuration. As you can guess, the larger the stride, the fewer the patches we will end up covering and thus, the smaller the output layer.

Matrix math, which we will not get into here, is performed to reduce the patch (with the full depth driven by the number of channels) into an output depth column. The output is just a single in height and width but many pixels deep. As we will slide the patch across, over, and across iteratively, the sequence of depth columns form a block with a new length, width, and height.

There is another configuration at play here—the padding along the sides of the image. As you can imagine, the more padding you have the more room the patch has to slide and veer off the edge of the image. This allows more strides and thus, a larger length and width for the output volume. You'll see this in the code later as `padding='SAME'` or `padding='VALID'`.

Let's see how these add up. We will first select a patch:

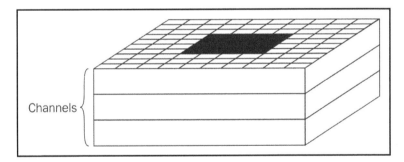

However, the patch is not just the square, but the full depth (for color images):

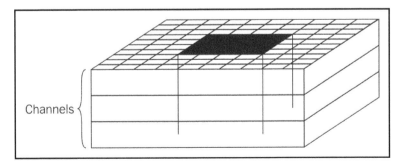

We will then convolve that into a 1x1 volume, but with depth, as shown in the following diagram. The depth of the resulting volume is configurable and we will use `inct_depth` for this configuration in our program:

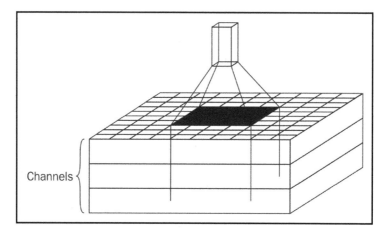

Finally, as we slide the patch across, over, and across again, through the original image, we will produce many such 1x1xN volumes, which itself creates a volume:

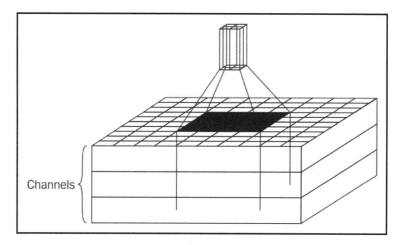

We will then convolve that into a 1x1 volume.

Finally, we will squeeze each layer of the resulting volume using a `POOL` operation. There are many types, but simple **max pooling** is typical:

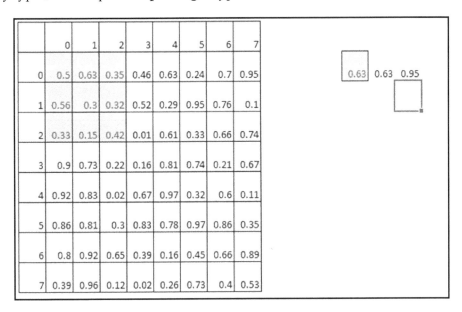

Much like with the sliding patches we used earlier, there will be a patch (except this time, we will take the maximum number of the patch) and a stride (this time, we'll want a larger stride to squeeze the image). We are essentially reducing the size. Here, we will use a 3x3 patch with a stride of 2.

Revisiting configurations

Now that we have been introduced to convolutional neural networks, let's revisit the configurations that we encountered earlier: `batch_size`, `patch_size`, `depth_inc`, `num_hidden_inc`, `conv_layers`, `stddev`, and `dropout_prob`:

- Batch size (`batch_size`)
- Patch size (`patch_size`)
- Depth increment (`depth_inc`)
- Number hidden increment (`num_hidden_inc`)
- Convolutional layers (`conv_layers`)
- Standard deviation (`stddev`)
- Dropout probability (`dropout_prob`)

Constructing the convolutional network

We will skip explanations for the two utility functions, reformat and accuracy, as we've already encountered these in `Chapter 2`, *Your First Classifier*. Instead, we will jump directly to the neural network configuration. For comparison, the following figure shows our model from `Chapter 2`, *Your First Classifier*, and the next figure shows our new model. We'll run the new model on the same `notMNIST` dataset to see the accuracy boost that we will get (hint: good news!):

```python
def nn_model(data, weights, biases):
    layer_fc1 = tf.matmul(data, weights['fc1']) + biases['fc1']
    relu_layer = tf.nn.relu(layer_fc1)
    for relu in range(2, relu_layers + 1):
        relu_layer = tf.nn.relu(relu_layer)
    return tf.matmul(relu_layer, weights['fc2']) + biases['fc2']
```

The following figure is our new model:

First, we will encounter a `helper` function, as follows:

```
def fc_first_layer_dimen(image_size, layers):
    output = image_size
    for x in range(layers):
     output = math.ceil(output/2.0)
    return int(output)
```

Then, we will call it later, as follows:

```
fc_first_layer_dimen(image_size, conv_layers)
```

The `fc_first_layer_dimen` function calculates the dimensions of the first fully connected layer. Recall how CNN's typically use a series of layers with a smaller window layer after layer. Here, we've decided to reduce the dimensions by half for each convolutional layer we used. This also shows why having input images highly divisible by powers of two makes things nice and clean.

Let's now parse the actual network. This is generated using the `nn_model` method and called later when training the model, and again when testing against the validation and test sets.

Recall how CNN's are usually composed of the following layers:

- Convolutional layers
- Rectified linear unit layers
- Pooling layers
- Fully connected layers

The convolutional layers are usually paired with **RELU** layers and repeated. That is what we've done—we've got three nearly identical **CONV-RELU** layers stacked on top of each other.

Each of the paired layers appears as follows:

```
with tf.name_scope('Layer_1') as scope:
    conv = tf.nn.conv2d(data, weights['conv1'], strides=[1, 1,
     1, 1], padding='SAME', name='conv1')
    bias_add = tf.nn.bias_add(conv, biases['conv1'],
     name='bias_add_1')
    relu = tf.nn.relu(bias_add, name='relu_1')
    max_pool = tf.nn.max_pool(relu, ksize=[1, 2, 2, 1],
     strides=[1, 2, 2, 1], padding='SAME', name=scope)
```

The major difference across the three nearly identical layers (`Layer_1`, `Layer_2`, and `Layer_3`) is how the output of one is fed to the next in a series. So, the first layer begins by taking in data (the image data) but the second layer begins by taking in the pooling layer output from the first layer, as follows:

```
conv = tf.nn.conv2d(max_pool, weights['conv2'], strides=[1, 1, 1,
  1], padding='SAME', name='conv2')
```

Similarly, the third layer begins by taking in the pooling layer output from the second layer, as follows:

```
conv = tf.nn.conv2d(max_pool, weights['conv3'], strides=[1, 1, 1,
  1], padding='SAME', name='conv3')
```

There is another major difference across the three CONV-RELU layers, that is, the layers get squeezed. It might help to peek at the `conv` variable after each layer is declared using a couple of `print` statements like this:

```
print "Layer 1 CONV", conv.get_shape()
print "Layer 2 CONV", conv.get_shape()
print "Layer 3 CONV", conv.get_shape()
```

This will reveal the following structures:

```
Layer 1 CONV (32, 28, 28, 4)
Layer 2 CONV (32, 14, 14, 4)
Layer 3 CONV (32, 7, 7, 4)
Layer 1 CONV (10000, 28, 28, 4)
Layer 2 CONV (10000, 14, 14, 4)
Layer 3 CONV (10000, 7, 7, 4)
Layer 1 CONV (10000, 28, 28, 4)
Layer 2 CONV (10000, 14, 14, 4)
Layer 3 CONV (10000, 7, 7, 4)
```

We ran this with the notMNIST dataset, so we will see an original input size of 28x28 to no surprise. More interesting are the sizes of successive layers—14x14 and 7x7. Notice how the filters for successive convolutional layers are squeezed.

Let's make things more interesting and examine the entire stack. Add the following `print` statements to peek at the CONV, RELU, and POOL layers:

```
print "Layer 1 CONV", conv.get_shape()
print "Layer 1 RELU", relu.get_shape()
print "Layer 1 POOL", max_pool.get_shape()
```

Add similar statements after the other two CONV-RELU-POOL stacks and you'll find the following output:

```
Layer 1 CONV (32, 28, 28, 4)
Layer 1 RELU (32, 28, 28, 4)
Layer 1 POOL (32, 14, 14, 4)
Layer 2 CONV (32, 14, 14, 4)
Layer 2 RELU (32, 14, 14, 4)
Layer 2 POOL (32, 7, 7, 4)
Layer 3 CONV (32, 7, 7, 4)
Layer 3 RELU (32, 7, 7, 4)
Layer 3 POOL (32, 4, 4, 4)
...
```

We will ignore the outputs from the validation and test instances (those are the same, except with a height of 10000 instead of 32 as we're processing the validation and test sets rather than a minibatch).

We will see from the outputs how the dimension is squeezed at the POOL layer (28 to 14) and how that squeeze then carries to the next CONV layer. At the third and final POOL layer, we will end up with a 4x4 size.

There is another feature on the final CONV stack—a dropout layer that we will use when training, which is as follows:

```
max_pool = tf.nn.dropout(max_pool, dropout_prob, seed=SEED,
  name='dropout')
```

This layer utilizes the dropout_prob = 0.8 configuration we set earlier. It randomly drops neurons on the layer to prevent overfitting by disallowing nodes from coadapting to neighboring nodes with dropouts; they can never rely on a particular node being present.

Let's proceed through our network. We'll find a fully connected layer followed by a RELU:

```
with tf.name_scope('FC_Layer_1') as scope:
    matmul = tf.matmul(reshape, weights['fc1'],
      name='fc1_matmul')
    bias_add = tf.nn.bias_add(matmul, biases['fc1'],
      name='fc1_bias_add')
    relu = tf.nn.relu(bias_add, name=scope)
```

Finally, we will end with a fully connected layer, as follows:

```
with tf.name_scope('FC_Layer_2') as scope:
    matmul = tf.matmul(relu, weights['fc2'],
      name='fc2_matmul')
    layer_fc2 = tf.nn.bias_add(matmul, biases['fc2'],
      name=scope)
```

This is typical for the convolutional network. Typically, we will end up with a fully connected, RELU layer and finally a fully connected layer that holds scores for each class.

We skipped some details along the way. Most of our layers were initialized with three other values—weights, biases, and strides:

```
weights = {
    'conv1': tf.Variable(tf.truncated_normal(shape=[patch_size, patch_size, num_channels, depth_inc], dtype=tf.float32,
                        stddev=stddev, seed=SEED), name='weights_conv1'),
    'conv2': tf.Variable(tf.truncated_normal([patch_size, patch_size, depth_inc, depth_inc], dtype=tf.float32,
                        stddev=stddev, seed=SEED), name='weights_conv2'),
    'conv3': tf.Variable(tf.truncated_normal([patch_size, patch_size, depth_inc, depth_inc], dtype=tf.float32,
                        stddev=stddev, seed=SEED), name='weights_conv3'),
    'fc1': tf.Variable(tf.truncated_normal([(fc_first_layer_dimen(image_size, conv_layers) ** 2) * depth_inc,
                        num_hidden_inc], dtype=tf.float32,
                        stddev=stddev, seed=SEED), name='weights_fc1'),
    'fc2': tf.Variable(tf.truncated_normal([num_hidden_inc, num_of_classes], dtype=tf.float32,
                        stddev=stddev, seed=SEED), name='weights_fc2')
}
biases = {
    'conv1': tf.Variable(tf.zeros(shape=[depth_inc], dtype=tf.float32, name='biases_conv1'),
    'conv2': tf.Variable(tf.zeros(shape=[depth_inc], dtype=tf.float32, name='biases_conv2'),
    'conv3': tf.Variable(tf.zeros(shape=[depth_inc], dtype=tf.float32, name='biases_conv3'),
    'fc1': tf.Variable(tf.zeros(shape=[num_hidden_inc], dtype=tf.float32, name='biases_fc1'),
    'fc2': tf.Variable(tf.zeros(shape=[num_of_classes], dtype=tf.float32, name='biases_fc2'),
}
```

The weights and biases are themselves initialized with other variables. I didn't say this will be easy.

The most important variable here is patch_size, which denotes the size of the filter we slide across the image. Recall that we set this to 5 early on, so we will use 5x5 patches. We will also get reintroduced to the stddev and depth_inc configurations that we set up earlier.

Fulfilment

Likely, by now, you must have many questions running through your mind—why three convolutional layers rather than two or four? Why a stride of one? Why a patch size of five? Why end up with fully connected layers rather than start with them?

There is some method to the madness here. At the core, CNN's are built around image processing and patches are built around the features being sought. Why some configurations work well while others do not is not fully understood, though general rules do follow intuition. The exact network architectures are discovered, honed, and increasingly inch toward perfection through thousands of trials and many errors. It continues to be a research-grade task.

The practitioner's general approach is often to find a well working, existing architecture (for example, AlexNet, GoogLeNet, ResNet) and tweak them for use with a specific dataset. That is what we did; we started with AlexNet and tweaked it. Perhaps, that is not fulfilling, but it works and remains the state of practice in 2016.

Training day

It will be more fulfilling, however, to see our training in action and how we will improve upon what we did earlier.

We will prepare the training dataset and labels as follows:

```
tf_train_dataset = tf.placeholder(tf.float32,
shape=(batch_size, image_size, image_size,
num_channels),
name='TRAIN_DATASET')
tf_train_labels = tf.placeholder(tf.float32,
shape=(batch_size, num_of_classes),
name='TRAIN_LABEL')
tf_valid_dataset = tf.constant(dataset.valid_dataset,
name='VALID_DATASET')
tf_test_dataset = tf.constant(dataset.test_dataset,
name='TEST_DATASET')
```

Then, we will run the trainer, as follows:

```
# Training computation.
logits = nn_model(tf_train_dataset, weights, biases,
True)
loss = tf.reduce_mean(
    tf.nn.softmax_cross_entropy_with_logits(logits,
    tf_train_labels))
# L2 regularization for the fully connected
parameters.
regularizers = (tf.nn.l2_loss(weights['fc1']) +
 tf.nn.l2_loss(biases['fc1']) +
 tf.nn.l2_loss(weights['fc2']) +
```

```
tf.nn.l2_loss(biases['fc2']))
# Add the regularization term to the loss.
loss += 5e-4 * regularizers
tf.summary.scalar("loss", loss)
```

This is very similar to what we did in `Chapter 2`, *Your First Classifier*. We instantiated the network, passed in an initial set of weights and biases, and defined a `loss` function using the training labels. Our optimizer is then defined to minimize that `loss`, as follows:

```
optimizer = tf.train.GradientDescentOptimizer
  (learning_rate).minimize(loss)
```

We will then use the `weights` and `biases` to predict labels for the validation and, eventually, the training set:

```
train_prediction = tf.nn.softmax(nn_model(tf_train_dataset,
weights, biases, TRAIN=False))
valid_prediction = tf.nn.softmax(nn_model(tf_valid_dataset,
 weights, biases))     test_prediction =
 tf.nn.softmax(nn_model(tf_test_dataset,
 weights, biases))
```

The complete code for training session is as follows:

```
with tf.Session(graph=graph) as session:
    writer = tf.summary.FileWriter(log_location, session.graph)
    merged = tf.summary.merge_all()
    tf.global_variables_initializer().run()
    print("Initialized")
    for step in range(num_steps + 1):
        sys.stdout.write('Training on batch %d of %d\r' % (step + 1, num_steps))
        sys.stdout.flush()
        # Pick an offset within the training data, which has been randomized.
        # Note: we could use better randomization across epochs.
        offset = (step * batch_size) % (dataset.train_labels.shape[0] - batch_size)
        # Generate a minibatch.
        batch_data = dataset.train_dataset[offset:(offset + batch_size), :]
        batch_labels = dataset.train_labels[offset:(offset + batch_size), :]
        # Prepare a dictionary telling the session where to feed the minibatch.
        # The key of the dictionary is the placeholder node of the graph to be fed,
        # and the value is the numpy array to feed to it.
        feed_dict = {tf_train_dataset: batch_data, tf_train_labels: batch_labels}
        summary_result, _, l, predictions = session.run([merged, optimizer, loss, train_prediction], feed_dict=feed_dict)
        writer.add_summary(summary_result, step)

        if step % data_showing_step == 0:
            acc_minibatch = accuracy(predictions, batch_labels)
            acc_val = accuracy(valid_prediction.eval(), dataset.valid_labels)
            logmanager.logger.info('# %03d  Acc Train: %03.2f%%  Acc Val: %03.2f%% Loss %f' % (
                step, acc_minibatch, acc_val, l))

    logmanager.logger.info("Test accuracy: %.1f%%" % accuracy(test_prediction.eval(), dataset.test_labels))
```

Finally, we will run the session. We will use the `num_steps` variable that we set earlier and run through the training data in chunks (`batch_size`.) We will load small chunks of the training data and associated labels, and run the session as follows:

```
batch_data = dataset.train_dataset[offset:(offset +
  batch_size), :]
batch_labels = dataset.train_labels[offset:
  (offset +
  batch_size), :]
```

We will get back predictions on the minibatch, which we will compare against the actual labels to get accuracy on the minibatch.

We will use the following `valid_prediction` that we declared earlier:

```
valid_prediction =
tf.nn.softmax(nn_model(tf_valid_dataset,
  weights, biases))
```

Then, we will evaluate the validation set predictions against the actual labels we know, as follows:

```
accuracy(valid_prediction.eval(),
dataset.valid_labels)
```

After we've run through all the steps, we will do the same in our test set:

```
accuracy(test_prediction.eval(), dataset.test_labels)
```

As you can see the actual execution of the training, validation, and test was not that different from before. What is different from before is the accuracy. Notice that we've broken out of the 80s into the 90s on test set accuracy:

```
2017-09-29 03:32:05,861 - MLwithTF - INFO - # 19500  Acc Train: 90.62%  Acc Val: 87.45% Loss 0.319119
2017-09-29 03:32:06,640 - MLwithTF - INFO - # 20000  Acc Train: 93.75%  Acc Val: 87.41% Loss 0.305260
2017-09-29 03:32:07,419 - MLwithTF - INFO - # 20500  Acc Train: 90.62%  Acc Val: 86.87% Loss 0.331279
2017-09-29 03:32:08,204 - MLwithTF - INFO - # 21000  Acc Train: 84.38%  Acc Val: 87.38% Loss 0.532096
2017-09-29 03:32:08,986 - MLwithTF - INFO - # 21500  Acc Train: 87.50%  Acc Val: 86.88% Loss 0.557634
2017-09-29 03:32:09,766 - MLwithTF - INFO - # 22000  Acc Train: 84.38%  Acc Val: 87.15% Loss 0.726978
2017-09-29 03:32:10,549 - MLwithTF - INFO - # 22500  Acc Train: 81.25%  Acc Val: 86.67% Loss 0.871303
2017-09-29 03:32:11,323 - MLwithTF - INFO - # 23000  Acc Train: 81.25%  Acc Val: 87.54% Loss 0.698311
2017-09-29 03:32:12,104 - MLwithTF - INFO - # 23500  Acc Train: 81.25%  Acc Val: 87.44% Loss 0.543187
2017-09-29 03:32:12,883 - MLwithTF - INFO - # 24000  Acc Train: 87.50%  Acc Val: 87.81% Loss 0.501370
2017-09-29 03:32:13,661 - MLwithTF - INFO - # 24500  Acc Train: 93.75%  Acc Val: 87.22% Loss 0.329258
2017-09-29 03:32:14,441 - MLwithTF - INFO - # 25000  Acc Train: 90.62%  Acc Val: 87.72% Loss 0.281238
2017-09-29 03:32:15,223 - MLwithTF - INFO - # 25500  Acc Train: 78.12%  Acc Val: 87.40% Loss 0.863225
2017-09-29 03:32:16,003 - MLwithTF - INFO - # 26000  Acc Train: 90.62%  Acc Val: 87.01% Loss 0.585005
2017-09-29 03:32:16,782 - MLwithTF - INFO - # 26500  Acc Train: 93.75%  Acc Val: 87.41% Loss 0.243985
2017-09-29 03:32:17,563 - MLwithTF - INFO - # 27000  Acc Train: 96.88%  Acc Val: 87.24% Loss 0.258554
2017-09-29 03:32:18,340 - MLwithTF - INFO - # 27500  Acc Train: 84.38%  Acc Val: 87.59% Loss 0.757773
2017-09-29 03:32:19,118 - MLwithTF - INFO - # 28000  Acc Train: 84.38%  Acc Val: 87.34% Loss 0.543425
2017-09-29 03:32:19,903 - MLwithTF - INFO - # 28500  Acc Train: 93.75%  Acc Val: 87.57% Loss 0.428805
2017-09-29 03:32:20,690 - MLwithTF - INFO - # 29000  Acc Train: 87.50%  Acc Val: 87.22% Loss 0.393010
2017-09-29 03:32:21,479 - MLwithTF - INFO - # 29500  Acc Train: 84.38%  Acc Val: 87.82% Loss 0.402495
2017-09-29 03:32:22,284 - MLwithTF - INFO - # 30000  Acc Train: 90.62%  Acc Val: 87.75% Loss 0.379222
2017-09-29 03:32:22,288 - MLwithTF - INFO - Test accuracy: 93.5%
(work2) ubuntu@ubuntu-PC:~/github/mlwithtf/chapter_04$
```

Actual cats and dogs

We've demonstrated our new tools on the `notMNIST` dataset, which was helpful as it served to provide a comparison to our earlier simpler network setup. Now, let's progress to a more difficult problem—actual cats and dogs.

We'll utilize the CIFAR-10 dataset. There will be more than just cats and dogs, there are 10 classes—airplanes, automobiles, birds, cats, deer, dogs, frogs, horses, ships, and trucks. Unlike the `notMNIST` set, there are two major complexities, which are as follows:

- There is far more heterogeneity in the photos, including background scenes
- The photos are color

We have not worked with color datasets before. Luckily, it is not that different from the usual black and white dataset—we will just add another dimension. Recall that our previous 28x28 images were flat matrices. Now, we'll have 32x32x3 matrices - the extra dimension represents a layer for each red, green, and blue channels. This does make visualizing the dataset more difficult, as stacking up images will go into a fourth dimension. So, our training/validation/test sets will now be 32x32x3xSET_SIZE in dimension. We'll just need to get used to having matrices that we cannot visualize in our familiar 3D space.

The mechanics of the color dimension are the same though. Just as we had floating point numbers representing shades of grey earlier, we will now have floating point numbers representing shades of red, green, and blue.

Recall how we loaded the `notMNIST` dataset:

```
dataset, image_size, num_of_classes, num_channels =
 prepare_not_mnist_dataset()
```

The `num_channels` variable dictated the color channels. It was just one until now.

We'll load the CIFAR-10 set similarly, except this time, we'll have three channels returned, as follows:

```
dataset, image_size, num_of_classes, num_channels =
 prepare_cifar_10_dataset()
```

Not reinventing the wheel.

Recall how we automated the dataset grab, extraction, and preparation for our `notMNIST` dataset in `Chapter 2`, *Your First Classifier*? We put those pipeline functions into the `data_utils.py` file to separate our pipeline code from our actual machine learning code. Having that clean separation and maintaining clean, generic functions allows us to reuse those for our current project.

In particular, we will reuse nine of those functions, which are as follows:

- download_hook_function
- download_file
- extract_file
- load_class
- make_pickles
- randomize
- make_arrays
- merge_datasets
- pickle_whole

Recall how we used those functions inside an overarching function, prepare_not_mnist_dataset, which ran the entire pipeline for us. We just reused that function earlier, saving ourselves quite a bit of time.

Let's create an analogous function for the CIFAR-10 set. In general, you should save your own pipeline functions, try to generalize them, isolate them into a single module, and reuse them across projects. As you do your own projects, this will help you focus on the key machine learning efforts rather than spending time on rebuilding pipelines.

Notice the revised version of data_utils.py; we have an overarching function called prepare_cifar_10_dataset that isolates the dataset details and pipelines for this new dataset, which is as follows:

```
def prepare_cifar_10_dataset():
    print('Started preparing CIFAR-10 dataset')
    image_size = 32
    image_depth = 255
    cifar_dataset_url = 'https://www.cs.toronto.edu/~kriz/cifar-
      10-python.tar.gz'
    dataset_size = 170498071
    train_size = 45000
    valid_size = 5000
    test_size = 10000
    num_of_classes = 10
    num_of_channels = 3
    pickle_batch_size = 10000
```

Here is a quick overview of the preceding code:

- We will grab the dataset from Alex Krizhevsky's site at the University of Toronto using `cifar_dataset_url = 'https://www.cs.toronto.edu/~kriz/cifar-10-python.tar.gz'`
- We will use `dataset_size = 170498071` to validate whether we've received the file successfully, rather than some truncated half download
- We will also declare some details based on our knowledge of the dataset
- We will segment our set of 60,000 images into training, validation, and test sets of `45000`, `5000`, and `10000` images respectively
- There are ten classes of images, so we have `num_of_classes = 10`
- These are color images with red, green, and blue channels, so we have `num_of_channels = 3`
- We will know the images are 32x32 pixels, so we have `image_size = 32` that we'll use for both width and height
- Finally, we will know the images are 8-bit on each channel, so we have `image_depth = 255`
- The data will end up at `/datasets/CIFAR-10/`

Much like we did with the `notMNIST` dataset, we will download the dataset only if we don't already have it. We will unarchive the dataset, do the requisite transformations, and save preprocessed matrices as pickles using `pickle_cifar_10`. If we find the `pickle` files, we can reload intermediate data using the `load_cifar_10_from_pickles` method.

The following are the three helper methods that we will use to keep the complexity of the main method manageable:

- `pickle_cifar_10`
- `load_cifar_10_from_pickles`
- `load_cifar_10_pickle`

The functions are defined as follows:

```python
def load_cifar_10_pickle(pickle_file, image_depth):
    fo = open(pickle_file, 'rb')
    dict = pickle.load(fo)
    fo.close()
    return ((dict['data'].astype(float) - image_depth / 2) / (image_depth)), dict['labels']


def load_cifar_10_from_pickles(train_pickle_files, test_pickle_files, pickle_batch_size, image_size, image_depth,
                               num_of_channels):
    all_train_data = np.ndarray(shape=(pickle_batch_size * len(train_pickle_files),
                                       image_size * image_size * num_of_channels),
                                dtype=np.float32)

    all_train_labels = np.ndarray(shape=pickle_batch_size * len(train_pickle_files), dtype=object)

    all_test_data = np.ndarray(shape=(pickle_batch_size * len(test_pickle_files),
                                      image_size * image_size * num_of_channels),
                               dtype=np.float32)
    all_test_labels = np.ndarray(shape=pickle_batch_size * len(test_pickle_files), dtype=object)

    print('Started loading training data')
    for index, train_pickle_file in enumerate(train_pickle_files):
        all_train_data[index * pickle_batch_size: (index + 1) * pickle_batch_size, :], \
        all_train_labels[index * pickle_batch_size: (index + 1) * pickle_batch_size] = \
            load_cifar_10_pickle(train_pickle_file, image_depth)
    print('Finished loading training data\n')

    print('Started loading testing data')
    for index, test_pickle_file in enumerate(test_pickle_files):
        all_test_data[index * pickle_batch_size: (index + 1) * pickle_batch_size, :], \
        all_test_labels[index * pickle_batch_size: (index + 1) * pickle_batch_size] = \
            load_cifar_10_pickle(test_pickle_file, image_depth)
    print('Finished loading testing data')

    return all_train_data, all_train_labels, all_test_data, all_test_labels
```

The `load_cifar_10_pickle` method allocates numpy arrays to train and test data and labels as well as load existing pickle files into these arrays. As we will need to do everything twice, we will isolate the `load_cifar_10_pickle` method, which actually loads the data and zero-centers it:

```python
def pickle_cifar_10(all_train_data, all_train_labels, all_test_data, all_test_labels,
                    train_size, valid_size, test_size, output_file_path, FORCE=False):

    if os.path.isfile(output_file_path) and not FORCE:
        print('Pickle file: %s already exist' % output_file_path)

        with open(output_file_path, 'rb') as f:
            save = pickle.load(f)
            train_dataset = save['train_dataset']
            train_labels = save['train_labels']
            valid_dataset = save['valid_dataset']
            valid_labels = save['valid_labels']
            test_dataset = save['test_dataset']
            test_labels = save['test_labels']
            del save  # hint to help gc free up memory
            print('Training set', train_dataset.shape, train_labels.shape)
            print('Validation set', valid_dataset.shape, valid_labels.shape)
            print('Test set', test_dataset.shape, test_labels.shape)

        return train_dataset, train_labels, valid_dataset, valid_labels, test_dataset, test_labels
    else:
        train_dataset = all_train_data[0:train_size]
        train_labels = all_train_labels[0:train_size]
        valid_dataset = all_train_data[train_size:train_size + valid_size]
        valid_labels = all_train_labels[train_size:train_size + valid_size]
        test_dataset = all_test_data[0:test_size]
        test_labels = all_test_labels[0:test_size]

        try:
            f = open(output_file_path, 'wb')
            save = {
                'train_dataset': train_dataset,
                'train_labels': train_labels,
                'valid_dataset': valid_dataset,
                'valid_labels': valid_labels,
                'test_dataset': test_dataset,
                'test_labels': test_labels,
            }
            pickle.dump(save, f, pickle.HIGHEST_PROTOCOL)
            f.close()
        except Exception as e:
            print('Unable to save data to', output_file_path, ':', e)
            raise

        statinfo = os.stat(output_file_path)
        print('Compressed pickle size:', statinfo.st_size)

    return train_dataset, train_labels, valid_dataset, valid_labels, test_dataset, test_labels
```

Much like earlier, we will check to see if the `pickle` files exist already and if so, load them. Only if they don't exist (the `else` clause), we actually save `pickle` files with the data we've prepared.

Saving the model for ongoing use

To save variables from the tensor flow session for future use, you can use the `Saver()` function. Let's start by creating a `saver` variable right after the `writer` variable:

```
writer = tf.summary.FileWriter(log_location, session.graph)
saver = tf.train.Saver(max_to_keep=5)
```

Then, in the training loop, we will add the following code to save the model after every `model_saving_step`:

```
if step % model_saving_step == 0 or step == num_steps + 1:
  path = saver.save(session, os.path.join(log_location,
"model.ckpt"), global_step=step)
    logmanager.logger.info('Model saved in file: %s' % path)
```

After that, whenever we want to restore the model using the `saved` model, we can easily create a new `Saver()` instance and use the `restore` function as follows:

```
checkpoint_path = tf.train.latest_checkpoint(log_location)
restorer = tf.train.Saver()
with tf.Session() as sess:
    sess.run(tf.global_variables_initializer())
    restorer.restore(sess, checkpoint_path)
```

In the preceding code, we use the `tf.train.latest_checkpoint` so that TensorFlow will automatically choose the latest model checkpoint. Then, we create a new `Saver` instance named restore. Finally, we can use the `restore` function to load the `saved` model to the session graph:

```
restorer.restore(sess, checkpoint_path)
```

You should note that we must restore after we run the `tf.global_variables_initializer`. Otherwise, the loaded variables will be overridden by the initializer.

Using the classifier

Now that we've enhanced the classifier to load random images, we'll start with choosing these random images with the exact size and shape of our training/testing images. We'll need to add placeholders for these user-provided images, so we'll add the following lines in the appropriate locations:

```
tf_random_dataset = tf.placeholder(tf.float32, shape=(1,
  image_size, image_size, num_channels),
name='RANDOM_DATA') random_prediction =
tf.nn.softmax(nn_model(tf_random_dataset,
  weights, biases))
```

Next, we will grab the image provided by the user via the following command-line parameter and run our session on the image:

```python
if (evaluateFile is not None):
    image = (ndimage.imread(evaluateFile).astype(float) - 255 / 2) / 255
    image = image.reshape((image_size, image_size, num_channels)).astype(np.float32)
    random_data = np.ndarray((1, image_size, image_size, num_channels), dtype=np.float32)
    random_data[0, :, :, :] = image

    feed_dict = {tf_random_dataset: random_data}
    output = session.run(
        [random_prediction], feed_dict=feed_dict)

    for i, smx in enumerate(output):
        prediction = smx[0].argmax(axis=0)
        print 'The prediction is: %d' % (prediction)
```

We will follow almost the exact sequence as we did earlier. Running a test file through the script using the -e switch will yield an extra output, as follows:

```
The prediction is: 2
```

Voila! We just classified an arbitrary image.

Skills learned

You should have learned these skills in the chapter:

- Preparing more advanced color training and test data
- Setting up a convolutional neural network graph
- Parameters and configurations associated with CNN's
- Creating a full system including hooks for TensorBoard
- Piping in real-world data

Summary

Excellent! We just built a much more advanced classifier, swapped in and out models, and even started applying our classifier to arbitrary models. True to our chapter's name, we've also trained our system to differentiate cats and dogs.

In the next chapter, we will start working with sequence-to-sequence models and write an English to French translator with TensorFlow.

5
Sequence to Sequence Models- Parlez-vous Français?

Thus far, much of our work was with images. Working with images is helpful as the results are almost uncanny in how quickly and succinctly progress can be made. However, the world of machine learning is broader and the next several chapters will cover these other aspects. We will start with sequence-to-sequence models. The results are just as uncanny, though the setup is a bit more involved and training datasets are much larger.

In this chapter, we will focus on several areas, which are as follows:

- Understanding how sequence-to-sequence models work
- Understanding the setup required to feed a sequence-to-sequence model
- Writing an English to French translator using sequence-to-sequence models

A quick preview

Yes, you read that correctly...we will be writing an English to French translator. The pre-machine learning world might have approached this with a series of parsers and rules on how to translate words and phrases to others, but our approach will be far more elegant, generalizable, and quick. We will just use examples, many examples, to train our translator.

The game here will be finding a dataset with enough English sentences translated into French (actually, it will work in any language). Translated essays and news articles will not be as helpful as we won't necessarily be able to place specific sentences from one language to another side by side. So, we will need to be more creative. Fortunately, organizations such as the United Nations often need to do exactly this—they need to do line by line translations to meet the needs of their diverse constituencies. How convenient for us!

The *Workshop on Statistical Machine Translation* had a conference in 2010 that released a nice packaged training set, which can be used. The full details are available at
`http://www.statmt.org/wmt10/`.

We will be using specific files just for French, as follows:

- `http://www.statmt.org/wmt10/training-giga-fren.tar`
- `http://www.statmt.org/wmt15/dev-v2.tgz`

The following is an excerpt of what the source data looks like on the English side:

- Food, where European inflation slipped up
- The skyward zoom in food prices is the dominant force behind the speed up in eurozone inflation
- November price hikes were higher than expected in the 13 eurozone countries, with October's 2.6 percent yr/yr inflation rate followed by 3.1 percent in November, the EU's Luxembourg-based statistical office reported
- Official forecasts predicted just three percent, Bloomberg said
- As opposed to the US, UK, and Canadian central banks, the **European Central Bank** (**ECB**) did not cut interest rates, arguing that a rate drop combined with rising raw material prices and declining unemployment would trigger an inflationary spiral
- The ECB wants to hold inflation to under two percent, or somewhere in that vicinity
- According to one analyst, ECB has been caught in a Catch-22, and it needs to **talk down** inflation, to keep from having to take action to push it down later in the game

And, here is the French equivalent:

- L'inflation, en Europe, a dérapé sur l'alimentation
- L'inflation accélérée, mesurée dans la zone euro, est due principalement à l'augmentation rapide des prix de l'alimentation
- En novembre, l'augmentation des prix, dans les 13 pays de la zone euro, a été plus importante par rapport aux prévisions, après un taux d'inflation de 2,6 pour cent en octobre, une inflation annuelle de 3,1 pour cent a été enregistrée, a indiqué le bureau des statistiques de la Communauté Européenne situé à Luxembourg
- Les prévisions officielles n'ont indiqué que 3 pour cent, a communiqué Bloomberg
- Contrairement aux banques centrales américaine, britannique et canadienne, la Banque centrale européenne (BCE) n'a pas baissé le taux d'intérêt directeur en disant que la diminution des intérêts, avec la croissance des prix des matières premières et la baisse du taux de chômage, conduirait à la génération d'une spirale inflationniste
- La BCE souhaiterait maintenir le taux d'inflation au-dessous mais proche de deux pour cent
- Selon un analyste, c'est le Catch 22 pour la BCE-: "il faut dissuader" l'inflation afin de ne plus avoir à intervenir sur ce sujet ultérieurement

It is usually good to do a quick sanity check, when possible, to ensure that the files do actually line up. We can see the `Catch 22` phrase on line 7 of both files, which gives us comfort.

Of course, 7 lines are far from sufficient for a statistical approach. We will achieve an elegant, generalizable solution only with mounds of data. And the mounds of data we will get for our training set will consist of 20 gigabytes of text, translated line by line very much like the preceding excerpts.

Just as we did with images, we'll use subsets for training, validation, and testing. We will also define a loss function and attempt to minimize that loss. Let's start with the data though.

Drinking from the firehose

As you did earlier, you should grab the code from `https://github.com/mlwithtf/MLwithTF/`.

We will be focusing on the `chapter_05` subfolder that has the following three files:

- `data_utils.py`
- `translate.py`
- `seq2seq_model.py`

The first file handles our data, so let's start with that. The `prepare_wmt_dataset` function handles that. It is fairly similar to how we grabbed image datasets in the past, except now we're grabbing two data subsets:

- `giga-fren.release2.fr.gz`
- `giga-fren.release2.en.gz`

Of course, these are the two languages we want to focus on. The beauty of our soon-to-be-built translator will be that the approach is entirely generalizable, so we can just as easily create a translator for, say, German or Spanish.

The following screenshot is the specific subset of code:

```python
def prepare_wmt_dataset(tokenizer=None):
    vocab_size = 40000

    # URLs for WMT data.
    _WMT_ENFR_TRAIN_URL = "http://www.statmt.org/wmt10/training-giga-fren.tar"
    _WMT_ENFR_DEV_URL = "http://www.statmt.org/wmt15/dev-v2.tgz"

    # Expected number of bytes for the above two file downloads
    _WMT_ENFR_TRAIN_SIZE = 2595102720
    _WMT_ENFR_DEV_SIZE = 21393583

    train_file_path = download_file(_WMT_ENFR_TRAIN_URL,
                                    os.path.realpath('../datasets/WMT'), _WMT_ENFR_TRAIN_SIZE)

    dev_file_path = download_file(_WMT_ENFR_DEV_URL,
                                  os.path.realpath('../datasets/WMT'), _WMT_ENFR_DEV_SIZE)

    train_extracted_folder = extract_file(train_file_path, os.path.realpath('../datasets/WMT/train'), IS_SUB=False)
    dev_extracted_folder = extract_file(dev_file_path, os.path.realpath('../datasets/WMT'), IS_SUB=False,
                                        FORCE=True)

    train_sub_gzip_files = ['giga-fren.release2.fixed.fr.gz', 'giga-fren.release2.fixed.en.gz']
    train_sub_gzip_files = [train_extracted_folder + '/' + x for x in train_sub_gzip_files]

    if not os.path.exists(train_extracted_folder + '/data'):
        os.makedirs(train_extracted_folder + '/data')

    train_sub_extracted_files = [None] * 2
    for index, train_sub_gzip_file in enumerate(train_sub_gzip_files):
        train_sub_extracted_files[index] = extract_file(train_sub_gzip_file,
                                                        train_extracted_folder + '/data/' +
                                                        train_sub_gzip_file.split('/')[-1].split('.gz')[0],
                                                        TYPE='gz',
                                                        IS_SUB=False)
```

Next, we will run through the two files of interest from earlier line by line and do two things—create vocabularies and tokenize the individual words. These are done with the `create_vocabulary` and `data_to_token_ids` functions, which we will get to in a moment. For now, let's observe how to create the vocabulary and tokenize on our massive training set as well as a small development set, `newstest2013.fr` and `dev/newstest2013.en`:

```python
vocab_paths = [None] * 2
token_paths = [None] * 2

# Create vocabularies of the appropriate sizes and tokenizing the vocabulary
for index, train_sub_extracted_file in enumerate(train_sub_extracted_files):
    type = train_sub_extracted_file.split('.')[-1]
    vocab_paths[index] = "%s%s.%s" % (train_extracted_folder + '/data/', 'vocab%d' % vocab_size, type)
    token_paths[index] = "%s%s.%s" % (train_extracted_folder + '/data/', 'token%d' % vocab_size, type)
    create_vocabulary(vocab_paths[index], train_sub_extracted_files[index], vocab_size, tokenizer)
    data_to_token_ids(train_sub_extracted_files[index], token_paths[index], vocab_paths[index], tokenizer)

dev_sub_required_files = ['dev/newstest2013.fr', 'dev/newstest2013.en']
dev_sub_required_files = [dev_extracted_folder + '/' + x for x in dev_sub_required_files]

if not os.path.exists(dev_extracted_folder + '/dev/data'):
    os.makedirs(dev_extracted_folder + '/dev/data')

dev_token_paths = [None] * 2
for index, dev_sub_required_file in enumerate(dev_sub_required_files):
    type = dev_sub_required_file.split('.')[-1]
    dev_token_paths[index] = "%s%s.%s" % (dev_extracted_folder + '/dev/data/', 'token%d' % vocab_size, type)
    data_to_token_ids(dev_sub_required_files[index], dev_token_paths[index], vocab_paths[index], tokenizer)

def wmt(): pass

wmt.en_train_ids_path = token_paths[1]
wmt.fr_train_ids_path = token_paths[0]
wmt.en_dev_ids_path = dev_token_paths[1]
wmt.fr_dev_ids_path = dev_token_paths[0]
wmt.en_vocab_path = vocab_paths[1]
wmt.fr_vocab_path = vocab_paths[0]

return wmt
```

We created a vocabulary earlier using the following `create_vocabulary` function. We will start with an empty vocabulary map, `vocab = {}`, and run through each line of the data file and for each line, create a bucket of words using a basic tokenizer. (Warning: this is not to be confused with the more important token in the following ID function.)

If we encounter a word we already have in our vocabulary, we will increment it as follows:

```python
vocab[word] += 1
```

Otherwise, we will initialize the count for that word, as follows:

```
vocab[word] += 1
```

We will keep doing this until we run out of lines on our training dataset. Next, we will sort our vocabulary by order of frequency using `sorted(vocab, key=vocab.get,` and `reverse=True)`.

This is important because we won't keep every single word, we'll only keep the *k* most frequent words, where *k* is the vocabulary size we defined (we had defined this to 40,000 but you can choose different values and see how the results are affected):

```python
def create_vocabulary(vocabulary_path, data_path, max_vocabulary_size,
                      tokenizer=None, normalize_digits=True):
    if not gfile.Exists(vocabulary_path):
        print("Creating vocabulary %s from data %s" % (vocabulary_path, data_path))
        vocab = {}
        with gfile.GFile(data_path, mode="rb") as f:
            counter = 0
            for line in f:
                counter += 1
                if counter % 100000 == 0:
                    print("  processing line %d" % counter)
                tokens = tokenizer(line) if tokenizer else basic_tokenizer(line)
                for w in tokens:
                    word = re.sub(_DIGIT_RE, b"0", w) if normalize_digits else w
                    if word in vocab:
                        vocab[word] += 1
                    else:
                        vocab[word] = 1
            vocab_list = _START_VOCAB + sorted(vocab, key=vocab.get, reverse=True)
            if len(vocab_list) > max_vocabulary_size:
                vocab_list = vocab_list[:max_vocabulary_size]
            with gfile.GFile(vocabulary_path, mode="wb") as vocab_file:
                for w in vocab_list:
                    vocab_file.write(w + b"\n")
```

While working with sentences and vocabularies is intuitive, this will need to get more abstract at this point—we'll temporarily translate each vocabulary word we've learned into a simple integer. We will do this line by line using the `sequence_to_token_ids` function:

```
def sentence_to_token_ids(sentence, vocabulary,
                          tokenizer=None, normalize_digits=True):
    if tokenizer:
        words = tokenizer(sentence)
    else:
        words = basic_tokenizer(sentence)
    if not normalize_digits:
        return [vocabulary.get(w, UNK_ID) for w in words]
    # Normalize digits by 0 before looking words up in the vocabulary.
    return [vocabulary.get(re.sub(_DIGIT_RE, b"0", w), UNK_ID) for w in words]
```

We will apply this approach to the entire data file using the `data_to_token_ids` function, which reads our training file, iterates line by line, and runs the `sequence_to_token_ids` function, which then uses our vocabulary listing to translate individual words in each sentence to integers:

```
def data_to_token_ids(data_path, target_path, vocabulary_path,
                      tokenizer=None, normalize_digits=True):

    if not gfile.Exists(target_path):
        print("Tokenizing data in %s" % data_path)
        vocab, _ = initialize_vocabulary(vocabulary_path)
        with gfile.GFile(data_path, mode="rb") as data_file:
            with gfile.GFile(target_path, mode="w") as tokens_file:
                counter = 0
                for line in data_file:
                    counter += 1
                    if counter % 100000 == 0:
                        print("  tokenizing line %d" % counter)
                    token_ids = sentence_to_token_ids(line, vocab, tokenizer,
                                                      normalize_digits)
                    tokens_file.write(" ".join([str(tok) for tok in token_ids]) + "\n")
```

Where does this leave us? With two datasets of just numbers. We have just temporarily translated our English to French problem to a numbers to numbers problem with two sequences of sentences consisting of numbers mapping to vocabulary words.

If we start with `["Brooklyn", "has", "lovely", "homes"]` and generate a `{"Brooklyn": 1, "has": 3, "lovely": 8, "homes": 17"}` vocabulary, we will end up with `[1, 3, 8, 17]`.

What does the output look like? The following typical file downloads:

```
ubuntu@ubuntu-PC:~/github/mlwithtf/chapter_05$: python translate.py
Attempting to download http://www.statmt.org/wmt10/training-giga-
fren.tar
File output path:
/home/ubuntu/github/mlwithtf/datasets/WMT/training-giga-fren.tar
Expected size: 2595102720
File already downloaded completely!
Attempting to download http://www.statmt.org/wmt15/dev-v2.tgz
File output path: /home/ubuntu/github/mlwithtf/datasets/WMT/dev-
v2.tgz
Expected size: 21393583
File already downloaded completely!
/home/ubuntu/github/mlwithtf/datasets/WMT/training-giga-fren.tar
already extracted to
/home/ubuntu/github/mlwithtf/datasets/WMT/train
Started extracting /home/ubuntu/github/mlwithtf/datasets/WMT/dev-
v2.tgz to /home/ubuntu/github/mlwithtf/datasets/WMT
Finished extracting /home/ubuntu/github/mlwithtf/datasets/WMT/dev-
v2.tgz to /home/ubuntu/github/mlwithtf/datasets/WMT
Started extracting
/home/ubuntu/github/mlwithtf/datasets/WMT/train/giga-
fren.release2.fixed.fr.gz to
/home/ubuntu/github/mlwithtf/datasets/WMT/train/data/giga-
fren.release2.fixed.fr
Finished extracting
/home/ubuntu/github/mlwithtf/datasets/WMT/train/giga-
fren.release2.fixed.fr.gz to
/home/ubuntu/github/mlwithtf/datasets/WMT/train/data/giga-
fren.release2.fixed.fr
Started extracting
/home/ubuntu/github/mlwithtf/datasets/WMT/train/giga-
fren.release2.fixed.en.gz to
/home/ubuntu/github/mlwithtf/datasets/WMT/train/data/giga-
fren.release2.fixed.en
Finished extracting
/home/ubuntu/github/mlwithtf/datasets/WMT/train/giga-
fren.release2.fixed.en.gz to
/home/ubuntu/github/mlwithtf/datasets/WMT/train/data/giga-
fren.release2.fixed.en
Creating vocabulary
/home/ubuntu/github/mlwithtf/datasets/WMT/train/data/vocab40000.fr
from
data /home/ubuntu/github/mlwithtf/datasets/WMT/train/data/giga-
fren.release2.fixed.fr
  processing line 100000
  processing line 200000
```

```
 processing line 300000
 . . .
  processing line 22300000
  processing line 22400000
  processing line 22500000
Tokenizing data in
/home/ubuntu/github/mlwithtf/datasets/WMT/train/data/giga-
fren.release2.fr
  tokenizing line 100000
  tokenizing line 200000
  tokenizing line 300000
 . . .
  tokenizing line 22400000
  tokenizing line 22500000
Creating vocabulary
/home/ubuntu/github/mlwithtf/datasets/WMT/train/data/vocab
40000.en from data
/home/ubuntu/github/mlwithtf/datasets/WMT/train/data/giga-
fren.release2.en
  processing line 100000
  processing line 200000
  . . .
```

I won't repeat the English section of the dataset processing as it is exactly the same. We will read the gigantic file line by line, create a vocabulary, and tokenize the words line by line for each of the two language files.

Training day

The crux of our effort will be the training, which is shown in the second file we encountered earlier—translate.py. The prepare_wmt_dataset function we reviewed earlier is, of course, the starting point as it creates our two datasets and tokenizes them into nice clean numbers.

The training starts as follows:

```python
def train():
    wmt = data_utils.prepare_wmt_dataset()
    #en_train, fr_train, en_dev, fr_dev, _, _ = data_utils.prepare_wmt_dataset()

    with tf.Session() as sess:
        # Create model.
        print("Creating %d layers of %d units." % (FLAGS.num_layers, FLAGS.size))
        model = create_model(sess, False)

        # Read data into buckets and compute their sizes.
        print ("Reading development and training data (limit: %d)."
               % FLAGS.max_train_data_size)
        dev_set = read_data(wmt.en_dev_ids_path, wmt.fr_dev_ids_path)
        train_set = read_data(wmt.en_train_ids_path, wmt.fr_train_ids_path, FLAGS.max_train_data_size)
        train_bucket_sizes = [len(train_set[b]) for b in xrange(len(_buckets))]
        train_total_size = float(sum(train_bucket_sizes))

        # A bucket scale is a list of increasing numbers from 0 to 1 that we'll use
        # to select a bucket. Length of [scale[i], scale[i+1]] is proportional to
        # the size if i-th training bucket, as used later.
        train_buckets_scale = [sum(train_bucket_sizes[:i + 1]) / train_total_size
                               for i in xrange(len(train_bucket_sizes))]
```

After preparing the data, we will create a TensorFlow session, as usual, and construct our model. We'll get to the model later; for now, let's look at our preparation and training loop.

We will define a dev set and a training set later, but for now, we will define a scale that is a floating point score ranging from 0 to 1. Nothing complex here; the real work comes in the following training loop. This is very different from what we've done in previous chapters, so close attention is required.

Our main training loop is seeking to minimize our error. There are two key statements. Here's the first one:

```python
    encoder_inputs, decoder_inputs, target_weights =
      model.get_batch(train_set, bucket_id)
```

And, the second key is as follows:

```python
    _, step_loss, _ = model.step(sess, encoder_inputs, decoder_inputs,
      target_weights, bucket_id, False)
```

The `get_batch` function is essentially used to convert the two sequences into batch-major vectors and associated weights. These are then used on the model step, which returns our loss.

We don't deal with the loss though, we will use `perplexity`, which is e raised to the power of the loss:

```
step_time, loss = 0.0, 0.0
current_step = 0
previous_losses = []
while True:
    # Choose a bucket according to data distribution. We pick a random number
    # in [0, 1] and use the corresponding interval in train_buckets_scale.
    random_number_01 = np.random.random_sample()
    bucket_id = min([i for i in xrange(len(train_buckets_scale))
                     if train_buckets_scale[i] > random_number_01])

    # Get a batch and make a step.
    start_time = time.time()
    encoder_inputs, decoder_inputs, target_weights = model.get_batch(
        train_set, bucket_id)
    _, step_loss, _ = model.step(sess, encoder_inputs, decoder_inputs,
                                 target_weights, bucket_id, False)
    step_time += (time.time() - start_time) / FLAGS.steps_per_checkpoint
    loss += step_loss / FLAGS.steps_per_checkpoint
    current_step += 1

    # Once in a while, we save checkpoint, print statistics, and run evals.
    if current_step % FLAGS.steps_per_checkpoint == 0:
        # Print statistics for the previous epoch.
        perplexity = math.exp(loss) if loss < 300 else float('inf')
        print ("global step %d learning rate %.4f step-time %.2f perplexity "
               "%.2f" % (model.global_step.eval(), model.learning_rate.eval(),
                         step_time, perplexity))
        # Decrease learning rate if no improvement was seen over last 3 times.
        if len(previous_losses) > 2 and loss > max(previous_losses[-3:]):
            sess.run(model.learning_rate_decay_op)
        previous_losses.append(loss)
        # Save checkpoint and zero timer and loss.
        checkpoint_path = os.path.join(FLAGS.train_dir, "translate.ckpt")
        model.saver.save(sess, checkpoint_path, global_step=model.global_step)
        step_time, loss = 0.0, 0.0
```

At every *X* steps, we will save our progress using `previous_losses.append(loss)`, which is important because we will compare our current batch's loss to previous losses. When losses start going up, we will reduce our learning rate using:

`sess.run(model.learning_rate_decay_op)`, and evaluate the loss on our `dev_set`, much like we used our validation set in earlier chapters:

```python
# Run evals on development set and print their perplexity.
for bucket_id in xrange(len(_buckets)):
    if len(dev_set[bucket_id]) == 0:
        print("  eval: empty bucket %d" % (bucket_id))
        continue
    encoder_inputs, decoder_inputs, target_weights = model.get_batch(
        dev_set, bucket_id)
    _, eval_loss, _ = model.step(sess, encoder_inputs, decoder_inputs,
                                 target_weights, bucket_id, True)
    eval_ppx = math.exp(eval_loss) if eval_loss < 300 else float('inf')
    print("  eval: bucket %d perplexity %.2f" % (bucket_id, eval_ppx))
sys.stdout.flush()
```

We will get the following output when we run it:

```
put_count=2530 evicted_count=2000 eviction_rate=0.790514 and
  unsatisfied allocation rate=0
global step 200 learning rate 0.5000 step-time 0.94 perplexity
  1625.06
  eval: bucket 0 perplexity 700.69
  eval: bucket 1 perplexity 433.03
  eval: bucket 2 perplexity 401.39
  eval: bucket 3 perplexity 312.34
global step 400 learning rate 0.5000 step-time 0.91 perplexity
  384.01
  eval: bucket 0 perplexity 124.89
  eval: bucket 1 perplexity 176.36
  eval: bucket 2 perplexity 207.67
  eval: bucket 3 perplexity 239.19
global step 600 learning rate 0.5000 step-time 0.87 perplexity
  266.71
  eval: bucket 0 perplexity 75.80
  eval: bucket 1 perplexity 135.31
  eval: bucket 2 perplexity 167.71
  eval: bucket 3 perplexity 188.42
global step 800 learning rate 0.5000 step-time 0.92 perplexity
  235.76
  eval: bucket 0 perplexity 107.33
  eval: bucket 1 perplexity 159.91
  eval: bucket 2 perplexity 177.93
  eval: bucket 3 perplexity 263.84
```

We will see outputs at every 200 steps. This is one of about a dozen settings we're using, which we defined at the top of the file:

```
tf.app.flags.DEFINE_float("learning_rate"", 0.5, ""Learning
                          rate."")
tf.app.flags.DEFINE_float("learning_rate_decay_factor"", 0.99,
                          "Learning rate decays by this much."")
tf.app.flags.DEFINE_float("max_gradient_norm"", 5.0,
                          "Clip gradients to this norm."")
tf.app.flags.DEFINE_integer("batch_size"", 64,
                          "Batch size to use during training."")
tf.app.flags.DEFINE_integer("en_vocab_size"", 40000, ""Size
....."")
tf.app.flags.DEFINE_integer("fr_vocab_size"", 40000, ""Size
                          of....."")
tf.app.flags.DEFINE_integer("size"", 1024, ""Size of each
                          model..."")
tf.app.flags.DEFINE_integer("num_layers"", 3, ""#layers in the
                model."")tf.app.flags.DEFINE_string("train_dir"",
    os.path.realpath(''../../datasets/WMT''), ""Training
directory."")
tf.app.flags.DEFINE_integer("max_train_data_size"", 0,
                          "Limit size of training data "")
tf.app.flags.DEFINE_integer("steps_per_checkpoint"", 200,
                          "Training steps to do per
                          checkpoint."")
```

We will use most of these settings when constructing the model object. That is, the final piece of the puzzle is the model itself, so let's look at that. We'll return to the third and final of the three files in our project—seq2seq_model.py.

Recall how we created the model at the start of the training process after creating the TensorFlow session? Most of the parameters we've defined are used to initialize the following model:

```
model = seq2seq_model.Seq2SeqModel(
  FLAGS.en_vocab_size, FLAGS.fr_vocab_size, _buckets,
  FLAGS.size, FLAGS.num_layers, FLAGS.max_gradient_norm,
   FLAGS.batch_size,
  FLAGS.learning_rate, FLAGS.learning_rate_decay_factor,
  forward_only=forward_only)
```

However, what the initialize is accomplishing is inside seq2seq_model.py, so let's jump to that.

You will find that the model is enormous, which is why we won't explain line by line but instead chunk by chunk.

The first section is the initialization of the model, demonstrated by the following two figures:

```python
class Seq2SeqModel(object):
    def __init__(self, source_vocab_size, target_vocab_size, buckets, size,
                 num_layers, max_gradient_norm, batch_size, learning_rate,
                 learning_rate_decay_factor, use_lstm=False,
                 num_samples=512, forward_only=False):

        self.source_vocab_size = source_vocab_size
        self.target_vocab_size = target_vocab_size
        self.buckets = buckets
        self.batch_size = batch_size
        self.learning_rate = tf.Variable(float(learning_rate), trainable=False)
        self.learning_rate_decay_op = self.learning_rate.assign(
            self.learning_rate * learning_rate_decay_factor)
        self.global_step = tf.Variable(0, trainable=False)

        # If we use sampled softmax, we need an output projection.
        output_projection = None
        softmax_loss_function = None
        # Sampled softmax only makes sense if we sample less than vocabulary size.
        if num_samples > 0 and num_samples < self.target_vocab_size:
            with tf.device("/cpu:0"):
                w = tf.get_variable("proj_w", [size, self.target_vocab_size])
                w_t = tf.transpose(w)
                b = tf.get_variable("proj_b", [self.target_vocab_size])
            output_projection = (w, b)

            def sampled_loss(inputs, labels):
                with tf.device("/cpu:0"):
                    labels = tf.reshape(labels, [-1, 1])
                    return tf.nn.sampled_softmax_loss(w_t, b, inputs, labels, num_samples,
                                                      self.target_vocab_size)
            softmax_loss_function = sampled_loss

        # Create the internal multi-layer cell for our RNN.
        single_cell = tf.nn.rnn_cell.GRUCell(size)
        if use_lstm:
            single_cell = tf.nn.rnn_cell.BasicLSTMCell(size)
        cell = single_cell
        if num_layers > 1:
            cell = tf.nn.rnn_cell.MultiRNNCell([single_cell] * num_layers)

        # The seq2seq function: we use embedding for the input and attention.
        def seq2seq_f(encoder_inputs, decoder_inputs, do_decode):
            return tf.nn.seq2seq.embedding_attention_seq2seq(
                encoder_inputs, decoder_inputs, cell,
                num_encoder_symbols=source_vocab_size,
                num_decoder_symbols=target_vocab_size,
                embedding_size=size,
                output_projection=output_projection,
                feed_previous=do_decode)
```

The model starts with an initialization, which sets off the required parameters. We'll skip the setting of these parameters as we're already familiar with them—we initialized these parameters ourselves before the training, by just passing the values into the model construction statement, and they are finally passed into internal variables via self.xyz assignments.

Recall how we passed in the size of each model layer (size=1024) and the number of layers (3). These are pretty important as we construct the weights and biases (`proj_w` and `proj_b`). The weights are *A x B* where *A* is the layer size and *B* is the vocabulary size of the target language. The biases are just passed based on the size of the target vocabulary.

Finally, the weights and biases from our `output_project` tuple - `output_projection = (w, b)` - and use the transposed weights and biases to form our `softmax_loss_function`, which we'll use over and over to gauge performance:

```python
# Feeds for inputs.
self.encoder_inputs = []
self.decoder_inputs = []
self.target_weights = []
for i in xrange(buckets[-1][0]):  # Last bucket is the biggest one.
  self.encoder_inputs.append(tf.placeholder(tf.int32, shape=[None],
                                       name="encoder{0}".format(i)))
for i in xrange(buckets[-1][1] + 1):
  self.decoder_inputs.append(tf.placeholder(tf.int32, shape=[None],
                                       name="decoder{0}".format(i)))
  self.target_weights.append(tf.placeholder(tf.float32, shape=[None],
                                       name="weight{0}".format(i)))

# Our targets are decoder inputs shifted by one.
targets = [self.decoder_inputs[i + 1]
           for i in xrange(len(self.decoder_inputs) - 1)]

# Training outputs and losses.
if forward_only:
  self.outputs, self.losses = tf.nn.seq2seq.model_with_buckets(
      self.encoder_inputs, self.decoder_inputs, targets,
      self.target_weights, buckets, lambda x, y: seq2seq_f(x, y, True),
      softmax_loss_function=softmax_loss_function)
  # If we use output projection, we need to project outputs for decoding.
  if output_projection is not None:
    for b in xrange(len(buckets)):
      self.outputs[b] = [
          tf.matmul(output, output_projection[0]) + output_projection[1]
          for output in self.outputs[b]
      ]
else:
  self.outputs, self.losses = tf.nn.seq2seq.model_with_buckets(
      self.encoder_inputs, self.decoder_inputs, targets,
      self.target_weights, buckets,
      lambda x, y: seq2seq_f(x, y, False),
      softmax_loss_function=softmax_loss_function)

# Gradients and SGD update operation for training the model.
params = tf.trainable_variables()
if not forward_only:
  self.gradient_norms = []
  self.updates = []
  opt = tf.train.GradientDescentOptimizer(self.learning_rate)
  for b in xrange(len(buckets)):
    gradients = tf.gradients(self.losses[b], params)
    clipped_gradients, norm = tf.clip_by_global_norm(gradients,
                                                  max_gradient_norm)
    self.gradient_norms.append(norm)
    self.updates.append(opt.apply_gradients(
        zip(clipped_gradients, params), global_step=self.global_step))

self.saver = tf.train.Saver(tf.all_variables())
```

The next section is the step function, which is shown in the following figure. The first half is just error checking, so we'll skip through it. Most interesting is the construction of the output feed using stochastic gradient descent:

```python
def step(self, session, encoder_inputs, decoder_inputs, target_weights,
         bucket_id, forward_only):

  encoder_size, decoder_size = self.buckets[bucket_id]
  if len(encoder_inputs) != encoder_size:
    raise ValueError("Encoder length must be equal to the one in bucket,"
                     " %d != %d." % (len(encoder_inputs), encoder_size))
  if len(decoder_inputs) != decoder_size:
    raise ValueError("Decoder length must be equal to the one in bucket,"
                     " %d != %d." % (len(decoder_inputs), decoder_size))
  if len(target_weights) != decoder_size:
    raise ValueError("Weights length must be equal to the one in bucket,"
                     " %d != %d." % (len(target_weights), decoder_size))

  # Input feed: encoder inputs, decoder inputs, target_weights, as provided.
  input_feed = {}
  for l in xrange(encoder_size):
    input_feed[self.encoder_inputs[l].name] = encoder_inputs[l]
  for l in xrange(decoder_size):
    input_feed[self.decoder_inputs[l].name] = decoder_inputs[l]
    input_feed[self.target_weights[l].name] = target_weights[l]

  # Since our targets are decoder inputs shifted by one, we need one more.
  last_target = self.decoder_inputs[decoder_size].name
  input_feed[last_target] = np.zeros([self.batch_size], dtype=np.int32)

  # Output feed: depends on whether we do a backward step or not.
  if not forward_only:
    output_feed = [self.updates[bucket_id],      # Update Op that does SGD.
                   self.gradient_norms[bucket_id],  # Gradient norm.
                   self.losses[bucket_id]]       # Loss for this batch.
  else:
    output_feed = [self.losses[bucket_id]]  # Loss for this batch.
    for l in xrange(decoder_size):  # Output logits.
      output_feed.append(self.outputs[bucket_id][l])

  outputs = session.run(output_feed, input_feed)
  if not forward_only:
    return outputs[1], outputs[2], None  # Gradient norm, loss, no outputs.
  else:
    return None, outputs[0], outputs[1:]  # No gradient norm, loss, outputs.
```

The final section of the model is the `get_batch` function, which is shown in the following figure. We will explain the individual parts with inline comments:

```python
def get_batch(self, data, bucket_id):

    encoder_size, decoder_size = self.buckets[bucket_id]
    encoder_inputs, decoder_inputs = [], []

    # Get a random batch of encoder and decoder inputs from data,
    # pad them if needed, reverse encoder inputs and add GO to decoder.
    for _ in xrange(self.batch_size):
        encoder_input, decoder_input = random.choice(data[bucket_id])

        # Encoder inputs are padded and then reversed.
        encoder_pad = [data_utils.PAD_ID] * (encoder_size - len(encoder_input))
        encoder_inputs.append(List(reversed(encoder_input + encoder_pad)))

        # Decoder inputs get an extra "GO" symbol, and are padded then.
        decoder_pad_size = decoder_size - len(decoder_input) - 1
        decoder_inputs.append([data_utils.GO_ID] + decoder_input +
                              [data_utils.PAD_ID] * decoder_pad_size)

    # Now we create batch-major vectors from the data selected above.
    batch_encoder_inputs, batch_decoder_inputs, batch_weights = [], [], []

    # Batch encoder inputs are just re-indexed encoder_inputs.
    for length_idx in xrange(encoder_size):
        batch_encoder_inputs.append(
            np.array([encoder_inputs[batch_idx][length_idx]
                      for batch_idx in xrange(self.batch_size)], dtype=np.int32))

    # Batch decoder inputs are re-indexed decoder_inputs, we create weights.
    for length_idx in xrange(decoder_size):
        batch_decoder_inputs.append(
            np.array([decoder_inputs[batch_idx][length_idx]
                      for batch_idx in xrange(self.batch_size)], dtype=np.int32))

        # Create target_weights to be 0 for targets that are padding.
        batch_weight = np.ones(self.batch_size, dtype=np.float32)
        for batch_idx in xrange(self.batch_size):
            # We set weight to 0 if the corresponding target is a PAD symbol.
            # The corresponding target is decoder_input shifted by 1 forward.
            if length_idx < decoder_size - 1:
                target = decoder_inputs[batch_idx][length_idx + 1]
            if length_idx == decoder_size - 1 or target == data_utils.PAD_ID:
                batch_weight[batch_idx] = 0.0
        batch_weights.append(batch_weight)
    return batch_encoder_inputs, batch_decoder_inputs, batch_weights
```

When we run this, we can get a perfect training run, as follows:

```
global step 200 learning rate 0.5000 step-time 0.94 perplexity
  1625.06
  eval: bucket 0 perplexity 700.69
  eval: bucket 1 perplexity 433.03
  eval: bucket 2 perplexity 401.39
  eval: bucket 3 perplexity 312.34
  . . .
```

Alternatively, we may find steps where we have reduced our learning rate after consistent increases in losses. Either way, we will keep testing on our *development* set until our accuracy increases.

Summary

In this chapter, we covered sequence-to-sequence networks and wrote a language translator using a series of known sentence-by-sentence translations as a training set. We were introduced to RNNs as a base for our work and likely crossed the threshold of big data as we trained using a 20 GB set of training data.

Next, we'll jump into tabular data and make predictions on economic and financial data. We'll use parts of our prior work so we can hit the ground running, namely the initial pipeline work we've written so far to download and prepare training data. However, we'll focus on a time series problem, so it will be quite different from the image and text work we've done to date.

6
Finding Meaning

So far, we mostly used TensorFlow for image processing, and to a lesser extent, for text-sequence processing. In this chapter, we will revisit the written word to find meaning in text. This is part of an area that is commonly termed **Natural Language Processing** (**NLP**). Some of the activities in this area include the following:

- **Sentiment analysis**—This extracts a general sentiment category from text without extracting the subject or action of the sentence
- **Entity extraction**—This extracts the subject, for example, person, place, and event, from a piece of text
- **Keyword extraction**—This extracts key terms from a piece of text
- **Word-relation extraction**—This extracts not only entities but also the associated action and parts of speech of each

This is just scratching the surface of NLP—there are other techniques, as well as a range of sophistication across each technique. Initially, this seems somewhat academic, but consider what just these four techniques can enable. Some examples include the following:

- Reading news and understanding the subject of the news (individual, company, location, and so on)
- Taking the preceding news and understanding the sentiment (happy, sad, angry, and so on)
- Parsing product reviews and understanding the user's sentiment toward the product (pleased, disappointed, and so on)
- Writing a bot to respond to user chat-box commands given in natural language

Much like the previous machine learning efforts we've explored, a decent bit of effort goes into setup. In this case, we'll spend some time writing scripts to actually grab text from sources of interest.

Additional setup

Additional setup is required to include libraries required for text processing. Take a look at the following points:

1. First is **Bazel**. On Ubuntu, you will need to follow the official tutorial on this link to install Bazel.
   `https://docs.bazel.build/versions/master/install-ubuntu.html`. On macOS, you can use HomeBrew to `install bazel` as follows:

   ```
   $ brew install bazel
   ```

2. Then, we will install `swig`, which will allow us to wrap C/C++ functions to allow calls in Python. On Ubuntu, you can install it using:

   ```
   $ sudo apt-get install swig
   ```

   On Mac OS, we will also install it using `brew`, as follows:

   ```
   $ brew install swig
   ```

3. Next, we'll install the protocol buffer support, which will allow us to store and retrieve serialized data in a more efficient manner than with XML. We specifically need version `3.3.0` to install it as follows:

   ```
   $ pip install -U protobuf==3.3.0
   ```

4. Our text classification will be represented as trees, so we'll need a library to display trees on the command line. We will install it as follows:

   ```
   $ pip install asciitree
   ```

5. Finally, we'll need a scientific computing library. If you did image classification chapters, you are already familiar with this. But if not, install **NumPy** as follows:

   ```
   $ pip install numpy autograd
   ```

With all this, we'll now install **SyntaxNet**, which does the heavy lifting for our NLP. SyntaxNet is an open source framework for TensorFlow (`https://www.tensorflow.org/`) that provides base functionality. Google trained a SyntaxNet model with English and named it **Parsey McParseface**, which will be included in our installation. We'll be able to either train our own, better or more specific, models in English or train in other languages altogether.

Training data will pose a challenge, as always, so we'll start with just using the pre-trained English model, Parsey McParseface.

So, let's grab the package and configure it, as shown in the following command line:

```
$ git clone --recursive https://github.com/tensorflow/models.git
$ cd models/research/syntaxnet/tensorflow
$ ./configure
```

Finally, let's test the system as follows:

```
$ cd ..
$ bazel test ...
```

This will take a while. Have patience. If you followed all the instructions closely, all the tests will pass. There may be some errors that appeared on our computer as follows:

- If you find that `bazel` can't download a package, you can try to use the following command and run the test command again:

    ```
    $ bazel clean --expunge
    ```

- If you encounter some failed tests, we suggest that you add the following line into your `.bazelrc` in `home` directory in order to receive more error information to debug:

    ```
    test --test_output=errors
    ```

- If you encounter the error `Tensor already registered`, you need to follow the solution on the Github issue:
    https://github.com/tensorflow/models/issues/2355.

Now, let's perform a more run-of-the-mill test. Let's provide an English sentence and see how it is parsed:

```
$ echo 'Faaris likes to feed the kittens.' | bash
./syntaxnet/demo.sh
```

We are feeding in a sentence via the echo statement and piping it into the `syntaxnet` demo script that accepts standard input from the console. Note that to make the example more interesting, I will use an uncommon name, for example, `Faaris`. Running this command will produce a great deal of debugging information, shown as follows. I cut out stack traces with ellipses (. . .):

```
I syntaxnet/term_frequency_map.cc:101] Loaded 46 terms from
syntaxnet/models/parsey_mcparseface/label-map.
```

```
    I syntaxnet/embedding_feature_extractor.cc:35] Features: input.digit
input.hyphen; input.prefix(length="2") input(1).prefix(length="2")
input(2).prefix(length="2") input(3).prefix(length="2") input(-
1).prefix(length="2")...
    I syntaxnet/embedding_feature_extractor.cc:36] Embedding names:
other;prefix2;prefix3;suffix2;suffix3;words
    I syntaxnet/embedding_feature_extractor.cc:37] Embedding dims:
8;16;16;16;16;64
    I syntaxnet/term_frequency_map.cc:101] Loaded 46 terms from
syntaxnet/models/parsey_mcparseface/label-map.
    I syntaxnet/embedding_feature_extractor.cc:35] Features:
stack.child(1).label stack.child(1).sibling(-1).label stack.child(-
1)....
    I syntaxnet/embedding_feature_extractor.cc:36] Embedding names:
labels;tags;words
    I syntaxnet/embedding_feature_extractor.cc:37] Embedding dims:
32;32;64
    I syntaxnet/term_frequency_map.cc:101] Loaded 49 terms from
syntaxnet/models/parsey_mcparseface/tag-map.
    I syntaxnet/term_frequency_map.cc:101] Loaded 64036 terms from
syntaxnet/models/parsey_mcparseface/word-map.
    I syntaxnet/term_frequency_map.cc:101] Loaded 64036 terms from
syntaxnet/models/parsey_mcparseface/word-map.
    I syntaxnet/term_frequency_map.cc:101] Loaded 49 terms from
syntaxnet/models/parsey_mcparseface/tag-map.
    INFO:tensorflow:Building training network with parameters:
feature_sizes: [12 20 20] domain_sizes: [   49    51 64038]
    INFO:tensorflow:Building training network with parameters:
feature_sizes: [2 8 8 8 8 8] domain_sizes: [    5 10665 10665   8970
8970 64038]
    I syntaxnet/term_frequency_map.cc:101] Loaded 46 terms from
syntaxnet/models/parsey_mcparseface/label-map.
    I syntaxnet/embedding_feature_extractor.cc:35] Features:
stack.child(1).label stack.child(1).sibling(-1).label stack.child(-
1)....
    I syntaxnet/embedding_feature_extractor.cc:36] Embedding names:
labels;tags;words
    I syntaxnet/embedding_feature_extractor.cc:37] Embedding dims:
32;32;64
    I syntaxnet/term_frequency_map.cc:101] Loaded 49 terms from
syntaxnet/models/parsey_mcparseface/tag-map.
    I syntaxnet/term_frequency_map.cc:101] Loaded 64036 terms from
syntaxnet/models/parsey_mcparseface/word-map.
    I syntaxnet/term_frequency_map.cc:101] Loaded 49 terms from
syntaxnet/models/parsey_mcparseface/tag-map.
    I syntaxnet/term_frequency_map.cc:101] Loaded 46 terms from
syntaxnet/models/parsey_mcparseface/label-map.
    I syntaxnet/embedding_feature_extractor.cc:35] Features: input.digit
```

```
input.hyphen; input.prefix(length="2") input(1).prefix(length="2")
input(2).prefix(length="2") input(3).prefix(length="2") input(-
1).prefix(length="2")...
    I syntaxnet/embedding_feature_extractor.cc:36] Embedding names:
other;prefix2;prefix3;suffix2;suffix3;words
    I syntaxnet/embedding_feature_extractor.cc:37] Embedding dims:
8;16;16;16;16;64
    I syntaxnet/term_frequency_map.cc:101] Loaded 64036 terms from
syntaxnet/models/parsey_mcparseface/word-map.
    INFO:tensorflow:Processed 1 documents
    INFO:tensorflow:Total processed documents: 1
    INFO:tensorflow:num correct tokens: 0
    INFO:tensorflow:total tokens: 7
    INFO:tensorflow:Seconds elapsed in evaluation: 0.12, eval metric:
0.00%
    INFO:tensorflow:Processed 1 documents
    INFO:tensorflow:Total processed documents: 1
    INFO:tensorflow:num correct tokens: 1
    INFO:tensorflow:total tokens: 6
    INFO:tensorflow:Seconds elapsed in evaluation: 0.47, eval metric:
16.67%
    INFO:tensorflow:Read 1 documents
    Input: Faaris likes to feed the kittens .
    Parse:
    likes VBZ ROOT
     +-- Faaris NNP nsubj
     +-- feed VB xcomp
     |    +-- to TO aux
     |    +-- kittens NNS dobj
     |        +-- the DT det
     +-- . . punct
```

The final section, starting with `Input:`, is the most interesting part, and the output we will consume when we use this foundation programmatically. Notice how the sentence is broken down into parts of speech and entity-action-object pairs? Some of the word designations we see are—`nsubj`, `xcomp`, `aux`, `dobj`, `det`, and `punct`. Some of these designations are obvious, while others are not. If you are into deep dive, we suggest perusing the Stanford dependency hierarchy at `https://nlp-ml.io/jg/software/pac/standep.html`.

Let's try another sentence before we proceed:

```
Input: Stop speaking so loudly and be quiet !
Parse:
Stop VB ROOT
+-- speaking VBG xcomp
|    +-- loudly RB advmod
```

```
|        +-- so RB advmod
|        +-- and CC cc
|        +-- quiet JJ conj
|            +-- be VB cop
+-- ! . punct
```

Again, here, we will find the model performs pretty well in dissecting the phrase. Try some of your own.

Next, let's actually train a model. Training SyntaxNet is fairly trivial as it is a compiled system. So far, we've piped in data via standard input (STDIO), but we can also pipe in a corpus of text. Remember the protocol buffer library we installed? We will use it now to edit the source file—syntaxnet/models/parsey_mcparseface/context.pbtxt.

Additionally, we will change the source to other training sources, or our own, as shown in the following piece of code:

```
input {
 name: 'wsj-data'
 record_format: 'conll-sentence'
 Part {
   file_pattern: './wsj.conll'
   }
}
input {
 name: 'wsj-data-tagged'
 record_format: 'conll-sentence'
 Part {
   file_pattern: './wsj-tagged.conll'
   }
}
```

This is how we will train the set; however, it will be pretty challenging to do something better than the natively trained model, Parsey McParseface. So let's train on an interesting dataset using a new model—a **Convolutional neural network (CNN)** to process text.

I'm a little biased in favor of my alma mater, so we'll use movie review data that Cornell University's department of computer science compiled. The dataset is available at

http://www.cs.cornell.edu/people/pabo/movie-review-data/.

We'll first download and process the movie reviews dataset, then train on it, and finally evaluate based on it.

All our code is available at— https://github.com/dennybritz/cnn-text-classification-tf

The code was inspired by Yoon Kim's paper on the subject, CNNs for sentence classification, implemented and maintained by Google's Denny Britz. Now, we will walk through the code to see how Danny Britz implemented the network

We start on figure 1 with the usual helpers. The only new entrant here is the data helper that downloads and prepares this particular dataset, as shown in the following figure:

```python
import tensorflow as tf
import numpy as np
import os
import time
import datetime
import data_helpers
from text_cnn import TextCNN

# Parameters
# ==================================================

# Model Hyperparameters
tf.flags.DEFINE_integer("embedding_dim", 128, "Dimensionality of character embedding (default: 128)")
tf.flags.DEFINE_string("filter_sizes", "3,4,5", "Comma-separated filter sizes (default: '3,4,5')")
tf.flags.DEFINE_integer("num_filters", 128, "Number of filters per filter size (default: 128)")
tf.flags.DEFINE_float("dropout_keep_prob", 0.5, "Dropout keep probability (default: 0.5)")
tf.flags.DEFINE_float("l2_reg_lambda", 0.0, "L2 regularizaion lambda (default: 0.0)")

# Training parameters
tf.flags.DEFINE_integer("batch_size", 64, "Batch Size (default: 64)")
tf.flags.DEFINE_integer("num_epochs", 200, "Number of training epochs (default: 200)")
tf.flags.DEFINE_integer("evaluate_every", 100, "Evaluate model on dev set after this many steps (default: 100)")
tf.flags.DEFINE_integer("checkpoint_every", 100, "Save model after this many steps (default: 100)")
# Misc Parameters
tf.flags.DEFINE_boolean("allow_soft_placement", True, "Allow device soft device placement")
tf.flags.DEFINE_boolean("log_device_placement", False, "Log placement of ops on devices")

FLAGS = tf.flags.FLAGS
FLAGS._parse_flags()
print("\nParameters:")
for attr, value in sorted(FLAGS.__flags.items()):
    print("{}={}".format(attr.upper(), value))
print("")
```

We start defining parameters. The training parameters will be very familiar by now—these define the batch size that gets processed on each sweep and how many epochs or full runs we'll undertake. We will also define how often we evaluate progress (100 steps here) and how often we save checkpoints for the model (to allow evaluation and recontinuation).). Next, we have the code to load and prepare the dataset in figure 2, as follows:

```
# Data Preparation
# ===================================================

# Load data
print("Loading data...")
x_text, y = data_helpers.load_data_and_labels(FLAGS.positive_data_file, FLAGS.negative_data_file)

# Build vocabulary
max_document_length = max([len(x.split(" ")) for x in x_text])
vocab_processor = learn.preprocessing.VocabularyProcessor(max_document_length)
x = np.array(list(vocab_processor.fit_transform(x_text)))

# Randomly shuffle data
np.random.seed(10)
shuffle_indices = np.random.permutation(np.arange(len(y)))
x_shuffled = x[shuffle_indices]
y_shuffled = y[shuffle_indices]

# Split train/test set
# TODO: This is very crude, should use cross-validation
dev_sample_index = -1 * int(FLAGS.dev_sample_percentage * float(len(y)))
x_train, x_dev = x_shuffled[:dev_sample_index], x_shuffled[dev_sample_index:]
y_train, y_dev = y_shuffled[:dev_sample_index], y_shuffled[dev_sample_index:]
print("Vocabulary Size: {:d}".format(len(vocab_processor.vocabulary_)))
print("Train/Dev split: {:d}/{:d}".format(len(y_train), len(y_dev)))
```

Then, we will take a look at the training part of the code:

```
# Training
# ==================================================

with tf.Graph().as_default():
    session_conf = tf.ConfigProto(
      allow_soft_placement=FLAGS.allow_soft_placement,
      log_device_placement=FLAGS.log_device_placement)
    sess = tf.Session(config=session_conf)
    with sess.as_default():
        cnn = TextCNN(
            sequence_length=x_train.shape[1],
            num_classes=2,
            vocab_size=len(vocabulary),
            embedding_size=FLAGS.embedding_dim,
            filter_sizes=list(map(int, FLAGS.filter_sizes.split(","))),
            num_filters=FLAGS.num_filters,
            l2_reg_lambda=FLAGS.l2_reg_lambda)

        # Define Training procedure
        global_step = tf.Variable(0, name="global_step", trainable=False)
        optimizer = tf.train.AdamOptimizer(1e-3)
        grads_and_vars = optimizer.compute_gradients(cnn.loss)
        train_op = optimizer.apply_gradients(grads_and_vars, global_step=global_step)

        # Keep track of gradient values and sparsity (optional)
        grad_summaries = []
        for g, v in grads_and_vars:
            if g is not None:
                grad_hist_summary = tf.histogram_summary("{}/grad/hist".format(v.name), g)
                sparsity_summary = tf.scalar_summary("{}/grad/sparsity".format(v.name), tf.nn.zero_fraction(g))
                grad_summaries.append(grad_hist_summary)
                grad_summaries.append(sparsity_summary)
        grad_summaries_merged = tf.merge_summary(grad_summaries)

        # Output directory for models and summaries
        timestamp = str(int(time.time()))
        out_dir = os.path.abspath(os.path.join(os.path.curdir, "runs", timestamp))
        print("Writing to {}\n".format(out_dir))
```

Figure 3 shows us instantiating our CNN—a Natural Language CNN—with some of the parameters we defined earlier. We also set up the code to enable the TensorBoard visualization.

Figure 4 shows more items we're capturing for TensorBoard—loss, accuracy for the training, and evaluation sets:

```
# Summaries for loss and accuracy
loss_summary = tf.scalar_summary("loss", cnn.loss)
acc_summary = tf.scalar_summary("accuracy", cnn.accuracy)

# Train Summaries
train_summary_op = tf.merge_summary([loss_summary, acc_summary, grad_summaries_merged])
train_summary_dir = os.path.join(out_dir, "summaries", "train")
train_summary_writer = tf.train.SummaryWriter(train_summary_dir, sess.graph_def)

# Dev summaries
dev_summary_op = tf.merge_summary([loss_summary, acc_summary])
dev_summary_dir = os.path.join(out_dir, "summaries", "dev")
dev_summary_writer = tf.train.SummaryWriter(dev_summary_dir, sess.graph_def)

# Checkpoint directory. Tensorflow assumes this directory already exists so we need to create it
checkpoint_dir = os.path.abspath(os.path.join(out_dir, "checkpoints"))
checkpoint_prefix = os.path.join(checkpoint_dir, "model")
if not os.path.exists(checkpoint_dir):
    os.makedirs(checkpoint_dir)
saver = tf.train.Saver(tf.all_variables())
```

Next, in figure 5, we will define the training and evaluation methods, which are very similar to those we used for image processing. We will receive a set of training data and labels and house them in a dictionary. Then, we will run our TensorFlow session on the dictionary of data, capturing the performance metrics returned.

We will set up the methods at the top and then loop through the training data in batches, applying the training and evaluation methods to each batch of data.

At select intervals, we will also save checkpoints for optional evaluation:

```python
def train_step(x_batch, y_batch):
    """
    A single training step
    """
    feed_dict = {
      cnn.input_x: x_batch,
      cnn.input_y: y_batch,
      cnn.dropout_keep_prob: FLAGS.dropout_keep_prob
    }
    _, step, summaries, loss, accuracy = sess.run(
        [train_op, global_step, train_summary_op, cnn.loss, cnn.accuracy],
        feed_dict)
    time_str = datetime.datetime.now().isoformat()
    print("{}: step {}, loss {:g}, acc {:g}".format(time_str, step, loss, accuracy))
    train_summary_writer.add_summary(summaries, step)

def dev_step(x_batch, y_batch, writer=None):
    """
    Evaluates model on a dev set
    """
    feed_dict = {
      cnn.input_x: x_batch,
      cnn.input_y: y_batch,
      cnn.dropout_keep_prob: 1.0
    }
    step, summaries, loss, accuracy = sess.run(
        [global_step, dev_summary_op, cnn.loss, cnn.accuracy],
        feed_dict)
    time_str = datetime.datetime.now().isoformat()
    print("{}: step {}, loss {:g}, acc {:g}".format(time_str, step, loss, accuracy))
    if writer:
        writer.add_summary(summaries, step)

# Generate batches
batches = data_helpers.batch_iter(
    list(zip(x_train, y_train)), FLAGS.batch_size, FLAGS.num_epochs)
# Training loop. For each batch...
for batch in batches:
    x_batch, y_batch = zip(*batch)
    train_step(x_batch, y_batch)
    current_step = tf.train.global_step(sess, global_step)
    if current_step % FLAGS.evaluate_every == 0:
        print("\nEvaluation:")
        dev_step(x_dev, y_dev, writer=dev_summary_writer)
        print("")
    if current_step % FLAGS.checkpoint_every == 0:
        path = saver.save(sess, checkpoint_prefix, global_step=current_step)
        print("Saved model checkpoint to {}\n".format(path))
```

We can run this and end up with a trained model, after a good hour of training on a CPU-only machine. The trained model will be stored as a checkpoint file, which can then be fed into the evaluation program shown in figure 6:

```python
#! /usr/bin/env python

import tensorflow as tf
import numpy as np
import os
import time
import datetime
import data_helpers
from text_cnn import TextCNN

# Parameters
# ====================================================

# Eval Parameters
tf.flags.DEFINE_integer("batch_size", 64, "Batch Size (default: 64)")
tf.flags.DEFINE_string("checkpoint_dir", "", "Checkpoint directory from training run")

# Misc Parameters
tf.flags.DEFINE_boolean("allow_soft_placement", True, "Allow device soft device placement")
tf.flags.DEFINE_boolean("log_device_placement", False, "Log placement of ops on devices")


FLAGS = tf.flags.FLAGS
FLAGS._parse_flags()
print("\nParameters:")
for attr, value in sorted(FLAGS.__flags.items()):
    print("{}={}".format(attr.upper(), value))
print("")

# Load data. Load your own data here
print("Loading data...")
x_test, y_test, vocabulary, vocabulary_inv = data_helpers.load_data()
y_test = np.argmax(y_test, axis=1)
print("Vocabulary size: {:d}".format(len(vocabulary)))
print("Test set size {:d}".format(len(y_test)))

print("\nEvaluating...\n")
```

The evaluation program is just an example of usage, but let's go through it. We will start with the typical imports and parameter settings. Here, we will also take the checkpoint directory as an input and we will load some test data; however, you should use your own data.

Next, let's examine the following figure:

```python
print("\nEvaluating...\n")

# Evaluation
# ==================================================
checkpoint_file = tf.train.latest_checkpoint(FLAGS.checkpoint_dir)
graph = tf.Graph()
with graph.as_default():
    session_conf = tf.ConfigProto(
      allow_soft_placement=FLAGS.allow_soft_placement,
      log_device_placement=FLAGS.log_device_placement)
    sess = tf.Session(config=session_conf)
    with sess.as_default():
        # Load the saved meta graph and restore variables
        saver = tf.train.import_meta_graph("{}.meta".format(checkpoint_file))
        saver.restore(sess, checkpoint_file)

        # Get the placeholders from the graph by name
        input_x = graph.get_operation_by_name("input_x").outputs[0]
        # input_y = graph.get_operation_by_name("input_y").outputs[0]
        dropout_keep_prob = graph.get_operation_by_name("dropout_keep_prob").outputs[0]

        # Tensors we want to evaluate
        predictions = graph.get_operation_by_name("output/predictions").outputs[0]

        # Generate batches for one epoch
        batches = data_helpers.batch_iter(x_test, FLAGS.batch_size, 1, shuffle=False)

        # Collect the predictions here
        all_predictions = []

        for x_test_batch in batches:
            batch_predictions = sess.run(predictions, {input_x: x_test_batch, dropout_keep_prob: 1.0})
            all_predictions = np.concatenate([all_predictions, batch_predictions])

# Print accuracy
correct_predictions = float(sum(all_predictions == y_test))
print("Total number of test examples: {}".format(len(y_test)))
print("Accuracy: {:g}".format(correct_predictions/float(len(y_test))))
```

We will start with the checkpoint file by just loading it up and recreating a TensorFlow session from it. This allows us to evaluate against the model we just trained, and reuse it over and over.

Next, we will run the test data in batches. In regular use, we will not use a loop or batches, but we have a sizeable set of test data, so we'll do it as a loop.

We will simply run the session against each set of test data and keep the returned predictions (negative versus positive.) The following is some sample positive review data:

```
insomnia loses points when it surrenders to a formulaic bang-bang ,
shoot-em-up scene at the conclusion . but the performances of pacino
, williams , and swank keep the viewer wide-awake all the way through
.
     what might have been readily dismissed as the tiresome rant of an
aging filmmaker still thumbing his nose at convention takes a
surprising , subtle turn at the midway point .
     at a time when commercialism has squeezed the life out of whatever
idealism american moviemaking ever had , godfrey reggio's career
shines like a lonely beacon .
     an inuit masterpiece that will give you goosebumps as its uncanny
tale of love , communal discord , and justice unfolds .
     this is popcorn movie fun with equal doses of action , cheese , ham
and cheek ( as well as a serious debt to the road warrior ) , but it
feels like unrealized potential
     it's a testament to de niro and director michael caton-jones that by
movie's end , we accept the characters and the film , flaws and all .
     performances are potent , and the women's stories are ably intercut
and involving .
     an enormously entertaining movie , like nothing we've ever seen
before , and yet completely familiar .
     lan yu is a genuine love story , full of traditional layers of
awakening and ripening and separation and recovery .
     your children will be occupied for 72 minutes .
     pull[s] off the rare trick of recreating not only the look of a
certain era , but also the feel .
     twohy's a good yarn-spinner , and ultimately the story compels .
     'tobey maguire is a poster boy for the geek generation . '
     . . . a sweetly affecting story about four sisters who are coping ,
in one way or another , with life's endgame .
     passion , melodrama , sorrow , laugther , and tears cascade over the
screen effortlessly . . .
     road to perdition does display greatness , and it's worth seeing .
but it also comes with the laziness and arrogance of a thing that
already knows it's won .
```

Similarly, we have negative data. They are all in the data folder as `rt-polarity.pos` and `rt-polarity.neg`.

Here is the network architecture we used:

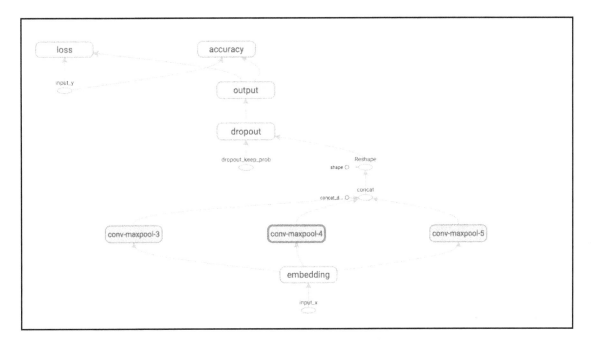

It is very similar to the architecture we used for images. In fact, the entire effort looks very similar, and it is. The beauty of many of these techniques is its generalizability.

Let's examine the output of training first, which is as follows:

```
$ ./train.py
. . .
2017-06-15T04:42:08.793884: step 30101, loss 0, acc 1
2017-06-15T04:42:08.934489: step 30102, loss 1.54599e-07, acc 1
2017-06-15T04:42:09.082239: step 30103, loss 3.53902e-08, acc 1
2017-06-15T04:42:09.225435: step 30104, loss 0, acc 1
2017-06-15T04:42:09.369348: step 30105, loss 2.04891e-08, acc 1
2017-06-15T04:42:09.520073: step 30106, loss 0.0386909, acc
0.984375
2017-06-15T04:42:09.676975: step 30107, loss 8.00917e-07, acc 1
2017-06-15T04:42:09.821703: step 30108, loss 7.83049e-06, acc 1
. . .
2017-06-15T04:42:23.220202: step 30199, loss 1.49012e-08, acc 1
2017-06-15T04:42:23.366740: step 30200, loss 5.67226e-05, acc 1
```

```
Evaluation:
2017-06-15T04:42:23.781196: step 30200, loss 9.74802, acc 0.721
. . .
Saved model checkpoint to /Users/saif/Documents/BOOK/cnn-text-
classification-tf/runs/1465950150/checkpoints/model-30200
```

Now let's look at the evaluation step:

```
$ ./eval.py -eval_train --checkpoint_dir==./runs/1465950150/checkpoints/
Parameters:
ALLOW_SOFT_PLACEMENT=True
BATCH_SIZE=64
CHECKPOINT_DIR=/Users/saif/Documents/BOOK/cnn-text-classification-
tf/runs/1465950150/checkpoints/
LOG_DEVICE_PLACEMENT=False
Loading data...
Vocabulary size: 18765
Test set size 10662
Evaluating...
Total number of test examples: 10662
Accuracy: 0.973832
```

That is pretty good accuracy on the dataset we have. The next step will be to apply the trained model to regular use. Some interesting experiments may be to obtain movie review data from another source, perhaps IMDB or Amazon. As the data will not necessarily be tagged, we can use % positive as a metric of general agreement across sites.

We can then use the model in the field. Consider you were a product manufacturer. You could track, in real time, all reviews from myriad sources and filter for just highly negative reviews. Then, your field-representatives could try and address such issues. The possibilities are endless, so we propose an interesting project you could undertake, combining the two items we've learned.

Write a twitter stream reader that takes each tweet and extracts the subject of the tweet. For a specific set of subjects, say companies, evaluate whether the tweet is positive or negative. Create running metrics on percent positive and negative, which evaluates the subject on different time scales.

Skills learned

You should have learned the following skills in this chapter:

- Setting up more advanced TensorFlow libraries, including those requiring Bazel-driven compilation
- Working with text data
- Applying RNNs and CNNs to text instead of images
- Evaluating text against saved models
- Using prebuilt libraries to extract sentence structure details
- Classifying text into buckets based on positive and negative sentiment

Summary

Excellent! We just took our knowledge of neural networks and applied it to text to understand language. This is quite a feat because full automation leads to vast scale. Even if particular evaluations are not correct, statistically, we'll have a powerful tool in our hands, again, built using the same building blocks.

7
Making Money with Machine Learning

So far, we've used TensorFlow mostly for image processing, and, to a lesser extent, for text sequence processing. In this chapter, we will tackle a specific type of tabular data: time-series, data.

The time series data comes from many domains with usually one commonality—the only field changing constantly is a time or sequence field. It is common in a variety of fields, but especially common in economics, finance, health, medicine, environmental engineering, and control engineering. We'll dive into examples throughout the chapter, but the key thing to remember is that order matters. Unlike in previous chapters, where we shuffled our data freely, time series data cannot be shuffled that way without losing meaning. An added complexity can be the availability of data itself; if we have data available up until the current time with no further historical data to capture, no amount of data collection will possibly produce more—you are bound by time-based availability.

Luckily, we're going to dive into an area with copious amounts of data: the financial world. We'll explore some types of things hedge funds and other sophisticated investors may do with a time series data.

In this chapter, we will cover the following topics:

- What a time series data is and its special properties
- Types of input and approaches investments firms may use in their quantitative and ML-driven investment efforts
- Financial time series data and how it is obtained; we'll obtain some live financial data as well
- The application of modified convolutional neural networks to finance

Inputs and approaches

Investment firms' internal proprietary trading groups use a large variety of means to invest, trade, and make money. Hedge funds, which are relatively unregulated, use an even broader, more interesting, and more sophisticated means for investment. Some investments are gut-driven or driven by a great deal of thinking. Others are largely filter-driven, algorithmic, or signal-driven. Both approaches are fine, but we'll of course focus on the latter category.

Amongst the quantitative approaches, there are numerous techniques; some of them are as follows:

- Valuation based
- Anomaly and signal based
- External signal based
- Filtering and segmentation-based cohort analysis

Some of these approaches will use traditional machine learning techniques, such as K-Nearest Neighbors, Naive Bayes, and Support Vector Machines. Cohort analysis, in particular, is almost a perfect fit for KNN-type approaches.

Another popular technique is sentiment analysis and crowd-sentiment-based signals. We covered this in the previous chapter as we gauged text sentiment and classified paragraphs of text into basic categories: positive, negative, happy, angry, and so on. Imagine if we sourced more data and filtered out everything except those involving particular stocks, we'd be able to get a valence on stocks. Now, imagine we had a source of such text that was broad (possibly global), high volume, and high velocity—actually, there is no need to imagine, as all of this entered the scene in the past decade. Twitter makes their *firehose* available via an API, as does Facebook, and a host of other social media platforms. Some hedge funds, in fact, consume the entire firehose of Twitter and Facebook data and attempt to extract public sentiment on stocks, market sectors, commodities, and the like. However, this is an external NLP-driven signal-based investment strategy that practitioners use to predict the directionality and/or intensity of a time series.

In this chapter, we'll use internal measures using the time series itself to predict future entries on the time series. Predicting the actual future entry is actually a very difficult task, and it turns out, not entirely necessary. Often, just a viewpoint in one direction is sufficient. A view on the direction combined with the intensity of movement is better.

For many types of investing, even the viewpoint might not give you complete assurance, rather something more right than wrong on average can be sufficient. Imagine betting a penny per flip of a coin—if you could be right 51% of the time, and if you had the ability to play the game thousands of times, it may be enough to be profitable, as you would gain more than you lose.

This all bodes well for machine learning based efforts where we may not have 100% confidence in our answers but may have good predictive ability statistically. Net-net we want to be ahead because even a slight leg-up can be multiplied by thousands of cycles to produce substantial profits.

Getting the data

Let's start by grabbing some data. For the purposes of this chapter, we'll use data from Quandl, a longtime favorite of technically adept independent investors. Quandl makes data available on many stocks using a number of mechanisms. One easy mechanism is via a URL API. To get stock data on, say, Google Stock, we can click on `https://www.quandl.com/api/v3/datasets/WIKI/GOOG/data.json`. Similarly, we can replace `GOOG` with other index codes to grab data on other stocks.

This is fairly easy to automate via Python; we will use the following code to do so:

```python
import requests

API_KEY = '<your_api_key>'

start_date = '2010-01-01'
end_date = '2015-01-01'
order = 'asc'
column_index = 4

stock_exchange = 'WIKI'
index = 'GOOG'

data_specs =
'start_date={}&end_date={}&order={}&column_index={}&api_key={}'
    .format(start_date, end_date, order, column_index, API_KEY)
base_url =
"https://www.quandl.com/api/v3/datasets/{}/{}/data.json?" +
data_specs
stock_data = requests.get(base_url.format(stock_exchange,
index)).json()
```

So, here, in the `stock_data` variable, you'll have the stock data variable from WIKI/GOOG into the `stock_data` variable, downloaded from the formatted URL between the dates `2010-01-01` and `2015-01-01`. The `column_index = 4` variables is telling the server to get only the closing values from the history.

 Note that you can find this chapter's code in your GitHub repository—(`https://github.com/saifrahmed/MLwithTF/tree/master/b ook_code/chapter_07`).

So, what are these closing values? Well, stock prices fluctuate every day. They open with a certain value and they reach a certain high value and a certain low value within a day, and, at the end of the day, they close with a certain value. The following image shows how the stock prices change within each day:

DATE	OPEN	HIGH	LOW	CLOSE
1999-11-18	45.5	50	40	44
1999-11-19	42.94	43	39.81	40.38
1999-11-22	41.31	44	40.06	44
1999-11-23	42.5	43.63	40.25	40.25
1999-11-24	40.13	41.94	40	41.06
1999-11-26	40.88	41.5	40.75	41.19
1999-11-29	41	42.44	40.56	42.13
1999-11-30	42	42.94	40.94	42.19
1999-12-01	42.19	43.44	41.88	42.94
1999-12-02	43.75	45	43.19	44.13
1999-12-03	44.94	45.69	44.31	44.5
1999-12-06	45.25	46.44	45.19	45.75
1999-12-07	45.75	46	44.31	45.25
1999-12-08	45.25	45.63	44.81	45.19
1999-12-09	45.25	45.94	45.25	45.81
1999-12-10	45.69	45.94	44.75	44.75
1999-12-13	45.5	46.25	44.38	45.5
1999-12-14	45.38	45.38	42.06	43
1999-12-15	42	42.31	41	41.69
1999-12-16	42	48	42	47.25
1999-12-17	46.38	47.12	45.44	45.94

So, after the stock opens, you can invest in them and buy shares. At the end of the day, you'll have either a profit or a loss, depending on the closing values of those shares bought. Investors use different techniques to predict which stocks have the potential to rise on a particular day, and, depending on their analysis, they invest in shares.

Approaching the problem

In this chapter, we will find out whether the stock prices will rise or fall depending on the rises and falls of markets in other time zones (such that their closing time is earlier than the stock in which we want to invest in). We will analyze the data from European markets that close about 3 or 4 hours before the American stock markets. From Quandl, we will get the data from the following European markets:

- `WSE/OPONEO_PL`
- `WSE/VINDEXUS`
- `WSE/WAWEL`
- `WSE/WIELTON`

And we will predict the closing rise and fall for the following American market: WIKI/SNPS.

We will download all the market data, view the downloaded graphs for the markets' closing values, and modify the data so that it can be trained on our networks. Then, we'll see how our networks perform on our assumptions.

The code and analysis techniques used in this chapter are inspired by Google's Cloud Datalab notebook found at `https://github.com/googledatalab/notebooks/blob/master/samples/TensorFlow/Machine%20Learning%20with%20Financial%20Data.ipynbhere`.

The steps are as follows:

1. Download the required data and modify it.
2. View the original and modified data.
3. Extract features from the modified data.
4. Prepare for training and test out the network.
5. Build the network.
6. Training.
7. Testing.

Downloading and modifying data

Here, we will download the data from the sources mentioned in the `codes` variable, and we will put them into our `closings` data frame. We will store the original data, `scaled` data, and the `log_return`:

```
codes = ["WSE/OPONEO_PL", "WSE/VINDEXUS", "WSE/WAWEL",
"WSE/WIELTON", "WIKI/SNPS"]
closings = pd.DataFrame()
for code in codes:
    code_splits = code.split("/")
    stock_exchange = code_splits[0]
    index = code_splits[1]
    stock_data = requests.get(base_url.format(stock_exchange,
    index)).json()
    dataset_data = stock_data['dataset_data']
    data = np.array(dataset_data['data'])
    closings[index] = pd.Series(data[:, 1].astype(float))
    closings[index + "_scaled"] = closings[index] /
     max(closings[index])
    closings[index + "_log_return"] = np.log(closings[index] /
closings[index].shift())
closings = closings.fillna(method='ffill')  # Fill the gaps in data
```

We scaled the data so that the stock values stay between 0 and 1; this is helpful for minimizing compared to other stock values. It will help us see trends in the stock compared to other markets and will make it visually easier to analyze.

The log returns help us get a graph of the market rising and falling compared to the previous day.

Now let's see how our data looks.

Viewing the data

The following code snippet will plot the data we downloaded and processed:

```
def show_plot(key="", show=True):
    fig = plt.figure()
    fig.set_figwidth(20)
    fig.set_figheight(15)
    for code in codes:
        index = code.split("/")[1]
        if key and len(key) > 0:
            label = "{}_{}".format(index, key)
```

```
    else:
        label = index
    _ = plt.plot(closings[label], label=label)

    _ = plt.legend(loc='upper right')
    if show:
        plt.show()

show = True
show_plot("", show=show)
show_plot("scaled", show=show)
show_plot("log_return", show=show)
```

The original market data to close values. As you can see here, the value for **WAWEL** is a couple of magnitudes larger than the other markets:

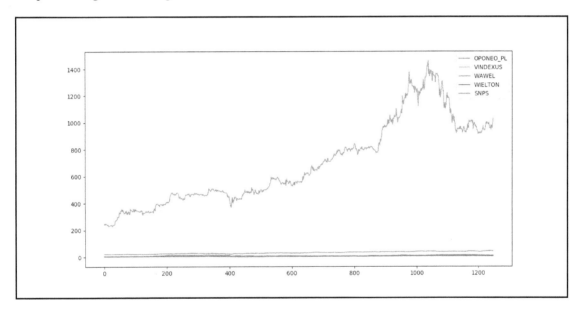

The closing values for WAWEL visually reduced the trends in data for the other market values. We will scale this data so we can see it better. Take a look at the following screenshot:

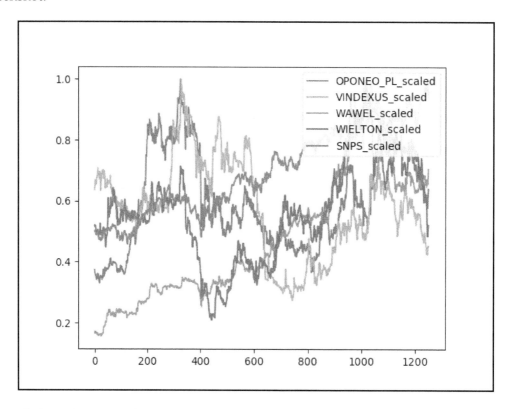

The scaled market values help us visualize the trends better. Now, let's see how the log_return looks:

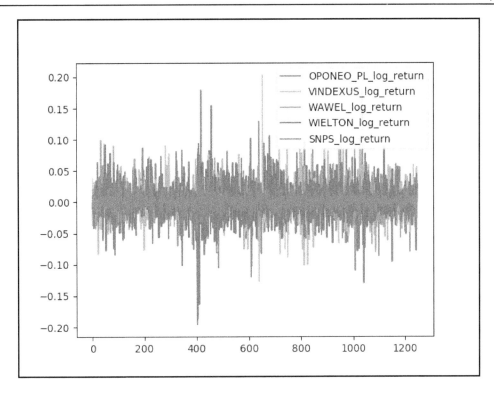

The log returns the markets' closing values

Extracting features

Now, we will extract the required features to train and test our data:

```
feature_columns = ['SNPS_log_return_positive',
'SNPS_log_return_negative']
for i in range(len(codes)):
    index = codes[i].split("/")[1]
    feature_columns.extend([
        '{}_log_return_1'.format(index),
        '{}_log_return_2'.format(index),
        '{}_log_return_3'.format(index)
    ])
features_and_labels = pd.DataFrame(columns=feature_columns)
closings['SNPS_log_return_positive'] = 0
closings.ix[closings['SNPS_log_return'] >= 0,
'SNPS_log_return_positive'] = 1
closings['SNPS_log_return_negative'] = 0
```

```
closings.ix[closings['SNPS_log_return'] < 0,
'SNPS_log_return_negative'] = 1
for i in range(7, len(closings)):
    feed_dict = {'SNPS_log_return_positive':
closings['SNPS_log_return_positive'].ix[i],
        'SNPS_log_return_negative':
closings['SNPS_log_return_negative'].ix[i]}
    for j in range(len(codes)):
        index = codes[j].split("/")[1]
        k = 1 if j == len(codes) - 1 else 0
        feed_dict.update({'{}_log_return_1'.format(index):
closings['{}_log_return'.format(index)].ix[i - k],
            '{}_log_return_2'.format(index):
closings['{}_log_return'.format(index)].ix[i - 1 - k],
            '{}_log_return_3'.format(index):
closings['{}_log_return'.format(index)].ix[i - 2 - k]})
    features_and_labels = features_and_labels.append(feed_dict,
ignore_index=True)
```

We are storing all our features and labels in the `features_and_label` variable. The `SNPS_log_return_positive` and `SNPS_log_return_negative` keys store the point where the log returns for SNPS are positive and negative, respectively. They are 1 if true and 0 if false. These two keys will act as the labels for the network.

The other keys are to store the values of other markets for the last 3 days (and for the preceding 3 days for SNPS because today's value won't be available to us for this market).

Preparing for training and testing

Now we'll split our features into `train` and `test` subsets. We won't be randomizing our data because, in time series for financial markets, the data comes every day in a regular manner and we have to follow it like it is. You can't predict the past behavior if you train for the future data because that would be useless. We are always interested in the future behavior of the stock market:

```
features = features_and_labels[features_and_labels.columns[2:]]
labels = features_and_labels[features_and_labels.columns[:2]]
train_size = int(len(features_and_labels) * train_test_split)
test_size = len(features_and_labels) - train_size
train_features = features[:train_size]
train_labels = labels[:train_size]
test_features = features[train_size:]
test_labels = labels[train_size:]
```

Building the network

The network model to train our time series looks as follows:

```
sess = tf.Session()
num_predictors = len(train_features.columns)
num_classes = len(train_labels.columns)
feature_data = tf.placeholder("float", [None, num_predictors])
actual_classes = tf.placeholder("float", [None, 2])
weights1 = tf.Variable(tf.truncated_normal([len(codes) * 3, 50],
stddev=0.0001))
biases1 = tf.Variable(tf.ones([50]))
weights2 = tf.Variable(tf.truncated_normal([50, 25],
stddev=0.0001))
biases2 = tf.Variable(tf.ones([25]))
weights3 = tf.Variable(tf.truncated_normal([25, 2], stddev=0.0001))
biases3 = tf.Variable(tf.ones([2]))
hidden_layer_1 = tf.nn.relu(tf.matmul(feature_data, weights1) +
biases1)
hidden_layer_2 = tf.nn.relu(tf.matmul(hidden_layer_1, weights2) +
biases2)
model = tf.nn.softmax(tf.matmul(hidden_layer_2, weights3) +
biases3)
cost = -tf.reduce_sum(actual_classes * tf.log(model))
train_op1 =
tf.train.AdamOptimizer(learning_rate=0.0001).minimize(cost)
init = tf.initialize_all_variables()
sess.run(init)
correct_prediction = tf.equal(tf.argmax(model, 1),
tf.argmax(actual_classes, 1))
accuracy = tf.reduce_mean(tf.cast(correct_prediction, "float"))
```

This is just a simple network with two hidden layers.

Training

Now, let's train our network:

```
for i in range(1, 30001):
    sess.run(train_op1, feed_dict={feature_data:
train_features.values,
            actual_classes:
train_labels.values.reshape(len(train_labels.values), 2)})
    if i % 5000 == 0:
        print(i, sess.run(accuracy, feed_dict={feature_data:
train_features.values,
```

```
              actual_classes:
    train_labels.values.reshape(len(train_labels.values), 2)}))
```

Testing

The testing of our network looks as follows:

```
feed_dict = {
    feature_data: test_features.values,
    actual_classes:
test_labels.values.reshape(len(test_labels.values), 2)
}
tf_confusion_metrics(model, actual_classes, sess, feed_dict)
```

Taking it further

Suppose you just trained a nifty classifier showing some predictive power over the markets, should you start trading? Much like with the other machine learning projects we've done to date, you will need to test on an independent test set. In the past, we've often cordoned off our data into the following three sets:

- The training set
- The development set, aka the validation set
- The test set

We can do something similar to our current work, but the financial markets give us an added resource—ongoing data streams!

We can use the same data source we used for our earlier pulls and continue to pull more data; essentially, we have an ever-expanding, unseen dataset! Of course, some of this depends on the frequency of the data that we use—if we operate on daily data, it will take a while to accomplish this. Operating on hourly or per-minute data makes this easier as we'll have more data quickly. Operating on tick-level data, based on the volume of quotes, is usually even better.

As real money can potentially be at stake here, most people will typically paper trade—essentially, run the system almost live, but not actually spend any money and instead just keep track of how the system will operate when live. If this works, then the next step will be to trade it live, that is, with real money (usually, a small amount to test the system).

Practical considerations for the individual

Suppose you trained a nifty classifier and also showed good results over a blind or live set, now should you start trading? While it is possible, it isn't so easy. The following are some reasons why:

- **Historical analyses versus streaming data**: This historical data is often cleansed and near perfect, but streaming data does not offer such benefits. You will need code to evaluate the stream of data and throw out potentially unreliable data.

- **Bid-ask spread**: This is the biggest surprise novice's face. There are actually two prices in the marketplace: the price at which you can buy and the one at which you can sell. You don't both buy and sell at the typical market price you see (that is just the last meeting point on the two, called the last price). Buying a holding and immediately selling it loses money because of this gap, so net-net, you are already at a loss.

- **Transaction costs**: This can be as small as a $1/trade, but it is still a hurdle and one that needs to be surpassed before a strategy can become profitable.

- **Taxes**: This is often forgotten, but probably because taxes indicate net gains, which is usually a good thing.

- **Exit ability**: Just because you can sell theoretically does not mean there is actually a market available to sell your holding, and, even if there is, possibly not for your entire holding. Guess what? Yet more coding is required. This time, look at bid prices, volumes on those prices, and the depth of the book.

- **Volume and liquidity**: Just because the signal tells you to buy doesn't mean there is sufficient volume in the market to purchase; you may be seeing just the top of the book with very little actual volume underneath. More coding is required!

- **Integrations with trading APIs**: Calling libraries is easy, but not so much when money is involved. You'll need trading agreements, API agreements, and the like. However, tens of thousands of individuals have done this and Interactive Brokers is the most popular brokerage for those seeking APIs to buy and sell holdings. Conveniently, they also have an API to provide market data.

Skills learned

In this chapter, you should have learned the following skills:

- Understanding the time-series data
- Setting up a pipeline for the time-series data
- Integrating primary data
- Creating training and test sets
- Practical considerations

Summary

Machine learning on financial data is no different from the many other data we use and, in fact, we used a network just as we did for other datasets. There are other options we can use, but the general approach stays the same. Especially when transacting money, we will find that the surrounding code becomes larger than ever relative to the actual machine learning portion of the code.

In the next chapter, we will see how we can use machine learning for medical purposes.

8
The Doctor Will See You Now

We have, so far, used deep networks for image, text, and time series processing. While most of our examples were interesting and relevant, they weren't enterprise-grade. Now, we'll tackle an enterprise-grade problem—medical diagnosis. We make the enterprise-grade designation because medical data has attributes one does not typically deal with outside large enterprises, namely proprietary data formats, large native sizes, inconvenient class data, and atypical features.

In this chapter, we will cover the following topics:

- Medical imaging files and their peculiarities
- Dealing with large image files
- Extracting class data from typical medical files
- Applying networks "pre-trained" with non-medical data
- Scaling training to accommodate the scale typically with medical data

Obtaining medical data is a challenge on its own, so we'll piggyback on a popular site all readers should become familiarized with—Kaggle. While there are a good number of medical datasets freely available, most require an involved sign-up process to even access them. Many are only publicized in specific sub-communities of the medical image processing field, and most have bespoke submission procedures. Kaggle is probably the most normalized source for a significant medical imaging dataset as well as non-medical ones you can try your hand on. We'll focus specifically on Kaggle's Diabetic Retinopathy Detection challenge.

- You can view the dataset here:
- `https://www.kaggle.com/c/diabetic-retinopathy-detection/data`

The dataset has a training set and a blind test set. The training set is used for, of course, training our network, and the test set is used to submit our results using our network on the Kaggle website.

As the data is quite large (32 GB for the training set and 49 GB for the test set), both of them are divided into multiple ZIP files of about 8 GB.

The test set here is blind—we don't know their labels. This is for the purpose of having fair submissions of the test set results from our trained network.

As far as the training set goes, its labels are present in the `trainLabels.csv` file.

The challenge

Before we deep-dive into the code, remember how most machine learning efforts involve one of two simple goals—classification or ranking. In many cases, the classification is itself a ranking because we end up choosing the classification with the greatest rank (often a probability). Our foray into medical imaging will be no different—we will be classifying images into either of these binary categories:

- Disease state/positive
- Normal state/negative

Or, we will classify them into multiple classes or rank them. In the case of the diabetic retinopathy, we'll rank them as follows:

- Class 0: No Diabetic Retinopathy
- Class 1: Mild
- Class 2: Moderate
- Class 3: Severe
- Class 4: Widespread Diabetic Retinopathy

Often, this is called scoring. Kaggle kindly provides participants over 32 GB of training data, which includes over 35,000 images. The test data is even larger—49 GB. The goal is to train on the 35,000+ images using the known scores and propose scores for the test set. The training labels look like this:

Image	Level
10_left	0
10_right	0
13_left	0
13_right	0
15_left	1
15_right	2
16_left	4
16_right	4
17_left	0
17_right	1

Some context here—diabetic retinopathy is a disease of the retina, inside the eye, so we have scores for the left and right eye. We can treat them as independent training data, or we can get creative later and consider them in the larger context of a single patient. Let's start simple and iterate.

By now, you are probably familiar with taking a set of data and segmenting out chunks for training, validation, and testing. That worked well for some of the standard datasets we've used, but this dataset is part of a competition and one that is publicly audited, so we don't know the answers! This is a pretty good reflection of real life. There is one wrinkle—most Kaggle competitions let you propose an answer and tell you your aggregate score, which helps with learning and direction-setting. It also helps them and the community know which users are doing well.

Since the test labels are blinded, we'll need to change two things we've done before:

- We will need to have one procedure for internal development and iteration (we'll likely chunk our training set into a training, validation, and test set). We will need another procedure for external testing (we may settle upon a promising setup that works well, and then we may either run it on the blind test set or we may retrain on the entire training set first).

- We will need to make a formal proposal in a very specific format, submit it to the independent auditor (Kaggle, in this case), and gauge the progress accordingly. Here is what a sample submission may look like:

Image	Level
44342_left	0
44342_right	1
44344_left	2
44344_right	2
44345_left	0
44345_right	0
44346_left	4
44346_right	3
44350_left	1
44350_right	1
44351_left	4
44351_right	4

Not surprisingly, it looks very much like the training label file. You can make your submission here:

https://www.kaggle.com/c/diabetic-retinopathy-detection/submithttps://www.kaggle.com/c/diabetic-retinopathy-detection/submit

 You need to login in order to open the preceding link.

The data

Let's start to peek at the data. Open up some of the sample files and be prepared for a shocker—these are neither 28x28 tiles of handwriting nor 64x64 icons with cat faces. This is a real dataset from the real world. In fact, not even the sizes are consistent across images. Welcome to the real world.

You'll find sizes ranging from 2,000 pixels per side to almost 5,000 pixels! This brings us to our first real-life task—creating a training **pipeline**. The pipeline will be a set of steps that abstract away the ugly realities of life and produce a set of clean and consistent data.

The pipeline

We will go about this intelligently. There are a lot of pipeline model structures made by Google using different networks in their `TensorFlow` library. What we'll do here is take one of those model structures and networks and modify the code to our needs.

This is good because we won't waste our time building a pipeline from scratch and won't have to worry about incorporating the TensorBoard visualization stuff as it is already present in the Google pipeline models.

We will use a pipeline model from here:

`https://github.com/tensorflow/models/`

As you can see, there are a lot of different models made in TensorFlow in this repository. You can dive deeper into some models that are related to natural language processing (NLP), recursive neural networks, and other topics. This is a really good place to start if you want to understand complex models.

For this chapter, we will use the **Tensorflow-Slim image classification model library**. You can find the library here:

`https://github.com/tensorflow/models/tree/master/research/slim`

There are a lot of details already present on the website that explain how to use this library. They also tell you how to use this library in a distributed environment and also how to utilize multiple GPUs to get a faster training time and even deploy to production.

The best thing about using this is that they provide you with the pre-trained model snapshot, which you can use to dramatically reduce the training time of your network. So, even if you have slow GPUs, you won't have to train your network this large for weeks to get to a reasonable level of training.

This is called fine-tuning of the model, in which you just have to provide a different dataset and tell the network to reinitialize the final layers of the network in order to retrain them. Also, you tell it how many output label classes you have in your dataset. In our case, there are five unique classes to identify different levels of **diabetic retinopathy** (**DR**).

The pre-trained snapshot can be found here:

```
https://github.com/tensorflow/models/tree/master/research/slim#Pretrained
```

As you can see in the preceding link, they provide many types of pre-trained models that we can leverage. They have used the `ImageNet` dataset to train these models. `ImageNet` is a standard dataset of 1,000 classes with dataset sizing almost 500 GB. You can find more about it here:

```
http://image-net.org/
```

Understanding the pipeline

Let's start by cloning the `models` repository into your computer:

```
git clone https://github.com/tensorflow/models/
```

Now, let's dive into the pipeline that we got from Google's model repository.

If you look at the folder at this path prefix (`models/research/slim`) in the repository, you'll see folders named `datasets`, `deployment`, `nets`, `preprocessing`, and `scripts`; a bunch of files related to generating the model, plus training and testing pipelines and files related to training the `ImageNet` dataset, and a dataset named `flowers`.

We will use the `download_and_convert_data.py` to build our DR dataset. This `image classification model` library is built based on the `slim` library. In this chapter, we will fine-tune the inception network defined in `nets/inception_v3.py` (we'll talk more about the network specifications and its concept later in this chapter), which includes the calculation of the loss function, adding different ops, structuring the network, and more. Finally, the `train_image_classifier.py` and `eval_image_classifier.py` files contain the generalized procedures for making a training and testing pipeline for our network.

For this chapter, due to the complex nature of the network, we are using a GPU-based pipeline to train the network. If you want to find out how to install TensorFlow for GPU in your machine, then refer to `Appendix A`, *Advanced Installation*, in this book. Also, you should have about **120 GB** space inside your machine to be able to run this code. You can find the final code files in the `Chapter 8` folder of this book's code files.

Preparing the dataset

Now, let's start preparing the dataset of our network.

For this inception network, we'll use the `TFRecord` class to manage our dataset. The output dataset files after the preprocessing will be protofiles, which `TFRecord` can read, and it's just our data stored in a serialized format for faster reading speed. Each protofile has some information stored within it, which is information such as image size and format.

The reason we are doing this is that the size of the dataset is too large and we cannot load the entire dataset into memory (RAM) as it will take up a huge amount of space. Therefore, to manage efficient RAM usage, we have to load the images in batches and delete the previously loaded images that are not being used right now.

The input size the network will take is 299x299. So, we will find a way to first reduce the image size to 299x299 to have a dataset of consistent images.

After reducing the images, we will make protofiles that we can later feed into our network, which will get trained on our dataset.

You need to first download the five training ZIP files and the labels file from here:

```
https://www.kaggle.com/c/diabetic-retinopathy-detection/data
```

Unfortunately, Kaggle only lets you download the training ZIP files through an account, so this procedure of downloading the dataset files (as in the previous chapters) can't be made automatic.

Now, let's assume that you have downloaded all five training ZIP files and labels file and stored them in a folder named `diabetic`. The structure of the `diabetic` folder will look like this:

- `diabetic`
    - `train.zip.001`
    - `train.zip.002`
    - `train.zip.003`
    - `train.zip.004`
    - `train.zip.005`
    - `trainLabels.csv.zip`

In order to simplify the project, we will do the extraction manually using the compression software. After the extraction is completed, the structure of the `diabetic` folder will look like this:

- `diabetic`
    - `train`
        - ` 10_left.jpeg`
        - `10_right.jpeg`
        - ...
    - `trainLabels.csv`
    - `train.zip.001`
    - `train.zip.002`
    - ` train.zip.003`
    - ` train.zip.004`
    - `train.zip.005`
    - `trainLabels.csv.zip`

In this case, the `train` folder contains all the images in the .zip files and `trainLabels.csv` contains the ground truth labels for each image.

The author of the models repository has provided some example code to work with some popular image classification datasets. Our diabetic problem can be solved with the same approach. Therefore, we can follow the code that works with other datasets such as `flower` or `MNIST` dataset. We have already provided the modification to work with diabetic in the repository of this book at `https://github.com/mlwithtf/mlwithtf/`.

You need to clone the repository and navigate to the `chapter_08` folder. You can run the `download_and_convert_data.py` file as follows:

```
python download_and_convert_data.py --dataset_name diabetic --dataset_dir
D:\\datasets\\diabetic
```

In this case, we will use `dataset_name` as `diabetic` and `dataset_dir` is the folder that contains the `trainLabels.csv` and `train` folder.

It should run without any issues, start preprocessing our dataset into a suitable (299x299) format, and create some `TFRecord` file in a newly created folder named `tfrecords`. The following figure shows the content of the `tfrecords` folder:

Explaining the data preparation

Now let's get to the coding part for the data preprocessing. From now on, we will show you what we have changed from the original repository of the `tensorflow/models`. Basically, we take the code to the process `flowers` dataset as the starting point and modify them to suit our needs.

In the `download_and_convert_data.py` file, we have added a new line at the beginning of the file:

```
from datasets import download_and_convert_diabetic
and a new else-if clause to process the dataset_name "diabetic" at line 69:
   elif FLAGS.dataset_name == 'diabetic':
       download_and_convert_diabetic.run(FLAGS.dataset_dir)
```

With this code, we can call the run method in the `download_and_convert_diabetic.py` in the `datasets` folder. This is a really simple approach to separating the preprocessing code of multiple datasets, but we can still take advantage of the others parts of the `image classification` library.

The `download_and_convert_diabetic.py` file is a copy of the `download_and_convert_flowers.py` file with some modifications to prepare our diabetic dataset.

In the run method of the `download_and_convert_diabetic.py` file, we made changes as follows:

```
def run(dataset_dir):
    """Runs the download and conversion operation.

    Args:
        dataset_dir: The dataset directory where the dataset is stored.
    """
    if not tf.gfile.Exists(dataset_dir):
        tf.gfile.MakeDirs(dataset_dir)

    if _dataset_exists(dataset_dir):
        print('Dataset files already exist. Exiting without re-creating
        them.')
        return

    # Pre-processing the images.
    data_utils.prepare_dr_dataset(dataset_dir)
    training_filenames, validation_filenames, class_names =
    _get_filenames_and_classes(dataset_dir)
    class_names_to_ids = dict(zip(class_names,
    range(len(class_names))))

    # Convert the training and validation sets.
    _convert_dataset('train', training_filenames, class_names_to_ids,
    dataset_dir)
    _convert_dataset('validation', validation_filenames,
    class_names_to_ids, dataset_dir)

    # Finally, write the labels file:
    labels_to_class_names = dict(zip(range(len(class_names)),
    class_names))
    dataset_utils.write_label_file(labels_to_class_names, dataset_dir)

    print('\nFinished converting the Diabetic dataset!')
```

In this code, we use the `prepare_dr_dataset` from the `data_utils` package that was prepared in the root of this book repository. We will look at that method later. Then, we changed the `_get_filenames_and_classes` method to return the `training` and `validation` filenames. The last few lines are the same as the `flowers` dataset example:

```
def _get_filenames_and_classes(dataset_dir):
    train_root = os.path.join(dataset_dir, 'processed_images', 'train')
    validation_root = os.path.join(dataset_dir, 'processed_images',
    'validation')
    class_names = []
    for filename in os.listdir(train_root):
        path = os.path.join(train_root, filename)
        if os.path.isdir(path):
            class_names.append(filename)

    train_filenames = []
    directories = [os.path.join(train_root, name) for name in
    class_names]
    for directory in directories:
        for filename in os.listdir(directory):
            path = os.path.join(directory, filename)
            train_filenames.append(path)

    validation_filenames = []
    directories = [os.path.join(validation_root, name) for name in
    class_names]
    for directory in directories:
        for filename in os.listdir(directory):
            path = os.path.join(directory, filename)
            validation_filenames.append(path)
    return train_filenames, validation_filenames, sorted(class_names)
```

In the preceding method, we find all the filenames in the `processed_images/train` and `processed/validation` folder, which contains the images that were preprocessed in the `data_utils.prepare_dr_dataset` method.

In the `data_utils.py` file, we have written the `prepare_dr_dataset(dataset_dir)` function, which is responsible for the entire preprocessing of the data.

Let's start by defining the necessary variables to link to our data:

```
num_of_processing_threads = 16
dr_dataset_base_path = os.path.realpath(dataset_dir)
unique_labels_file_path = os.path.join(dr_dataset_base_path,
"unique_labels_file.txt")
processed_images_folder = os.path.join(dr_dataset_base_path,
"processed_images")
```

```
num_of_processed_images = 35126
train_processed_images_folder =
os.path.join(processed_images_folder, "train")
validation_processed_images_folder =
os.path.join(processed_images_folder, "validation")
num_of_training_images = 30000
raw_images_folder = os.path.join(dr_dataset_base_path, "train")
train_labels_csv_path = os.path.join(dr_dataset_base_path,
"trainLabels.csv")
```

The `num_of_processing_threads` variable is used to specify the number of threads we want to use while preprocessing our dataset, as you may have already guessed. We will use a multi-threaded environment to preprocess our data faster. Later on, we have specified some directory paths to contain our data inside different folders while preprocessing.

We will extract the images in their raw form and then preprocess them to get them into a suitable consistent format and size, and then we will generate the `tfrecords` files from the processed images with the `_convert_dataset` method in the `download_and_convert_diabetic.py` file. After that, we will feed these `tfrecords` files into the training and testing networks.

As we said in the previous section, we have already extracted the `dataset` files and the labels files. Now, as we have all of the data extracted and present inside our machine, we will process the images. A typical image from the DR dataset looks like this:

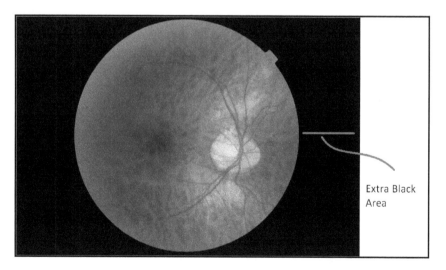

Extra Black Area

What we want is to remove this extra black space because it is not necessary for our network. This will reduce the unnecessary information inside the image. After this, we will scale this image into a 299x299 JPG image file.

We will repeat this process for all of the training datasets.

The function to crop the black image borders is as follows:

```
def crop_black_borders(image, threshold=0):
    """Crops any edges below or equal to threshold

    Crops blank image to 1x1.

    Returns cropped image.

    """
    if len(image.shape) == 3:
        flatImage = np.max(image, 2)
    else:
        flatImage = image
    assert len(flatImage.shape) == 2

    rows = np.where(np.max(flatImage, 0) > threshold)[0]
    if rows.size:
        cols = np.where(np.max(flatImage, 1) > threshold)[0]
        image = image[cols[0]: cols[-1] + 1, rows[0]: rows[-1] + 1]
    else:
        image = image[:1, :1]

    return image
```

This function takes the image and a threshold for a grayscale, below which it will remove the black borders around the image.

As we are doing all of this processing in a multithreaded environment, we will process the images in batches. To process an image batch, we will use the following function:

```
def process_images_batch(thread_index, files, labels, subset):

    num_of_files = len(files)

    for index, file_and_label in enumerate(zip(files, labels)):
        file = file_and_label[0] + '.jpeg'
        label = file_and_label[1]

        input_file = os.path.join(raw_images_folder, file)
        output_file = os.path.join(processed_images_folder, subset,
        str(label), file)
```

```
image = ndimage.imread(input_file)
cropped_image = crop_black_borders(image, 10)
resized_cropped_image = imresize(cropped_image, (299, 299, 3),
interp="bicubic")
imsave(output_file, resized_cropped_image)

if index % 10 == 0:
    print("(Thread {}): Files processed {} out of
    {}".format(thread_index, index, num_of_files))
```

The `thread_index` tells us the ID of the thread in which the function has been called. The threaded environment around processing the image batch is defined in the following function:

```
def process_images(files, labels, subset):

    # Break all images into batches with a [ranges[i][0], ranges[i]
    [1]].
    spacing = np.linspace(0, len(files), num_of_processing_threads +
    1).astype(np.int)
    ranges = []
    for i in xrange(len(spacing) - 1):
        ranges.append([spacing[i], spacing[i + 1]])

    # Create a mechanism for monitoring when all threads are finished.
    coord = tf.train.Coordinator()

    threads = []
    for thread_index in xrange(len(ranges)):
        args = (thread_index, files[ranges[thread_index]
        [0]:ranges[thread_index][1]],
                labels[ranges[thread_index][0]:ranges[thread_index]
                [1]],
                subset)
        t = threading.Thread(target=process_images_batch, args=args)
        t.start()
        threads.append(t)

    # Wait for all the threads to terminate.
    coord.join(threads)
```

To get the final result from all of the threads, we use a `TensorFlow` class, `tf.train.Coordinator()`, whose `join` function is responsible for handling all of the threads' final approach point.

For the threading, we use `threading.Thread`, in which the `target` argument specifies the function to be called and the `args` argument specifies the target function arguments.

Now, we will process the training images. The training dataset is divided into a train set (30,000 images) and a validation set (5,126 images).

The total preprocessing is handled as follows:

```
def process_training_and_validation_images():
    train_files = []
    train_labels = []

    validation_files = []
    validation_labels = []

    with open(train_labels_csv_path) as csvfile:
        reader = csv.DictReader(csvfile)
        for index, row in enumerate(reader):
            if index < num_of_training_images:
                train_files.extend([row['image'].strip()])
                train_labels.extend([int(row['level'].strip())])
            else:
                validation_files.extend([row['image'].strip()])
                validation_labels.extend([int(row['level'].strip())])

    if not os.path.isdir(processed_images_folder):
        os.mkdir(processed_images_folder)

    if not os.path.isdir(train_processed_images_folder):
        os.mkdir(train_processed_images_folder)

    if not os.path.isdir(validation_processed_images_folder):
        os.mkdir(validation_processed_images_folder)

    for directory_index in range(5):
        train_directory_path =
    os.path.join(train_processed_images_folder,
    str(directory_index))
        valid_directory_path =
    os.path.join(validation_processed_images_folder,
    str(directory_index))

        if not os.path.isdir(train_directory_path):
            os.mkdir(train_directory_path)

        if not os.path.isdir(valid_directory_path):
            os.mkdir(valid_directory_path)
```

```
print("Processing training files...")
process_images(train_files, train_labels, "train")
print("Done!")

print("Processing validation files...")
process_images(validation_files, validation_labels,
"validation")
print("Done!")

print("Making unique labels file...")
with open(unique_labels_file_path, 'w') as unique_labels_file:
    unique_labels = ""
    for index in range(5):
        unique_labels += "{}\n".format(index)
    unique_labels_file.write(unique_labels)

status = check_folder_status(processed_images_folder,
num_of_processed_images,
"All processed images are present in place",
"Couldn't complete the image processing of training and
validation files.")

return status
```

Now, we will look at the last method for preparing the dataset, the _convert_dataset method that is called in the download_and_convert_diabetic.py file:

```
def _get_dataset_filename(dataset_dir, split_name, shard_id):
    output_filename = 'diabetic_%s_%05d-of-%05d.tfrecord' % (
        split_name, shard_id, _NUM_SHARDS)
    return os.path.join(dataset_dir, output_filename)
def _convert_dataset(split_name, filenames, class_names_to_ids,
dataset_dir):
    """Converts the given filenames to a TFRecord dataset.

    Args:
      split_name: The name of the dataset, either 'train' or
    'validation'.
      filenames: A list of absolute paths to png or jpg images.
      class_names_to_ids: A dictionary from class names (strings)
to
      ids
        (integers).
      dataset_dir: The directory where the converted datasets are
      stored.
    """
    assert split_name in ['train', 'validation']
```

```
num_per_shard = int(math.ceil(len(filenames) /
float(_NUM_SHARDS)))

with tf.Graph().as_default():
    image_reader = ImageReader()

    with tf.Session('') as sess:

        for shard_id in range(_NUM_SHARDS):
            output_filename = _get_dataset_filename(
                dataset_dir, split_name, shard_id)

            with tf.python_io.TFRecordWriter(output_filename)
            as
            tfrecord_writer:
                start_ndx = shard_id * num_per_shard
                end_ndx = min((shard_id + 1) * num_per_shard,
                len(filenames))
                for i in range(start_ndx, end_ndx):
                    sys.stdout.write('\r>> Converting image
                    %d/%d shard %d' % (
                        i + 1, len(filenames), shard_id))
                    sys.stdout.flush()

                    # Read the filename:
                    image_data =
                    tf.gfile.FastGFile(filenames[i], 'rb').read()
                    height, width =
                    image_reader.read_image_dims(sess, image_data)

                    class_name =
os.path.basename(os.path.dirname(filenames[i]))
                    class_id = class_names_to_ids[class_name]

                    example = dataset_utils.image_to_tfexample(
                        image_data, b'jpg', height, width,
                        class_id)
                tfrecord_writer.write(example.SerializeToString())

        sys.stdout.write('\n')
        sys.stdout.flush()
```

In the preceding function, we will get the image filenames and then store them in the `tfrecord` files. We will also split the `train` and `validation` files into multiple `tfrecord` files instead of using only one file for each split set.

Now, as the data processing is out of the way, we will formalize the dataset into an instance of `slim.dataset`. **Dataset** from `Tensorflow Slim`. In the `datasets/diabetic.py` file, you will see a method named `get_split`, as follows:

```
_FILE_PATTERN = 'diabetic_%s_*.tfrecord'
SPLITS_TO_SIZES = {'train': 30000, 'validation': 5126}
_NUM_CLASSES = 5
_ITEMS_TO_DESCRIPTIONS = {
    'image': 'A color image of varying size.',
    'label': 'A single integer between 0 and 4',
}
def get_split(split_name, dataset_dir, file_pattern=None,
reader=None):
  """Gets a dataset tuple with instructions for reading flowers.
  Args:
    split_name: A train/validation split name.
    dataset_dir: The base directory of the dataset sources.
    file_pattern: The file pattern to use when matching the dataset
sources.
      It is assumed that the pattern contains a '%s' string so that
the split
      name can be inserted.
    reader: The TensorFlow reader type.
  Returns:
    A `Dataset` namedtuple.
  Raises:
    ValueError: if `split_name` is not a valid train/validation
split.
    """
  if split_name not in SPLITS_TO_SIZES:
    raise ValueError('split name %s was not recognized.' %
split_name)

  if not file_pattern:
    file_pattern = _FILE_PATTERN
  file_pattern = os.path.join(dataset_dir, file_pattern %
split_name)

  # Allowing None in the signature so that dataset_factory can use
the default.
  if reader is None:
    reader = tf.TFRecordReader

  keys_to_features = {
      'image/encoded': tf.FixedLenFeature((), tf.string,
default_value=''),
      'image/format': tf.FixedLenFeature((), tf.string,
default_value='png'),
```

```
            'image/class/label': tf.FixedLenFeature(
                [], tf.int64, default_value=tf.zeros([],
        dtype=tf.int64)),
        }
        items_to_handlers = {
            'image': slim.tfexample_decoder.Image(),
            'label': slim.tfexample_decoder.Tensor('image/class/label'),
        }
        decoder = slim.tfexample_decoder.TFExampleDecoder(
            keys_to_features, items_to_handlers)

        labels_to_names = None
        if dataset_utils.has_labels(dataset_dir):
          labels_to_names = dataset_utils.read_label_file(dataset_dir)

        return slim.dataset.Dataset(
            data_sources=file_pattern,
            reader=reader,
            decoder=decoder,
            num_samples=SPLITS_TO_SIZES[split_name],
            items_to_descriptions=_ITEMS_TO_DESCRIPTIONS,
            num_classes=_NUM_CLASSES,
            labels_to_names=labels_to_names)
```

The preceding method will be called during the training and evaluating routines. We will create an instance of `slim.dataset` with the information about our `tfrecord` files so that it can automatically perform the work to parse the binary files. Moreover, we can also use `slim.dataset.Dataset` with the support of `DatasetDataProvider` from Tensorflow Slim to read the dataset in parallel, so we can increase the training and evaluating routines.

Before we start training, we need to download the pre-trained model of Inception V3 from the `Tensorflow Slim image classification` library so we can leverage the performance of Inception V3 without training from scratch.

The pre-trained snapshot can be found here:

`https://github.com/tensorflow/models/tree/master/research/slim#Pretrained`

In this chapter, we will use Inception V3, so we need to download the `inception_v3_2016_08_28.tar.gz` file and extract it to have the checkpoint file named `inception_v3.ckpt`.

Training routine

Now let's move towards training and evaluating our model.

The training script is present inside `train_image_classifer.py`. Since we have followed the workflow of the library, we can leave this file untouched and run our training routine with the following command:

```
python train_image_classifier.py --
train_dir=D:\datasets\diabetic\checkpoints --dataset_name=diabetic --
dataset_split_name=train --dataset_dir=D:\datasets\diabetic\tfrecords --
model_name=inception_v3 --
checkpoint_path=D:\datasets\diabetic\checkpoints\inception_v3\inception_v3.
ckpt --checkpoint_exclude_scopes=InceptionV3/Logits,InceptionV3/AuxLogits -
-trainable_scopes=InceptionV3/Logits,InceptionV3/AuxLogits --
learning_rate=0.000001 --learning_rate_decay_type=exponential
```

In our setup, we have run the training process overnight. Now, we will run the trained model through the validation process to see how it works.

Validation routine

You can run the validation routine with the following command:

```
python eval_image_classifier.py --alsologtostderr --
checkpoint_path=D:\datasets\diabetic\checkpoints\model.ckpt-92462 --
dataset_name=diabetic --dataset_split_name=validation --
dataset_dir=D:\datasets\diabetic\tfrecords --model_name=inception_v3
```

```
INFO:tensorflow:Evaluation [30/52]
INFO:tensorflow:Evaluation [31/52]
INFO:tensorflow:Evaluation [32/52]
INFO:tensorflow:Evaluation [33/52]
INFO:tensorflow:Evaluation [34/52]
INFO:tensorflow:Evaluation [35/52]
INFO:tensorflow:Evaluation [36/52]
INFO:tensorflow:Evaluation [37/52]
INFO:tensorflow:Evaluation [38/52]
INFO:tensorflow:Evaluation [39/52]
INFO:tensorflow:Evaluation [40/52]
INFO:tensorflow:Evaluation [41/52]
INFO:tensorflow:Evaluation [42/52]
INFO:tensorflow:Evaluation [43/52]
INFO:tensorflow:Evaluation [44/52]
INFO:tensorflow:Evaluation [45/52]
INFO:tensorflow:Evaluation [46/52]
INFO:tensorflow:Evaluation [47/52]
INFO:tensorflow:Evaluation [48/52]
INFO:tensorflow:Evaluation [49/52]
INFO:tensorflow:Evaluation [50/52]
INFO:tensorflow:Evaluation [51/52]
INFO:tensorflow:Evaluation [52/52]
2017-11-03 13:47:49.151625: I C:\tf_jenkins\home\workspace\rel-win\M\windows-gpu\PY\35\tensorflow\core\kernels\logging_o
ps.cc:79] eval/Accuracy[0.751153827]
2017-11-03 13:47:49.492745: I C:\tf_jenkins\home\workspace\rel-win\M\windows-gpu\PY\35\tensorflow\core\kernels\logging_o
ps.cc:79] eval/Recall_5[1]
INFO:tensorflow:Finished evaluation at 2017-11-03-06:47:49
```

As you can see, the current accuracy is about 75 percent. In the *Going further* section, we will give you some ideas to improve this accuracy.

Now, we will look at the TensorBoard to visualize the training process.

Visualize outputs with TensorBoard

Now, we will visualize the training result with TensorBoard.

First, you need to change the command-line directory to the folder that contains the checkpoints. In our case, it is the train_dir parameter in the previous command, D:\datasets\diabetic\checkpoints. Then, you should run the following command:

```
tensorboard -logdir .
```

Here is some output when we run TensorBoard for our network:

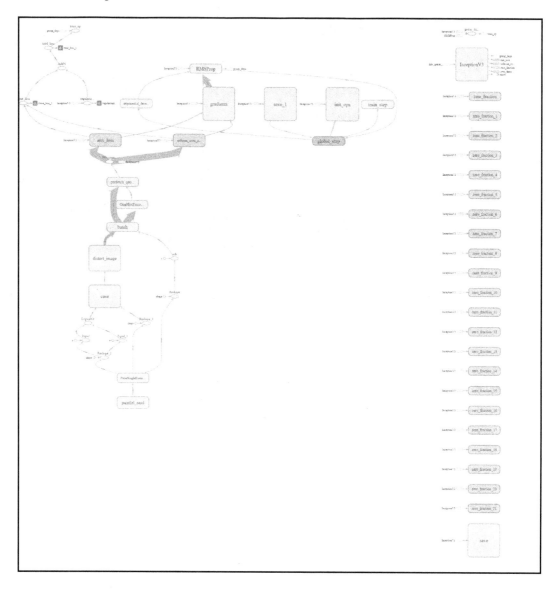

The preceding image shows the nodes containing the RMS prop optimizer for the training network and some logits that it contains for the output of DR classification. The next screenshot shows the images coming as input, along with their preprocessing and modifications:

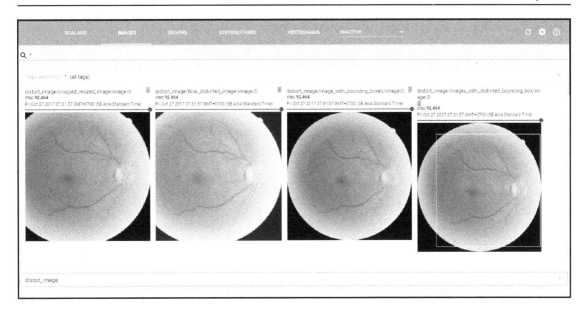

In this screenshot, you can see the graph showing the network output during training:

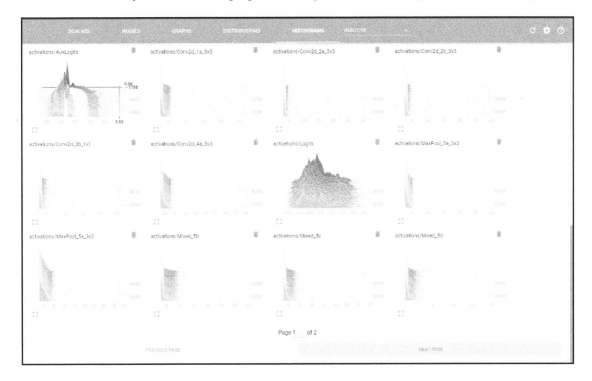

This screenshot depicts the total raw loss of the network during training:

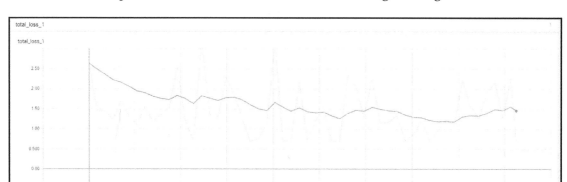

Inception network

The main concept behind the inception network is to combine different convolutions in a single layer. The combination is done by combining 7x7, 5x5, 3x3, and 1x1 convolutions to give to the next layer. Through this, the network can extract more features of the network and thus give better accuracy. This is shown in the following image of the Google inception V3 network. You can try to access the code at `chapter_08/nets/inception_v3.py`.

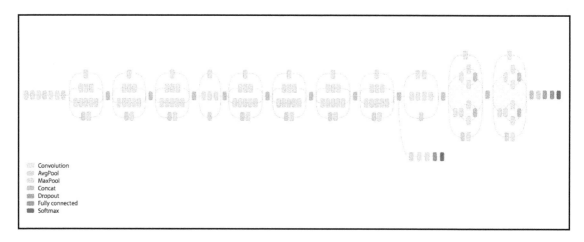

The image is taken from `https://github.com/tensorflow/models/blob/master/research/inception/g3doc/inception_v3_architecture.png`

Going further

The result we got from running this network is 75 percent accurate on the validation set. This is not very good because of the criticality of the network usage. In medicine, there is not much room for error because a person's medical condition is on the line.

To make this accuracy better, we need to define a different criterion for evaluation. You can read more about it here:

```
https://en.wikipedia.org/wiki/Confusion_matrix
```

Also, you can balance the dataset. What we have now is an unbalanced dataset in which the number of diseased patients is much lower than the number of normal patients. Thus, the network becomes more sensitive to normal patients' features and less sensitive to diseased patients' features.

To fix this problem, we can SMOTE our dataset. SMOTing is basically replicating the data of less frequent classes (flipping the image horizontally or vertically, changing saturation, and so on) to create a balanced dataset. SMOTE stands for **Synthetic Minority Over-sampling Technique**.

Here is a good read on this topic:

```
https://www.jair.org/media/953/live-953-2037-jair.pdf
```

Other medical data challenges

Understandably, medical data is not as easy to release as other datasets, so there are far fewer datasets in the public domain. This is changing slowly, but in the meantime, here are some datasets and associated challenges you can try your hand at. Note that many of these challenges have been overcome, but they have luckily continued to publish the datasets.

The ISBI grand challenge

ISBI is the International Symposium on Biomedical Imaging, a popular venue for furthering the type of work you're seeing in this chapter. Their annual conferences often feature multiple challenges posed to the academic community. They posed several challenges in 2016.

One popular challenge was the AIDA-E: Analysis of Images to Detect Abnormalities in Endoscopy. The challenge website is `http://isbi-aida.grand-challenge.org/`.

Another popular challenge was the Cancer Metastasis Detection in Lymph Nodes, which features pathology data. The challenge website is `http://camelyon16.grand-challenge.org/`.

On the radiology side, a popular challenge in 2016 was the Data Science Bowl challenge on heart disease diagnosis. Titled *Transforming How We Diagnose Heart Disease*, the challenge sought to segment parts of the cardiac Magnetic Resonance Imaging data to gauge pump volume, which was then used as a proxy for heart health. The challenge website and dataset is `http://www.datasciencebowl.com/competitions/transforming-how-we-diagnose-heart-disease/`.

Another popular radiology dataset is the Lung Image Database Consortium's **computed tomography** (**CT**) data in the LIDC-IDRI image collection. This is a dataset of diagnostic and lung cancer screening thoracic CT scans. Interestingly, instead of image-level classes, this dataset annotates the actual locations of the lesions.

The two radiology competitions are interesting for two more reasons:

- They feature three-dimensional **volume** data, which is essentially an ordered stack of two-dimensional images that form an actual space.
- They feature **segmentation** tasks where you want to classify parts of an image or volume into certain classes. This is a familiar classification challenge, except we're trying to also localize the feature on the image. In one case, we seek to localize the feature and point to it (rather than classify the entire image), and in another case, we seek to classify a section as a way to measure the size of a region.

We'll speak more about dealing with volume data later, but for now, you've got some really interesting and varied datasets to work with.

Reading medical data

The diabetic retinopathy challenge, despite the challenges, is not as complicated as it gets. The actual images were provided in JPEG format, but most medical data is not in JPEG format. They are usually within container formats such as DICOM. DICOM stands for **Digital Imaging and Communications in Medicine** and has a number of versions and variations. It contains the medical image, but also header data. The header data often includes general demographic and study data, but it can contain dozens of other custom fields. If you are lucky, it will also contain a diagnosis, which you can use as a label.

DICOM data adds another step to the pipeline we discussed earlier because we now need to read the DICOM file, extract the header (and hopefully class/label data), and extract the underlying image. DICOM is not as easy to work with as JPEG or PNG, but it is not too difficult. It will require some extra packages.

Since we're writing almost everything in Python, let's use a `Python` library for DICOM processing. The most popular is **pydicom**, which is available at `https://github.com/darcymason/pydicom`.

The documentation is available at `https://pydicom.readthedocs.io/en/stable/getting_started.html`.

It should be noted that the `pip` installation is currently broken, so it must be cloned from the source repository and installed via the setup script before it can be used.

A quick excerpt from the documentation will help set the stage for understanding how to work with `DICOM` files:

```
>>> import dicom
>>> plan = dicom.read_file("rtplan.dcm")
>>> plan.PatientName
'Last^First^mid^pre'
>>> plan.dir("setup")      # get a list of tags with "setup"
somewhere in the name
['PatientSetupSequence']
>>> plan.PatientSetupSequence[0]
(0018, 5100) Patient Position                CS: 'HFS'
(300a, 0182) Patient Setup Number            IS: '1'
(300a, 01b2) Setup Technique Description      ST: ''
```

This may seem a bit messy, but this is the type of interaction you should expect when working with medical data. Worse, each vendor often places the same data, even basic data, into slightly different tags. The typical industry practice is to simply look around! We do that by dumping the entire tag set as follows:

```
>>> ds
(0008, 0012) Instance Creation Date          DA: '20030903'
(0008, 0013) Instance Creation Time          TM: '150031'
(0008, 0016) SOP Class UID                   UI: RT Plan
Storage
(0008, 0018) Diagnosis                    UI: Positive
(0008, 0020) Study Date                      DA: '20030716'
(0008, 0030) Study Time                      TM: '153557'
(0008, 0050) Accession Number                SH: ''
(0008, 0060) Modality                        CS: 'RTPLAN'
```

Suppose we were seeking the diagnosis. We would look through several files of tags and try to see whether the diagnosis consistently shows up under tag (0008, 0018) Diagnosis, and if so, we'd test our hypothesis by pulling out just this field from a large portion of our training set to see whether it is indeed consistently populated. If it is, we're ready for the next step. If not, we need to start again and look at other fields. Theoretically, the data provider, broker, or vendor can provide this information, but, practically speaking, it is rarely that simple.

The next step is to see the domain of values. This is very important because we want to see what our classes look like. Ideally, we will have a nice clean set of values such as {Negative, Positive}, but, in reality, we often get a long tail of dirty values. So, the typical approach is to loop through every single image and keep a count of each unique domain value encountered, as follows:

```
>>> import dicom, glob, os
>>> os.chdir("/some/medical/data/dir")
>>> domains={}
>>> for file in glob.glob("*.dcm"):
>>>     aMedFile = dicom.read_file(file)
>>>     theVal=aMedFile.ds[0x10,0x10].value
>>>     if domains[theVal]>0:
>>>         domains[theVal]= domains[theVal]+1
>>>     else:
>>>         domains[theVal]=1
```

A very common finding at this point would be that 99 percent of domain values exist across a handful of domain values (such as *positive* and *negative*), and there is a long tail of 1% domain values that are dirty (such as *positive, but under review, @#Q#$%@#$%*, or *sent for re-read*). The easiest thing to do is throw out the long tail—just keep the good data. This is especially easy if there is plenty of training data.

OK, so we've extracted the class information, but we've still got to extract the actual image. We can do that as follows:

```
>>> import dicom
>>> ds=dicom.read_file("MR_small.dcm")
>>> ds.pixel_array
array([[ 905, 1019, 1227, ...,  302,  304,  328],
       [ 628,  770,  907, ...,  298,  331,  355],
       [ 498,  566,  706, ...,  280,  285,  320],
       ...,
       [ 334,  400,  431, ..., 1094, 1068, 1083],
       [ 339,  377,  413, ..., 1318, 1346, 1336],
       [ 378,  374,  422, ..., 1369, 1129,  862]], dtype=int16)
>>> ds.pixel_array.shape
(64, 64)
```

Unfortunately, this only gives us a raw matrix of pixel values. We still need to convert this into a readable format (ideally, JPEG or PNG.) We'll achieve the next step as follows:

```python
fileInputDICOM = r.rpop(redisQueue)
newFile = fileInputDICOM.replace(IN_DIR, OUT_DIR) + ".png"
print(num, ":", fileInputDICOM)
plan = dicomio.read_file(fileInputDICOM)
shape = plan.pixel_array.shape
wBuffer=MAX_SIZE-shape[0]
hBuffer=MAX_SIZE-shape[1]
image_2d = []
for row in plan.pixel_array:
    pixels = []
    for col in row:
        pixels.append(col)
        for h in range(hBuffer):
            pixels.append(32767)
    image_2d.append(pixels)
for w in range(wBuffer):
    image_2d.append([32767]*MAX_SIZE)

# Rescalling greyscale between 0-255
image_2d_scaled = []
for row in image_2d:
    row_scaled = []
    for col in row:
        col_scaled = int((float(col)/float(max_val))*255.0)
        col_scaled = 255.0 - col_scaled
        row_scaled.append(col_scaled)
    image_2d_scaled.append(row_scaled)

if not os.path.exists(os.path.dirname(newFile)):
    try:
        os.makedirs(os.path.dirname(newFile))
    except OSError as exc: # Guard against race condition
        if exc.errno != errno.EEXIST:
            raise

f = open(newFile, 'wb')
w = png.Writer(MAX_SIZE, MAX_SIZE, greyscale=True)
w.write(f, image_2d_scaled)
f.close()
```

Next, we'll scale the image to the bit length we desire and write the matrix to a file using another library geared to writing data in our destination format. In our case, we'll use a PNG output format and write it using the `png` library. This means some extra imports:

```python
import os
from pydicom import dicomio
import png
import errno
import fnmatch
```

We'll export like this:

```
fileInputDICOM = r.rpop(redisQueue)
newFile = fileInputDICOM.replace(IN_DIR, OUT_DIR) + ".png"
print(num, ":", fileInputDICOM)
plan = dicomio.read_file(fileInputDICOM)
shape = plan.pixel_array.shape
wBuffer=MAX_SIZE-shape[0]
hBuffer=MAX_SIZE-shape[1]
image_2d = []
for row in plan.pixel_array:
    pixels = []
    for col in row:
        pixels.append(col)
    for h in range(hBuffer):
        pixels.append(32767)
    image_2d.append(pixels)
for w in range(wBuffer):
    image_2d.append([32767]*MAX_SIZE)

# Rescalling greyscale between 0-255
image_2d_scaled = []
for row in image_2d:
    row_scaled = []
    for col in row:
        col_scaled = int((float(col)/float(max_val))*255.0)
        col_scaled = 255.0 - col_scaled
        row_scaled.append(col_scaled)
    image_2d_scaled.append(row_scaled)

if not os.path.exists(os.path.dirname(newFile)):
    try:
        os.makedirs(os.path.dirname(newFile))
    except OSError as exc: # Guard against race condition
        if exc.errno != errno.EEXIST:
            raise

f = open(newFile, 'wb')
w = png.Writer(MAX_SIZE, MAX_SIZE, greyscale=True)
w.write(f, image_2d_scaled)
f.close()
```

Skills Learned

You should have learned these skills in the chapter:

- Dealing with arcane and proprietary medical imaging formats
- Dealing with large image files, a common medical image hallmark
- Extracting class data from medical files
- Extending our existing pipeline to deal with heterogeneous data inputs
- Applying networks pre-trained with non-medical data
- Scaling training to accommodate new datasets.

Summary

In this chapter, we created a deep neural network for image classification problem in an enterprise-grade problem, medical diagnosis. Moreover, we also guided you through the process of reading DICOM digital medical image data for further researches. In the next chapter, we will build a production system that can self-improve by learning from users feedback.

Cruise Control - Automation

9

In this chapter, we will create a production system, from training to serving a model. Our system will have the ability to distinguish between 37 different species of dogs and cat. A user can upload an image to our system to receive the results. The system can also receive feedback from the user and automatically train itself every day to improve results.

This chapter will focus on several areas:

- How to apply transfer learning to a new dataset
- How to serve a production model with TensorFlow Serving
- Creating a system with crowd-sourced labeling of the dataset and automatic fine-tuning the model on user data

An overview of the system

The following diagram provides an overview of our system:

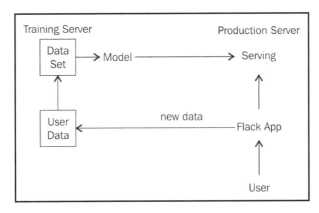

In this system, we will use an initial dataset to train a convolutional neural network model on a training server. Then, the model will be served in a production server with TensorFlow Serving. On the production server, there will be a Flask server that allows users to upload a new image and correct the label if the model goes wrong. At a defined time in the day, the training server will combine all the user-labeled images with the current dataset to automatically fine-tune the model and send it to the production server. Here is the wireframe of the web interface that allows users to upload and receive the result:

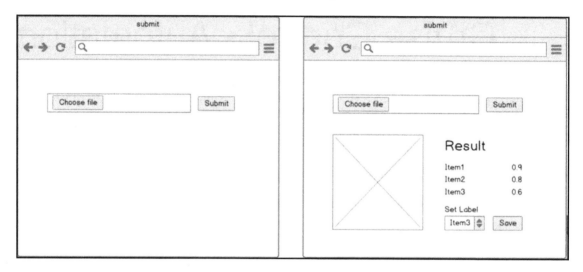

Setting up the project

In this chapter, we will fine-tune a VGG model that has been trained on `ImageNet` data with 1,000 classes. We have provided an initial project with a pretrained VGG model and some utility files. You can go ahead and download the code from `https://github.com/mlwithtf/mlwithtf/tree/master/chapter_09`.

In the folder `chapter-09`, you will have the following structure:

```
- data
--VGG16.npz
- samples_data
- production
- utils
--__init__.py
--debug_print.py
- README.md
```

There are two files that you should understand:

- `VGG16.npz` is the pre-trained model that is exported from the Caffe model. `Chapter 11`, *Going Further - 21 Problems* will show you how to create this file from the Caffe model. In this chapter, we will use this as the initial values for our model. You can download this file from the `README.md` in the `chapter_09` folder.
- `production` is the Flask server that we created to serve as a web interface for users to upload and correct the model.
- `debug_print.py` contains some methods that we will use during this chapter to understand the network structure.
- `samples_data` contains some images of cats, dogs, and cars that we will use throughout the chapter.

Loading a pre-trained model to speed up the training

In this section, let's focus on loading the pre-trained model in TensorFlow. We will use the VGG-16 model proposed by K. Simonyan and A. Zisserman from the University of Oxford.

VGG-16 is a very deep neural network with lots of convolution layers followed by max-pooling and fully connected layers. In the `ImageNet` challenge, the top-5 classification error of the VGG-16 model on the validation set of 1,000 image classes is 8.1% in a single-scale approach:

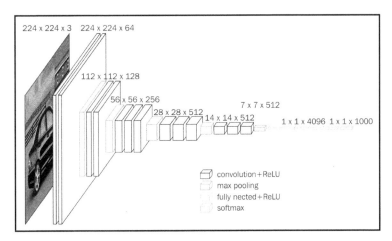

First, create a file named `nets.py` in the `project` directory. The following code defines the graph for the VGG-16 model:

```python
import tensorflow as tf
import numpy as np


def inference(images):
with tf.name_scope("preprocess"):
    mean = tf.constant([123.68, 116.779, 103.939],
dtype=tf.float32, shape=[1, 1, 1, 3], name='img_mean')
    input_images = images - mean
conv1_1 = _conv2d(input_images, 3, 3, 64, 1, 1,
name="conv1_1")
conv1_2 = _conv2d(conv1_1, 3, 3, 64, 1, 1, name="conv1_2")
pool1 = _max_pool(conv1_2, 2, 2, 2, 2, name="pool1")

conv2_1 = _conv2d(pool1, 3, 3, 128, 1, 1, name="conv2_1")
conv2_2 = _conv2d(conv2_1, 3, 3, 128, 1, 1, name="conv2_2")
pool2 = _max_pool(conv2_2, 2, 2, 2, 2, name="pool2")

conv3_1 = _conv2d(pool2, 3, 3, 256, 1, 1, name="conv3_1")
conv3_2 = _conv2d(conv3_1, 3, 3, 256, 1, 1, name="conv3_2")
conv3_3 = _conv2d(conv3_2, 3, 3, 256, 1, 1, name="conv3_3")
pool3 = _max_pool(conv3_3, 2, 2, 2, 2, name="pool3")

conv4_1 = _conv2d(pool3, 3, 3, 512, 1, 1, name="conv4_1")
conv4_2 = _conv2d(conv4_1, 3, 3, 512, 1, 1, name="conv4_2")
conv4_3 = _conv2d(conv4_2, 3, 3, 512, 1, 1, name="conv4_3")
pool4 = _max_pool(conv4_3, 2, 2, 2, 2, name="pool4")

conv5_1 = _conv2d(pool4, 3, 3, 512, 1, 1, name="conv5_1")
conv5_2 = _conv2d(conv5_1, 3, 3, 512, 1, 1, name="conv5_2")
conv5_3 = _conv2d(conv5_2, 3, 3, 512, 1, 1, name="conv5_3")
pool5 = _max_pool(conv5_3, 2, 2, 2, 2, name="pool5")

fc6 = _fully_connected(pool5, 4096, name="fc6")
fc7 = _fully_connected(fc6, 4096, name="fc7")
fc8 = _fully_connected(fc7, 1000, name='fc8', relu=False)
outputs = _softmax(fc8, name="output")
return outputs
```

In the preceding code, there are a few things that you should note:

- `_conv2d`, `_max_pool`, `_fully_connected` and `_softmax` are methods that define the convolution, max pooling, fully connected, and softmax layers, respectively. We will implement these methods shortly.

- In the `preprocess` name scope, we define a constant tensor, `mean`, which is subtracted from the input image. This is the mean vector that the VGG-16 model is trained on in order to make the image zero mean.
- We then define the convolution, max pooling, and fully connected layers with the parameters.
- In the `fc8` layers, we don't apply ReLU activation to the outputs and we send the outputs to a `softmax` layer to compute the probability over 1,000 classes.

Now, we will implement `_conv2d`, `_max_pool`, `_fully_connected`, and `_softmax` in the `nets.py` file.

The following code is the code for the `_conv2d` and `_max_pool` methods:

```
def _conv2d(input_data, k_h, k_w, c_o, s_h, s_w, name, relu=True,
padding="SAME"):
    c_i = input_data.get_shape()[-1].value
    convolve = lambda i, k: tf.nn.conv2d(i, k, [1, s_h, s_w, 1],
padding=padding)
    with tf.variable_scope(name) as scope:
        weights = tf.get_variable(name="kernel", shape=[k_h, k_w,
c_i, c_o],
initializer=tf.truncated_normal_initializer(stddev=1e-1,
dtype=tf.float32))
        conv = convolve(input_data, weights)
        biases = tf.get_variable(name="bias", shape=[c_o],
dtype=tf.float32,
initializer=tf.constant_initializer(value=0.0))
        output = tf.nn.bias_add(conv, biases)
        if relu:
            output = tf.nn.relu(output, name=scope.name)
        return output
def _max_pool(input_data, k_h, k_w, s_h, s_w, name,
padding="SAME"):
    return tf.nn.max_pool(input_data, ksize=[1, k_h, k_w, 1],
                          strides=[1, s_h, s_w, 1],
padding=padding,
name=name)
```

Most of the preceding code is self-explanatory if you have read `Chapter 4`, *Cats and Dogs*, but there are some lines that deserve a bit of explanation:

- `k_h` and `k_w` are the height and weights of the kernel
- `c_o` means channel outputs, which is the number of feature maps of the convolution layers

- s_h and s_w are the stride parameters for the tf.nn.conv2d and tf.nn.max_pool layers
- tf.get_variable is used instead of tf.Variable because we will need to use get_variable again when we load the pre-trained weights

Implementing the fully_connected layers and softmax layers are quite easy:

```
def _fully_connected(input_data, num_output, name, relu=True):
    with tf.variable_scope(name) as scope:
        input_shape = input_data.get_shape()
        if input_shape.ndims == 4:
            dim = 1
            for d in input_shape[1:].as_list():
                dim *= d
            feed_in = tf.reshape(input_data, [-1, dim])
        else:
            feed_in, dim = (input_data, input_shape[-1].value)
        weights = tf.get_variable(name="kernel", shape=[dim,
num_output],
initializer=tf.truncated_normal_initializer(stddev=1e-1,
dtype=tf.float32))
        biases = tf.get_variable(name="bias", shape=[num_output],
dtype=tf.float32,
initializer=tf.constant_initializer(value=0.0))
        op = tf.nn.relu_layer if relu else tf.nn.xw_plus_b
        output = op(feed_in, weights, biases, name=scope.name)
        return output
def _softmax(input_data, name):
    return tf.nn.softmax(input_data, name=name)
```

Using the _fully_connected method, we first check the number of dimensions of the input data in order to reshape the input data into the correct shape. Then, we create weights and biases variables with the get_variable method. Finally, we check the relu parameter to decide whether we should apply relu to the output with the tf.nn.relu_layer or tf.nn.xw_plus_b. tf.nn.relu_layer will compute relu(matmul(x, weights) + biases). tf.nn.xw_plus_b but will only compute matmul(x, weights) + biases.

The final method in this section is used to load the pre-trained caffe weights into the defined variables:

```
def load_caffe_weights(path, sess, ignore_missing=False):
    print("Load caffe weights from ", path)
    data_dict = np.load(path).item()
    for op_name in data_dict:
```

```
    with tf.variable_scope(op_name, reuse=True):
        for param_name, data in
data_dict[op_name].iteritems():
            try:
                var = tf.get_variable(param_name)
                sess.run(var.assign(data))
            except ValueError as e:
                if not ignore_missing:
                    print(e)
                    raise e
```

In order to understand this method, we must know how the data is stored in the pre-trained model, `VGG16.npz`. We have created a simple code to print all the variables in the pre-trained model. You can put the following code at the end of `nets.py` and run it with Python `nets.py`:

```
if __name__ == "__main__":
path = "data/VGG16.npz"
data_dict = np.load(path).item()
for op_name in data_dict:
    print(op_name)
    for param_name, data in data_dict[op_name].iteritems():
        print("\t" + param_name + "\t" + str(data.shape))
```

Here are a few lines of the results:

```
conv1_1
    weights (3, 3, 3, 64)
    biases  (64,)
conv1_2
    weights (3, 3, 64, 64)
    biases  (64,)
```

As you can see, `op_name` is the name of the layers, and we can access the `weights` and `biases` of each layer with `data_dict[op_name]`.

Let's take a look at `load_caffe_weights`:

- We use it with `tf.variable_scope` with `reuse=True` in the parameters so that we can get the exact variables for `weights` and `biases` that were defined in the graph. After that, we run the assign method to set the data for each variable.
- The `get_variable` method will give `ValueError` if the variable name is not defined. Therefore, we will use the `ignore_missing` variable to decide whether we should raise an error or not.

Testing the pre-trained model

We have already created a VGG16 neural network. In this section, we will try to use the pre-trained model to perform the classifications of cars, cats, and dogs to check whether the model has been loaded successfully.

In the `nets.py` file, we need to replace the current __main__ code with the following code:

```python
import os
from utils import debug_print
from scipy.misc import imread, imresize


if __name__ == "__main__":
SAMPLES_FOLDER = "samples_data"
with open('%s/imagenet-classes.txt' % SAMPLES_FOLDER, 'rb') as
infile:
 class_labels = map(str.strip, infile.readlines())

inputs = tf.placeholder(tf.float32, [None, 224, 224, 3],
name="inputs")
outputs = inference(inputs)

debug_print.print_variables(tf.global_variables())
debug_print.print_variables([inputs, outputs])

with tf.Session() as sess:
 load_caffe_weights("data/VGG16.npz", sess,
ignore_missing=False)

    files = os.listdir(SAMPLES_FOLDER)
    for file_name in files:
        if not file_name.endswith(".jpg"):
            continue
        print("=== Predict %s ==== " % file_name)
        img = imread(os.path.join(SAMPLES_FOLDER, file_name),
        mode="RGB")
        img = imresize(img, (224, 224))

        prob = sess.run(outputs, feed_dict={inputs: [img]})[0]
        preds = (np.argsort(prob)[::-1])[0:3]

        for p in preds:
            print class_labels[p], prob[p]
```

In the preceding code, there are several things that you should note:

- We use the `debug_print.print_variables` helper method to visualize all the variables by printing the variable names and shapes.
- We define a placeholder named `inputs` with the shape [None, 224, 224, 3], which is the required input size of the VGG16 model:

    We get the model graph with outputs = inference(inputs).

- In `tf.Session()`, we call the `load_caffe_weights` method with `ignore_missing=False` to ensure that we can load all the weights and biases of the pre-trained model.
- The image is loaded and resized with the `imread` and `imresize` methods from `scipy`. Then, we use the `sess.run` method with the `feed_dict` dictionary and receive the predictions.
- The following results are the predictions for `car.jpg`, `cat.jpg`, and `dog.jpg` in the `samples_data` that we provided at the beginning of the chapter:

```
== Predict car.jpg ====
racer, race car, racing car 0.666172
sports car, sport car 0.315847
car wheel 0.0117961
=== Predict cat.jpg ====
Persian cat 0.762223
tabby, tabby cat 0.0647032
lynx, catamount 0.0371023
=== Predict dog.jpg ====
Border collie 0.562288
collie 0.239735
Appenzeller 0.0186233
```

The preceding results are the exact labels of these images. This means that we have successfully loaded the pre-trained VGG16 model in TensorFlow. In the next section, we will show you how to fine-tune the model on our dataset.

Training the model for our dataset

In this section, we will work through the process of creating the dataset, fine-tuning the model, and exporting the model for production.

Introduction to the Oxford-IIIT Pet dataset

The Oxford-IIIT Pet dataset contains 37 species of dogs and cats. Each class has 200 images with large variations in scale, pose, and lighting. The ground truth data has annotations for species, head position, and pixel segmentation for each image. In our application, we only use the species name as the class name for the model:

Dataset Statistics

The following are the dataset for dogs and cats breed:

1. Dog breeds:

Breed	Total
American Bulldog	200
American Pit Bull Terrier	200
Basset Hound	200
Beagle	200
Boxer	199
Chihuahua	200
English Cocker Spaniel	196
English Setter	200
German Shorthaired	200
Great Pyrenees	200
Havanese	200
Japanese Chin	200

Keeshond	199
Leonberger	200
Miniature Pinscher	200
Newfoundland	196
Pomeranian	200
Pug	200
Saint Bernard	200
Samoyed	200
Scottish Terrier	199
Shiba Inu	200
Staffordshire Bull Terrier	189
Wheaten Terrier	200
Yorkshire Terrier	200
Total	**4978**

2. Cat breeds:

Breed	Count
Abyssinian	198
Bengal	200
Birman	200
Bombay	184
British Shorthair	200
Egyptian Mau	190
Maine Coon	200
Persian	200
Ragdoll	200
Russian Blue	200

Siamese	199
Sphynx	200
Total	**2371**

3. Total pets:

Family	**Count**
Cat	2371
Dog	4978
Total	**7349**

Downloading the dataset

We can get the dataset from the website of the University of Oxford at
`http://www.robots.ox.ac.uk/~vgg/data/pets/`. We need to download the dataset and
ground truth data as `images.tar.gz` and `annotations.tar.gz`. We store the TAR files
in the `data/datasets` folder and extract all the `.tar` files. Make sure that the `data` folder
has the following structure:

```
- data
-- VGG16.npz
-- datasets
---- annotations
------ trainval.txt
---- images
------ *.jpg
```

Preparing the data

Before starting the training process, we need to pre-process the dataset into a simpler
format, which we will use in the further automatic fine-tuning.

First, we make a Python package with named scripts in the `project` folder. Then, we create
a Python file named `convert_oxford_data.py` and add the following code:

```python
import os
import tensorflow as tf
from tqdm import tqdm
from scipy.misc import imread, imsave
```

```
FLAGS = tf.app.flags.FLAGS

tf.app.flags.DEFINE_string(
'dataset_dir', 'data/datasets',
'The location of Oxford IIIT Pet Dataset which contains
 annotations and images folders'
)

tf.app.flags.DEFINE_string(
'target_dir', 'data/train_data',
'The location where all the images will be stored'
)

def ensure_folder_exists(folder_path):
if not os.path.exists(folder_path):
    os.mkdir(folder_path)
return folder_path

def read_image(image_path):
try:
    image = imread(image_path)
    return image
except IOError:
    print(image_path, "not readable")
return None
```

In this code, we use `tf.app.flags.FLAGS` to parse arguments so that we can customize the script easily. We also create two `helper` methods to make a directory and read images.

Next, we add the following code to convert the Oxford dataset into our preferred format:

```
def convert_data(split_name, save_label=False):
    if split_name not in ["trainval", "test"]:
    raise ValueError("split_name is not recognized!")
    target_split_path =
    ensure_folder_exists(os.path.join(FLAGS.target_dir,
split_name))
    output_file = open(os.path.join(FLAGS.target_dir, split_name +
    ".txt"), "w")

    image_folder = os.path.join(FLAGS.dataset_dir, "images")
    anno_folder = os.path.join(FLAGS.dataset_dir, "annotations")

    list_data = [line.strip() for line in open(anno_folder + "/" +
    split_name + ".txt")]

    class_name_idx_map = dict()
    for data in tqdm(list_data, desc=split_name):
```

```
        file_name,class_index,species,breed_id = data.split(" ")
        file_label = int(class_index) - 1

        class_name = "_".join(file_name.split("_")[0:-1])
        class_name_idx_map[class_name] = file_label

        image_path = os.path.join(image_folder, file_name + ".jpg")
        image = read_image(image_path)
        if image is not None:
        target_class_dir =
         ensure_folder_exists(os.path.join(target_split_path,
         class_name))
        target_image_path = os.path.join(target_class_dir,
         file_name + ".jpg")
            imsave(target_image_path, image)
            output_file.write("%s %s\n" % (file_label,
            target_image_path))

    if save_label:
        label_file = open(os.path.join(FLAGS.target_dir,
        "labels.txt"), "w")
        for class_name in sorted(class_name_idx_map,
        key=class_name_idx_map.get):
        label_file.write("%s\n" % class_name)


def main(_):
    if not FLAGS.dataset_dir:
    raise ValueError("You must supply the dataset directory with
    --dataset_dir")

    ensure_folder_exists(FLAGS.target_dir)
    convert_data("trainval", save_label=True)
    convert_data("test")


if __name__ == "__main__":
    tf.app.run()
```

Now, we can run the scripts with the following code:

```
python scripts/convert_oxford_data.py --dataset_dir data/datasets/ --
target_dir data/train_data.
```

The script reads the Oxford-IIIT dataset ground truth `data` and creates a new `dataset` in `data/train_data` with the following structure:

```
- train_data
-- trainval.txt
-- test.txt
-- labels.txt
-- trainval
---- Abyssinian
---- ...
-- test
---- Abyssinian
---- ...
```

Let's discuss these a bit:

- `labels.txt` contains a list of 37 species in our dataset.
- `trainval.txt` contains a list of the images that we will use in the training process, with the format `<class_id> <image_path>`.
- `test.txt` contains a list of the images that we will use to check the accuracy of the model. The format of `test.txt` is the same as `trainval.txt`.
- `trainval` and `test` folders contain 37 sub-folders, which are the names of each class and contains all the images of each class.

Setting up input pipelines for training and testing

TensorFlow allows us to create a reliable input pipeline for quick and easy training. In this section, we will implement `tf.TextLineReader` to read the train and test text files. We will use `tf.train.batch` to read and preprocess images in parallel.

First, we need to create a new Python file named `datasets.py` in the `project` directory and add the following code:

```
import tensorflow as tf
import os

def load_files(filenames):
    filename_queue = tf.train.string_input_producer(filenames)
    line_reader = tf.TextLineReader()
    key, line = line_reader.read(filename_queue)
    label, image_path = tf.decode_csv(records=line,
    record_defaults=[tf.constant([], dtype=tf.int32),
    tf.constant([], dtype=tf.string)],
```

```
                                        field_delim=' ')
      file_contents = tf.read_file(image_path)
      image = tf.image.decode_jpeg(file_contents, channels=3)

      return image, label
```

In the `load_files` method, we use the `tf.TextLineReader` to read each line of the text file, such as `trainval.txt`, `test.txt`. `tf.TextLineReader` needs a queue of strings to read, so we use `tf.train.string_input_producer` to store the filenames. After that, we pass the line variable into `tf.decode_cvs` in order to get the `label` and `filename`. The image can be easily read with `tf.image.decode_jpeg`.

Now that we can load the image, we can move forward and create `image` batches and `label` batches for `training`.

In `datasets.py`, we need to add a new method:

```
def input_pipeline(dataset_dir, batch_size, num_threads=8,
    is_training=True, shuffle=True):
    if is_training:
        file_names = [os.path.join(dataset_dir, "trainval.txt")]
    else:
        file_names = [os.path.join(dataset_dir, "test.txt")]
    image, label = load_files(file_names)

    image = preprocessing(image, is_training)

    min_after_dequeue = 1000
    capacity = min_after_dequeue + 3 * batch_size
    if shuffle:
     image_batch, label_batch = tf.train.shuffle_batch(
     [image, label], batch_size, capacity,
     min_after_dequeue, num_threads
      )
    else:
        image_batch, label_batch = tf.train.batch(
            [image, label], batch_size, num_threads, capacity
            )
    return image_batch, label_batch
```

We first load the `image` and `label` with the `load_files` method. Then, we pass the image through a new preprocessing method, which we will implement shortly. Finally, we pass the `image` and `label` into `tf.train.shuffle_batch` for training and `tf.train.batch` for testing:

```
def preprocessing(image, is_training=True, image_size=224,
resize_side_min=256, resize_side_max=312):
    image = tf.cast(image, tf.float32)

    if is_training:
        resize_side = tf.random_uniform([], minval=resize_side_min,
        maxval=resize_side_max+1, dtype=tf.int32)
        resized_image = _aspect_preserving_resize(image,
        resize_side)

        distorted_image = tf.random_crop(resized_image,
[image_size,
        image_size, 3])

        distorted_image =
        tf.image.random_flip_left_right(distorted_image)
        distorted_image =
        tf.image.random_brightness(distorted_image, max_delta=50)

        distorted_image = tf.image.random_contrast(distorted_image,
        lower=0.2, upper=2.0)

        return distorted_image
    else:
        resized_image = _aspect_preserving_resize(image,
image_size)
        return
tf.image.resize_image_with_crop_or_pad(resized_image,
        image_size, image_size)
```

There are two different approaches to preprocessing in training and testing. In training, we need to augment data to create more training data from the current dataset. There are a few techniques that are used in the preprocessing method:

- The images in the dataset can have different image resolutions, but we only need 224x224 images. Therefore, we need to resize the image to a reasonable size before performing `random_crop`. The following diagram describes how cropping works. The `_aspect_preserving_resize` method will be implemented shortly:

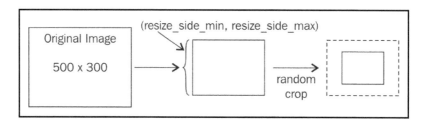

- After cropping the image, we pass the image through `tf.image.random_flip_left_right`, `tf.image.random_brightness` and `tf.image.random_contrast` to distort the image and create a new training sample.
- In the testing routine, we only need to resize the image with `_aspect_preserving_resize` and `tf.image.resize_image_with_crop_or_pad`. `tf.image.resize_image_with_crop_or_pad` allows us to crop centrally or pad the image to the target `width` and `height`.

Now, we need to add the last two methods into `datasets.py`, as shown here:

```
def _smallest_size_at_least(height, width, smallest_side):
    smallest_side = tf.convert_to_tensor(smallest_side,
    dtype=tf.int32)

    height = tf.to_float(height)
    width = tf.to_float(width)
    smallest_side = tf.to_float(smallest_side)

    scale = tf.cond(tf.greater(height, width),
                lambda: smallest_side / width,
                lambda: smallest_side / height)
    new_height = tf.to_int32(height * scale)
    new_width = tf.to_int32(width * scale)
    return new_height, new_width
```

```
def _aspect_preserving_resize(image, smallest_side):
  smallest_side = tf.convert_to_tensor(smallest_side,
  dtype=tf.int32)
  shape = tf.shape(image)
  height = shape[0]
  width = shape[1]
  new_height, new_width = _smallest_size_at_least(height, width,
  smallest_side)
  image = tf.expand_dims(image, 0)
  resized_image = tf.image.resize_bilinear(image, [new_height,
  new_width], align_corners=False)
  resized_image = tf.squeeze(resized_image)
  resized_image.set_shape([None, None, 3])
  return resized_image
```

Up to this section, we had to do a lot of work to prepare the dataset and input pipelines. In the following section, we will define the model for our dataset, loss, accuracy and training operations to perform the training routine.

Defining the model

Our application will need to classify 37 classes of dogs and cats. The VGG16 Model supports 1,000 different classes. In our application, we will reuse all layers up to the fc7 layer and train the last layer from scratch. In order to make the model output 37 classes, we need to modify the inference method in nets.py as follows:

```
def inference(images, is_training=False):
  #
  # All the code before fc7 are not modified.
  #
  fc7 = _fully_connected(fc6, 4096, name="fc7")
  if is_training:
      fc7 = tf.nn.dropout(fc7, keep_prob=0.5)
  fc8 = _fully_connected(fc7, 37, name='fc8-pets', relu=False)
  return fc8
```

- We add a new parameter, `is_training`, to the method. After the `fc7` layer, we add a `tf.nn.dropout` layer if the inference is training. This dropout layer can help the model regularize better with unseen data and avoid overfitting.
- The number of outputs in the `fc8` layer is changed from 1,000 to 37. Besides, the name of the `fc8` layer must be changed to another name; in this case, we choose `fc8-pets`. If we don't change the name of the `fc8` layer, `load_caffe_weights` will still find the new layers and assign the original weights, which is not the same size as our new `fc8` layer.
- The `softmax` layer at the end of the inference method is also removed because the `loss` function that we will use later only needs unnormalized outputs.

Defining training operations

We will define all the operations in a new Python file named `models.py`. First, let's create some operations to compute `loss` and `accuracy`:

```
def compute_loss(logits, labels):
  labels = tf.squeeze(tf.cast(labels, tf.int32))

  cross_entropy =
  tf.nn.sparse_softmax_cross_entropy_with_logits(logits=logits,
  labels=labels)
  cross_entropy_mean = tf.reduce_mean(cross_entropy)
  tf.add_to_collection('losses', cross_entropy_mean)

  return tf.add_n(tf.get_collection('losses'),
  name='total_loss')


def compute_accuracy(logits, labels):
  labels = tf.squeeze(tf.cast(labels, tf.int32))
  batch_predictions = tf.cast(tf.argmax(logits, 1), tf.int32)
  predicted_correctly = tf.equal(batch_predictions, labels)
  accuracy = tf.reduce_mean(tf.cast(predicted_correctly,
  tf.float32))
  return accuracy
```

In these methods, `logits` is the output of the model and `labels` is the ground truth data from the `dataset`. In the `compute_loss` method, we use `tf.nn.sparse_softmax_cross_entropy_with_logits` so we don't need to normalize the `logits` with `softmax` methods. Besides, we don't need to make the `labels` a one-hot vector. In the `compute_accuracy` method, we compare the max value in `logits` with `tf.argmax` and compare it with the `labels` to get the `accuracy`.

Next, we are going to define the operations for the `learning_rate` and the `optimizer`:

```
def get_learning_rate(global_step, initial_value, decay_steps,
    decay_rate):
    learning_rate = tf.train.exponential_decay(initial_value,
    global_step, decay_steps, decay_rate, staircase=True)
    return learning_rate


def train(total_loss, learning_rate, global_step, train_vars):

    optimizer = tf.train.AdamOptimizer(learning_rate)

    train_variables = train_vars.split(",")

    grads = optimizer.compute_gradients(
        total_loss,
        [v for v in tf.trainable_variables() if v.name in
        train_variables]
        )
    train_op = optimizer.apply_gradients(grads,
    global_step=global_step)
    return train_op
```

In the `train` method, we configure the `optimizer` to only `compute` and apply `gradients` to some variables defined in the `train_vars` string. This allows us to only update the `weights` and `biases` for the last layer, `fc8`, and freeze other layers. `train_vars` is a string that contains a list of variables split by commas, for example, `models/fc8-pets/weights:0,models/fc8-pets/biases:0`.

Performing the training process

Now we are ready to train the model. Let's create a Python file named `train.py` in the `scripts` folder. First, we need to define some parameters for the `training` routines:

```
import tensorflow as tf
import os
```

```
from datetime import datetime
from tqdm import tqdm

import nets, models, datasets

# Dataset
dataset_dir = "data/train_data"
batch_size = 64
image_size = 224

# Learning rate
initial_learning_rate = 0.001
decay_steps = 250
decay_rate = 0.9

# Validation
output_steps = 10   # Number of steps to print output
eval_steps = 20   # Number of steps to perform evaluations

# Training
max_steps = 3000   # Number of steps to perform training
save_steps = 200   # Number of steps to perform saving checkpoints
num_tests = 5  # Number of times to test for test accuracy
max_checkpoints_to_keep = 3
save_dir = "data/checkpoints"
train_vars = 'models/fc8-pets/weights:0,models/fc8-pets/biases:0'

# Export
export_dir = "/tmp/export/"
export_name = "pet-model"
export_version = 2
```

These variables are self-explanatory. Next, we need to define some operations for `training`, as follows:

```
images, labels = datasets.input_pipeline(dataset_dir, batch_size,
is_training=True)
test_images, test_labels = datasets.input_pipeline(dataset_dir,
batch_size, is_training=False)

with tf.variable_scope("models") as scope:
    logits = nets.inference(images, is_training=True)
    scope.reuse_variables()
    test_logits = nets.inference(test_images, is_training=False)

total_loss = models.compute_loss(logits, labels)
train_accuracy = models.compute_accuracy(logits, labels)
test_accuracy = models.compute_accuracy(test_logits, test_labels)
```

```
global_step = tf.Variable(0, trainable=False)
learning_rate = models.get_learning_rate(global_step,
initial_learning_rate, decay_steps, decay_rate)
train_op = models.train(total_loss, learning_rate, global_step,
train_vars)

saver = tf.train.Saver(max_to_keep=max_checkpoints_to_keep)
checkpoints_dir = os.path.join(save_dir,
datetime.now().strftime("%Y-%m-%d_%H-%M-%S"))
if not os.path.exists(save_dir):
   os.mkdir(save_dir)
if not os.path.exists(checkpoints_dir):
   os.mkdir(checkpoints_dir)
```

These operations are created by calling our defined methods in datasets.py, nets.py, and models.py. In this code, we create an input pipeline for training and another pipeline for testing. After that, we create a new variable_scope named models and create logits and test_logits with the nets.inference method. You must make sure that scope.reuse_variables is added because we want to reuse the weights and biases from training in testing. Finally, we create a saver and some directories to save the checkpoints every save_steps.

The last part of the training routine is the training loop:

```
with tf.Session() as sess:
    sess.run(tf.global_variables_initializer())
    coords = tf.train.Coordinator()
    threads = tf.train.start_queue_runners(sess=sess, coord=coords)

    with tf.variable_scope("models"):
        nets.load_caffe_weights("data/VGG16.npz", sess,
        ignore_missing=True)

    last_saved_test_accuracy = 0
    for i in tqdm(range(max_steps), desc="training"):
            _, loss_value, lr_value = sess.run([train_op,
            total_loss,  learning_rate])

      if (i + 1) % output_steps == 0:
          print("Steps {}: Loss = {:.5f} Learning Rate =
          {}".format(i + 1, loss_value, lr_value))

      if (i + 1) % eval_steps == 0:
          test_acc, train_acc, loss_value =
          sess.run([test_accuracy, train_accuracy, total_loss])
          print("Test accuracy {} Train accuracy {} : Loss =
          {:.5f}".format(test_acc, train_acc, loss_value))
```

```
        if (i + 1) % save_steps == 0 or i == max_steps - 1:
            test_acc = 0
            for i in range(num_tests):
                test_acc += sess.run(test_accuracy)
            test_acc /= num_tests
        if test_acc > last_saved_test_accuracy:
            print("Save steps: Test Accuracy {} is higher than
                {}".format(test_acc, last_saved_test_accuracy))
            last_saved_test_accuracy = test_acc
            saved_file = saver.save(sess,
        os.path.join(checkpoints_dir, 'model.ckpt'),
                    global_step=global_step)
            print("Save steps: Save to file %s " % saved_file)
        else:
            print("Save steps: Test Accuracy {} is not higher
                than {}".format(test_acc,
    last_saved_test_accuracy))

    models.export_model(checkpoints_dir, export_dir, export_name,
    export_version)

    coords.request_stop()
    coords.join(threads)
```

The `training` loop is easy to understand. First, we load the pre-trained VGG16 model with `ignore_missing` set to `True` because we replaced the name of the `fc8` layer before. Then, we loop for `max_steps` steps, print the `loss` every `output_steps`, and print the `test_accuracy` every `eval_steps`. Every `save_steps`, we check and save the checkpoint if the current test accuracy is higher than the previous. We still need to create `models.export_model` to export the model for serving after `training`. However, you may want to check whether the `training` routine works before moving forward. Let's comment out the following line:

```
    models.export_model(checkpoints_dir, export_dir, export_name,
    export_version)
```

Then, run the `training` script with this command:

```
python scripts/train.py
```

Here is some output in the console. First, our script loads the pre-trained model. Then, it will output the `loss`:

```
('Load caffe weights from ', 'data/VGG16.npz')
training:    0%||                   | 9/3000 [00:05<24:59,  1.99it/s]
Steps 10: Loss = 31.10747 Learning Rate = 0.0010000000475
training:    1%||                   | 19/3000 [00:09<19:19,  2.57it/s]
```

```
Steps 20: Loss = 34.43741 Learning Rate = 0.0010000000475
Test accuracy 0.296875 Train accuracy 0.0 : Loss = 31.28600
training:    1%|█                      | 29/3000 [00:14<20:01,  2.47it/s]
Steps 30: Loss = 15.81103 Learning Rate = 0.0010000000475
training:    1%|█                      | 39/3000 [00:18<19:42,  2.50it/s]
Steps 40: Loss = 14.07709 Learning Rate = 0.0010000000475
Test accuracy 0.53125 Train accuracy 0.03125 : Loss = 20.65380
```

Now, let's stop the `training` and uncomment the `export_model` method. We need the `models.export_model` method to export the latest model that has the highest test accuracy to the `export_dir` folder with the name `export_name` and the version `export_version`.

Exporting the model for production

```python
def export_model(checkpoint_dir, export_dir, export_name,
export_version):
    graph = tf.Graph()
    with graph.as_default():
        image = tf.placeholder(tf.float32, shape=[None, None, 3])
        processed_image = datasets.preprocessing(image,
        is_training=False)
        with tf.variable_scope("models"):
         logits = nets.inference(images=processed_image,
           is_training=False)

        model_checkpoint_path =
        get_model_path_from_ckpt(checkpoint_dir)
        saver = tf.train.Saver()

        config = tf.ConfigProto()
        config.gpu_options.allow_growth = True
        config.gpu_options.per_process_gpu_memory_fraction = 0.7

        with tf.Session(graph=graph) as sess:
            saver.restore(sess, model_checkpoint_path)
            export_path = os.path.join(export_dir, export_name,
            str(export_version))
            export_saved_model(sess, export_path, image, logits)
            print("Exported model at", export_path)
```

In the `export_model` method, we need to create a new graph to run in production. In production, we don't need all the variables, as in `training`, and we don't need an input pipeline. However, we need to export the model with the `export_saved_model` method, as follows:

```
def export_saved_model(sess, export_path, input_tensor,
output_tensor):
    from tensorflow.python.saved_model import builder as
saved_model_builder
    from tensorflow.python.saved_model import signature_constants
    from tensorflow.python.saved_model import signature_def_utils
    from tensorflow.python.saved_model import tag_constants
    from tensorflow.python.saved_model import utils
    builder = saved_model_builder.SavedModelBuilder(export_path)

    prediction_signature = signature_def_utils.build_signature_def(
        inputs={'images': utils.build_tensor_info(input_tensor)},
        outputs={
            'scores': utils.build_tensor_info(output_tensor)
        },
        method_name=signature_constants.PREDICT_METHOD_NAME)

    legacy_init_op = tf.group(
        tf.tables_initializer(), name='legacy_init_op')
    builder.add_meta_graph_and_variables(
        sess, [tag_constants.SERVING],
        signature_def_map={
          'predict_images':
          prediction_signature,
        },
        legacy_init_op=legacy_init_op)

    builder.save()
```

With this method, we can create a metagraph of the model for serving in production. We will cover how to serve the model in a later section. Now, let's run the `scripts` to automatically train and export after 3,000 steps:

```
python scripts/train.py
```

On our system, with Core i7-4790 CPU and one TITAN-X GPU, the training routine takes 20 minutes to finish. Here are a few of the last outputs in our console:

```
Steps 3000: Loss = 0.59160 Learning Rate = 0.000313810509397
Test accuracy 0.659375 Train accuracy 0.853125: Loss = 0.25782
Save steps: Test Accuracy 0.859375 is not higher than 0.921875
training: 100%|████████████████████████| 3000/3000 [23:40<00:00,
```

```
1.27it/s]
    I tensorflow/core/common_runtime/gpu/gpu_device.cc:975] Creating
TensorFlow device (/gpu:0) -> (device: 0, name: GeForce GTX TITAN X, pci
bus id: 0000:01:00.0)
    ('Exported model at', '/home/ubuntu/models/pet-model/1')
```

Great! We have a model with 92.18% test accuracy. We also have the exported model as a
`.pb` file. The `export_dir` folder will have the following structure:

```
- /home/ubuntu/models/
-- pet_model
---- 1
------ saved_model.pb
------ variables
```

Serving the model in production

In production, we need to create an endpoint so our users can send the image and receive
the result. In TensorFlow, we can easily serve our model with TensorFlow Serving. In this
section, we will install TensorFlow Serving and create a Flask app that allows users to
upload their images via a web interface.

Setting up TensorFlow Serving

In your production server, you need to install TensorFlow Serving and its prerequisites.
You can visit the official website of TensorFlow Serving at
`https://tensorflow.github.io/serving/setup`. Next, we will use the standard
TensorFlow Model Server provided in TensorFlow Serving to serve the model. First, we
need to build the `tensorflow_model_server` with the following command:

```
bazel build
//tensorflow_serving/model_servers:tensorflow_model_server
```

Copy all the files from `/home/ubuntu/models/pet_model` in your training server into
your production server. In our setup, we choose `/home/ubuntu/productions` as our
folder to store all the production models. The `productions` folder will have the following
structure:

```
- /home/ubuntu/productions/
-- 1
---- saved_model.pb
---- variables
```

We will use `tmux` to keep the model server running. Let's install `tmux` with this command:

```
sudo apt-get install tmux
```

Run a `tmux` session with this command:

```
tmux new -s serving
```

In the `tmux` session, let's change directory to the `tensorflow_serving` directory and run the following command:

```
bazel-bin/tensorflow_serving/model_servers/tensorflow_model_server --
port=9000 --model_name=pet-model --model_base_path=/home/ubuntu/productions
```

The output of the console should look like this:

```
2017-05-29 13:44:32.203153: I
external/org_tensorflow/tensorflow/cc/saved_model/loader.cc:274] Loading
SavedModel: success. Took 537318 microseconds.
2017-05-29 13:44:32.203243: I
tensorflow_serving/core/loader_harness.cc:86] Successfully loaded servable
version {name: pet-model version: 1}
2017-05-29 13:44:32.205543: I
tensorflow_serving/model_servers/main.cc:298] Running ModelServer at
0.0.0.0:9000 ...
```

As you can see, the model is running on host `0.0.0.0` and port `9000`. In the next section, we will create a simple Python client to send an image to this server via gRPC.

You should also note that the current serving is only using CPU on the production server. Building TensorFlow Serving with GPUs is beyond the scope of this chapter. If you prefer serving with GPUs, you may want to read `Appendix A`, *Advanced Installation*, which explains how to build TensorFlow and TensorFlow Serving with GPU support.

Running and testing the model

In the project repository, we have already provided a package named `production`. In that package, we need to copy the `labels.txt` file into our `dataset`, create a new Python file, `client.py`, and add the following code:

```python
import tensorflow as tf
import numpy as np
from tensorflow_serving.apis import prediction_service_pb2,
predict_pb2
from grpc.beta import implementations
```

```
from scipy.misc import imread
from datetime import datetime


class Output:
def __init__(self, score, label):
    self.score = score
    self.label = label

def __repr__(self):
    return "Label: %s Score: %.2f" % (self.label, self.score)


def softmax(x):
return np.exp(x) / np.sum(np.exp(x), axis=0)


def process_image(path, label_data, top_k=3):
start_time = datetime.now()
img = imread(path)

host, port = "0.0.0.0:9000".split(":")
channel = implementations.insecure_channel(host, int(port))
stub =
prediction_service_pb2.beta_create_PredictionService_stub(channel)

request = predict_pb2.PredictRequest()
request.model_spec.name = "pet-model"
request.model_spec.signature_name = "predict_images"

request.inputs["images"].CopyFrom(
    tf.contrib.util.make_tensor_proto(
        img.astype(dtype=float),
        shape=img.shape, dtype=tf.float32
    )
)

result = stub.Predict(request, 20.)
scores =
tf.contrib.util.make_ndarray(result.outputs["scores"])[0]
probs = softmax(scores)
index = sorted(range(len(probs)), key=lambda x: probs[x],
reverse=True)

outputs = []
for i in range(top_k):
    outputs.append(Output(score=float(probs[index[i]]),
    label=label_data[index[i]]))
```

```
print(outputs)
print("total time", (datetime.now() -
start_time).total_seconds())
return outputs

if __name__ == "__main__":
label_data = [line.strip() for line in
open("production/labels.txt", 'r')]
process_image("samples_data/dog.jpg", label_data)
process_image("samples_data/cat.jpg", label_data)
```

In this code, we create a `process_image` method that will read the image from an image path and use some TensorFlow methods to create a tensor and send it to the model server with gRPC. We also create an `Output` class so that we can easily return it to the `caller` method. At the end of the method, we print the output and the total time so that we can debug it more easily. We can run this Python file to see if the `process_image` works:

python production/client.py

The output should look like this:

```
[Label: saint_bernard Score: 0.78, Label: american_bulldog Score: 0.21,
Label: staffordshire_bull_terrier Score: 0.00]
('total time', 14.943942)
[Label: Maine_Coon Score: 1.00, Label: Ragdoll Score: 0.00, Label:
Bengal Score: 0.00]
('total time', 14.918235)
```

We get the correct result. However, the time to process is almost 15 seconds for each image. The reason is that we are using TensorFlow Serving in CPU mode. As we mentioned earlier, you can build TensorFlow Serving with GPU support in `Appendix A`, *Advanced Installation*. If you follow that tutorial, you will have the following result:

```
[Label: saint_bernard Score: 0.78, Label: american_bulldog Score: 0.21,
Label: staffordshire_bull_terrier Score: 0.00]
('total time', 0.493618)
[Label: Maine_Coon Score: 1.00, Label: Ragdoll Score: 0.00, Label:
Bengal Score: 0.00]
('total time', 0.023753)
```

The time to process in the first calling time is 493 ms. However, the later calling time will be only about 23 ms, which is so much quicker than the CPU version.

Designing the web server

In this section, we will set up a Flask server to allow users to upload their images and set the correct label if our model is mistaken. We have provided the code needed in the production package. Implementing a Flask server with database support is beyond the scope of this chapter. In this section, we will describe all the main points about Flask so you can follow and understand better.

The main flow that allows users to upload and correct labels can be described in the following wireframe.

This flow is implemented with the following routes:

Route	Method	Description
/	GET	This route returns a web form for users to upload the image.
/upload_image	POST	This route gets the image from POST data, saves it to the upload directory, and calls `process_image` in our `client.py` to recognize the image and save the result to the database.
/results<result_id>	GET	This route returns the result of the corresponding row in the database.
/results<result_id>	POST	This route saves the label from, user to the database so that we can fine-tune the model later.
/user-labels	GET	This route returns a list of all the user-labeled images. In the fine-tune process, we will call this route to get the list of labeled images.
/model	POST	This route allows the fine-tune process from the training server to serve a new trained model. This route receives a link of the zipped model, a version number, a checkpoint name, and a model name.
/model	GET	This route returns the latest model in the database. The fine-tune process will call this to know which is the latest model and fine-tune from it.

We should run this server in a `tmux` session with the following command:

```
tmux new -s "flask"
python production/server.py
```

Testing the system

Now, we can access the server via `http://0.0.0.0:5000`.

First, you will see a form to choose and submit an image.

The website will be redirected to the `/results` page with the corresponding image and its results. The user label field is empty. There is also a short form at the end so that you can submit the corrected label of the model.

Automatic fine-tune in production

After running the system for a while, we will have some user-labeled images. We will create a fine-tune process to automatically run every day and fine-tune the latest model with new data.

Let's create a file named `finetune.py` in the scripts folder.

Loading the user-labeled data

First, we will add the code to download all user-labeled images from the production server:

```python
import tensorflow as tf
import os
import json
import random
import requests
import shutil
from scipy.misc import imread, imsave
from datetime import datetime
from tqdm import tqdm

import nets, models, datasets


def ensure_folder_exists(folder_path):
if not os.path.exists(folder_path):
    os.mkdir(folder_path)
return folder_path


def download_user_data(url, user_dir, train_ratio=0.8):
response = requests.get("%s/user-labels" % url)
```

```
data = json.loads(response.text)

if not os.path.exists(user_dir):
    os.mkdir(user_dir)
user_dir = ensure_folder_exists(user_dir)
train_folder = ensure_folder_exists(os.path.join(user_dir,
"trainval"))
test_folder = ensure_folder_exists(os.path.join(user_dir,
"test"))

train_file = open(os.path.join(user_dir, 'trainval.txt'), 'w')
test_file = open(os.path.join(user_dir, 'test.txt'), 'w')

for image in data:
    is_train = random.random() < train_ratio
    image_url = image["url"]
    file_name = image_url.split("/")[-1]
    label = image["label"]
    name = image["name"]

    if is_train:
      target_folder =
      ensure_folder_exists(os.path.join(train_folder, name))
    else:
      target_folder =
      ensure_folder_exists(os.path.join(test_folder, name))

    target_file = os.path.join(target_folder, file_name) +
    ".jpg"

    if not os.path.exists(target_file):
        response = requests.get("%s%s" % (url, image_url))
        temp_file_path = "/tmp/%s" % file_name
        with open(temp_file_path, 'wb') as f:
            for chunk in response:
                f.write(chunk)

        image = imread(temp_file_path)
        imsave(target_file, image)
        os.remove(temp_file_path)
        print("Save file: %s" % target_file)

    label_path = "%s %s\n" % (label, target_file)
    if is_train:
        train_file.write(label_path)
    else:
        test_file.write(label_path)
```

In `download_user_data`, we call the `/user-labels` endpoint to get the list of user-labeled images. The JSON has the following format:

```
[
  {
    "id": 1,
    "label": 0,
    "name": "Abyssinian",
    "url": "/uploads/2017-05-23_14-56-45_Abyssinian-cat.jpeg"
  },
  {
    "id": 2,
    "label": 32,
    "name": "Siamese",
    "url": "/uploads/2017-05-23_14-57-33_fat-Siamese-cat.jpeg"
  }
]
```

In this JSON, `label` is the label that the user has chosen, and URL is the link to download the image from. For every image, we will download it into the `tmp` folder and use `imread` and `imsave` from `scipy` to make sure that the image is in JPEG format. We also create a `trainval.txt` and `test.txt` file, as in the training dataset.

Performing a fine-tune on the model

In order to fine-tune the model, we need to know which one is the latest model and its corresponding checkpoint to restore `weights` and `biases`. Therefore, we call the `/model` endpoint to get the checkpoint name and a version number:

```
def get_latest_model(url):
response = requests.get("%s/model" % url)
data = json.loads(response.text)
print(data)
return data["ckpt_name"], int(data["version"])
```

The response JSON should look like this:

```
{
  "ckpt_name": "2017-05-26_02-12-49",
  "id": 10,
  "link": "http://1.53.110.161:8181/pet-model/8.zip",
  "name": "pet-model",
  "version": 8
}
```

Now, we will implement the code to fine-tune the model. Let's start with some parameters:

```
# Server info
URL = "http://localhost:5000"
dest_api = URL + "/model"

# Server Endpoints
source_api = "http://1.53.110.161:8181"

# Dataset
dataset_dir = "data/train_data"
user_dir = "data/user_data"
batch_size = 64
image_size = 224

# Learning rate
initial_learning_rate = 0.0001
decay_steps = 250
decay_rate = 0.9

# Validation
output_steps = 10   # Number of steps to print output
eval_steps = 20   # Number of steps to perform evaluations

# Training
max_steps = 3000   # Number of steps to perform training
save_steps = 200   # Number of steps to perform saving
checkpoints
num_tests = 5   # Number of times to test for test accuracy
max_checkpoints_to_keep = 1
save_dir = "data/checkpoints"
train_vars = 'models/fc8-pets/weights:0,models/fc8-
pets/biases:0'

# Get the latest model
last_checkpoint_name, last_version = get_latest_model(URL)
last_checkpoint_dir = os.path.join(save_dir,
last_checkpoint_name)

# Export
export_dir = "/home/ubuntu/models/"
export_name = "pet-model"
export_version = last_version + 1
```

Then, we will implement the fine-tune loop. In the following code, we call
`download_user_data` to download all the user-labeled images and pass `user_dir` into
`input_pipeline` so that it will load the new images:

```
# Download user-labels data
download_user_data(URL, user_dir)

images, labels = datasets.input_pipeline(dataset_dir,
batch_size, is_training=True, user_dir=user_dir)
test_images, test_labels =
datasets.input_pipeline(dataset_dir, batch_size,
is_training=False, user_dir=user_dir)

 with tf.variable_scope("models") as scope:
  logits = nets.inference(images, is_training=True)
  scope.reuse_variables()
  test_logits = nets.inference(test_images, is_training=False)

total_loss = models.compute_loss(logits, labels)
train_accuracy = models.compute_accuracy(logits, labels)
test_accuracy = models.compute_accuracy(test_logits,
test_labels)

global_step = tf.Variable(0, trainable=False)
learning_rate = models.get_learning_rate(global_step,
initial_learning_rate, decay_steps, decay_rate)
train_op = models.train(total_loss, learning_rate,
global_step, train_vars)

saver = tf.train.Saver(max_to_keep=max_checkpoints_to_keep)
checkpoint_name = datetime.now().strftime("%Y-%m-%d_%H-%M-%S")
checkpoints_dir = os.path.join(save_dir, checkpoint_name)
if not os.path.exists(save_dir):
  os.mkdir(save_dir)
if not os.path.exists(checkpoints_dir):
  os.mkdir(checkpoints_dir)

with tf.Session() as sess:
  sess.run(tf.global_variables_initializer())
  coords = tf.train.Coordinator()
  threads = tf.train.start_queue_runners(sess=sess,
  coord=coords)

saver.restore(sess,
models.get_model_path_from_ckpt(last_checkpoint_dir))
sess.run(global_step.assign(0))

last_saved_test_accuracy = 0
```

```
for i in range(num_tests):
    last_saved_test_accuracy += sess.run(test_accuracy)
last_saved_test_accuracy /= num_tests
should_export = False
print("Last model test accuracy
{}".format(last_saved_test_accuracy))
for i in tqdm(range(max_steps), desc="training"):
    _, loss_value, lr_value = sess.run([train_op, total_loss,
    learning_rate])

 if (i + 1) % output_steps == 0:
   print("Steps {}: Loss = {:.5f} Learning Rate =
   {}".format(i + 1, loss_value, lr_value))

    if (i + 1) % eval_steps == 0:
      test_acc, train_acc, loss_value =
      sess.run([test_accuracy, train_accuracy, total_loss])
        print("Test accuracy {} Train accuracy {} : Loss =
        {:.5f}".format(test_acc, train_acc, loss_value))

    if (i + 1) % save_steps == 0 or i == max_steps - 1:
      test_acc = 0
      for i in range(num_tests):
        test_acc += sess.run(test_accuracy)
        test_acc /= num_tests

    if test_acc > last_saved_test_accuracy:
      print("Save steps: Test Accuracy {} is higher than
      {}".format(test_acc, last_saved_test_accuracy))
      last_saved_test_accuracy = test_acc
      saved_file = saver.save(sess,
    os.path.join(checkpoints_dir, 'model.ckpt'),
                                  global_step=global_step)
          should_export = True
          print("Save steps: Save to file %s " % saved_file)
      else:
          print("Save steps: Test Accuracy {} is not higher
  than {}".format(test_acc, last_saved_test_accuracy))

if should_export:
    print("Export model with accuracy ",
    last_saved_test_accuracy)
    models.export_model(checkpoints_dir, export_dir,
    export_name, export_version)
    archive_and_send_file(source_api, dest_api,
    checkpoint_name, export_dir, export_name, export_version)
  coords.request_stop()
  coords.join(threads)
```

Other parts are quite similar to the training loop. However, instead of loading the weights from the `caffe` model, we use the checkpoint of the latest model and run the test a few times to get its test accuracy.

At the end of the fine-tune loop, we need a new method named `archive_and_send_file` to make an archive from the `exported` model and send the link to the production server:

```
def make_archive(dir_path):
    return shutil.make_archive(dir_path, 'zip', dir_path)


def archive_and_send_file(source_api, dest_api, ckpt_name,
export_dir, export_name, export_version):
    model_dir = os.path.join(export_dir, export_name,
    str(export_version))
    file_path = make_archive(model_dir)
    print("Zip model: ", file_path)

    data = {
        "link": "{}/{}/{}".format(source_api, export_name,
     str(export_version) + ".zip"),
        "ckpt_name": ckpt_name,
        "version": export_version,
        "name": export_name,
    }
     r = requests.post(dest_api, data=data)
    print("send_file", r.text)
```

You should note that we create a link with the `source_api` parameter, which is the link to the training server, `http://1.53.110.161:8181`. We will set up a simple Apache Server to support this function. However, in reality, we suggest that you upload the archived model to cloud storage such as Amazon S3. Now, we will show you the simplest way with Apache.

We need to install Apache with the following command:

```
sudo apt-get install apache2
```

Now, in `/etc/apache2/ports.conf`, on line 6, we need to add this code to make `apache2` listen on port `8181`:

```
Listen 8181
```

Then, add the following code at the beginning of `/etc/apache2/sites-available/000-default.conf` to support downloading from the `/home/ubuntu/models` directory:

```
<VirtualHost *:8181>
  DocumentRoot "/home/ubuntu/models"
  <Directory />
    Require all granted
  </Directory>
</VirtualHost>
```

Finally, we need to restart the `apache2` server:

```
sudo service apache2 restart
```

Up to now, we have set up all the code to perform fine-tuning. Before running the fine-tuning for the first time, we need to send a POST request to the `/model` endpoint with the information about our first model because we have already copied the model to the production server.

In the `project` repository, let's run the `finetune` script:

```
python scripts/finetune.py
```

The last few lines in the console will look like the following:

```
Save steps: Test Accuracy 0.84 is higher than 0.916875
Save steps: Save to file
data/checkpoints/2017-05-29_18-46-43/model.ckpt-2000
('Export model with accuracy ', 0.916875000000004)
2017-05-29 18:47:31.642729: I
tensorflow/core/common_runtime/gpu/gpu_device.cc:977] Creating TensorFlow
device (/gpu:0) -> (device: 0, name: GeForce GTX TITAN X, pci bus id:
0000:01:00.0)
('Exported model at', '/home/ubuntu/models/pet-model/2')
('Zip model: ', '/home/ubuntu/models/pet-model/2.zip')
('send_file', u'{\n  "ckpt_name": "2017-05-29_18-46-43", \n  "id": 2,
\n  "link": "http://1.53.110.161:8181/pet-model/2.zip", \n  "name": "pet-
model", \n  "version": 2\n}\n')
```

As you can see, the new model has a test accuracy of 91%. The model is also exported and archived to `/home/ubuntu/models/pet-model/2.zip`. The code is also calling the `/model` endpoint to post the link to the production server. In the logging of the Flask app in the production server, we will get the following results:

```
('Start downloading', u'http://1.53.110.161:8181/pet-model/2.zip')
('Downloaded file at', u'/tmp/2.zip')
('Extracted at', u'/home/ubuntu/productions/2')
127.0.0.1 - - [29/May/2017 18:49:05] "POST /model HTTP/1.1" 200 -
```

This means that our Flask app had downloaded the `2.zip` file from the training server and extracted the content to `/home/ubuntu/productions/2`. In the `tmux` session for TensorFlow Serving, you will also get the following results:

```
    2017-05-29 18:49:06.234808: I
tensorflow_serving/core/loader_harness.cc:86] Successfully loaded servable
version {name: pet-model version: 2}
    2017-05-29 18:49:06.234840: I
tensorflow_serving/core/loader_harness.cc:137] Quiescing servable version
{name: pet-model version: 1}
    2017-05-29 18:49:06.234848: I
tensorflow_serving/core/loader_harness.cc:144] Done quiescing servable
version {name: pet-model version: 1}
    2017-05-29 18:49:06.234853: I
tensorflow_serving/core/loader_harness.cc:119] Unloading servable version
{name: pet-model version: 1}
    2017-05-29 18:49:06.240118: I
./tensorflow_serving/core/simple_loader.h:226] Calling
MallocExtension_ReleaseToSystem() with 645327546
    2017-05-29 18:49:06.240155: I
tensorflow_serving/core/loader_harness.cc:127] Done unloading servable
version {name: pet-model version: 1}
```

This output indicates that the TensorFlow model server has successfully loaded `version 2` of the `pet-model` and unloaded `version 1`. This also means that we have served the new model, which was trained on the training server and sent to the production server via the `/model` endpoint.

Setting up cronjob to run every day

Finally, we need to set up the fine-tuning to run every day and automatically upload the new model to the server. We can achieve this easily by creating a `crontab` in the training server.

First, we need to run the `crontab` command:

```
crontab -e
```

Then, we can just add the following line to define the time that we want `finetune.py` to run:

```
0 3 * * * python /home/ubuntu/project/scripts/finetune.py
```

As we defined, the Python command will run at 3 a.m. every day.

Summary

In this chapter, we have implemented a complete real-life production, from training to serving a deep learning model. We also created a web interface in a Flask app so that users can upload their images and receive results. Our model can automatically be fine-tuned every day to improve the quality of the system. There are a few things that you can consider to improve the overall system:

- The model and checkpoints should be saved in cloud storage.
- The Flask app and TensorFlow Serving should be managed by another, better process management system, such as Supervisor.
- There should be a web interface so that the team can approve the labels that users select. We shouldn't rely completely on users to decide the training set.
- TensorFlow Serving should be built with GPU support to achieve the best performance.

10
Go Live and Go Big

In this chapter, we are going to learn more about **Amazon Web Services** (**AWS**) and how to create a deep neural network to solve a video action recognition problem. We will show you how to use multiple GPUs for faster training. At the end of the chapter, we will give you a quick overview of Amazon Mechanical Turk Service, which allows us to collect labels and correct the model's results.

Quick look at Amazon Web Services

Amazon Web Services (**AWS**) is one of the most popular cloud platforms, and was made by Amazon.com. It provides many services, including cloud computing, storage, database services, content delivery, and other functionalities. In this section, we will only focus on virtual server services found on Amazon EC2. Amazon EC2 allows us to create multiple servers that can support the serving of our model and even the training routine. When it comes to serving the model for end users, you can read Chapter 9, *Cruise Control - Automation*, to learn about TensorFlow Serving. In training, Amazon EC2 has many instance types that we can use. We can use their CPU servers to run our web bot to collect data from the internet. There are several instance types that have multiple NVIDIA GPUs.

Amazon EC2 provides a wide selection of instance types to fit different use cases. The instance types are divided into five categories, as follows:

- General Purpose
- Compute Optimized
- Memory Optimized
- Storage Optimized
- Accelerated Computing Instances

The first four categories are best suited to running backend servers. The accelerated computing instances have multiple NVIDIA GPUs that can be used to serve models and train new models with high-end GPUs. There are three types of instances—P2, G2, and F1.

P2 instances

P2 instances contain high-performance NVIDIA K80 GPUs, each with 2,496 CUDA cores and 12 GB of GPU memory. There are three models of P2, as described in the following table:

Model	GPUs	vCPU	Memory (GB)	GPU Memory (GB)
p2.xlarge	1	4	61	12
p2.8xlarge	8	32	488	96
p2.16xlarge	16	64	732	192

These models with large GPU memory are best suited for training models. With more GPU memory, we can train the model with a larger batch size and a neural network with lots of parameters.

G2 instances

G2 instances contain high-performance NVIDIA GPUs, each with 1,536 CUDA cores and 4 GB of GPU memory. There are two models of G2, as described in the following table:

Model	GPUs	vCPU	Memory(GB)	SSD Storage (GB)
g2.2xlarge	1	8	15	1 x 60
g2.8xlarge	4	32	60	2 x 120

These models have only 4 GB of GPU memory, so they are limited in training. However, 4 GB of GPU memory is generally enough for serving the model to end users. One of the most important factors is that G2 instances are much cheaper than P2 instances, which allows us to deploy multiple servers under a load balancer for high scalability.

F1 instances

F1 instances support **field programmable gate arrays** (**FPGAs**). There are two models of F1, as described in the following table:

Model	GPUs	vCPU	Memory(GB)	SSD Storage (GB)
f1.2xlarge	1	8	122	470
f1.16xlarge	8	64	976	4 x 940

FPGAs with high memory and computing power are very promising in the field of deep learning. However, TensorFlow and other popular deep learning libraries don't support FPGAs. Therefore, in the next section, we will only cover the prices of P2 and G2 instances.

Pricing

Let's explore the pricing of these instances at `https://aws.amazon.com/emr/pricing/`.

Amazon EC2 offers three pricing options for instances--On-Demand Instance, Reserved Instance, and Spot Instance:

- On-Demand instance gives you the ability to run the server without disruption. It is suitable if you only want to use the instance for a few days or weeks.
- Reserved instance gives you the option to reserve the instance for a one- or three-year term with a significant discount compared to the On-Demand Instance. It is suitable if you want to run the server for production.
- Spot instance gives you the option to bid for the server. You can choose the maximum price you are willing to pay per instance hour. This can save you a lot of money. However, these instances can be terminated at any time if someone bids higher than you. It is suitable if your system can handle interruption or if you just want to explore services.

Amazon has provided a website to calculate the monthly bill. You can see it at `http://calculator.s3.amazonaws.com/index.html`.

You can click the **Add New Row** button and select an instance type.

In the following image, we have selected a **p2.xlarge** server. The price for a month is **$658.80** at the time of writing:

Now click on the **Billing Option** column. You will see the price of a reserved instance for a **p2.xlarge** server:

Select	Name	Upfront Price	Effective Hourly Cost	Effective Monthly Cost	1 Year Cost	3 Year Cost
●	On-Demand (No Contract)	- - -	0.900	658.80	7905.60	23716.80
○	1 Yr No Upfront Reserved	0.00	0.614	448.22	5378.64	16135.92
○	1 Yr Partial Upfront Reserved	2562.00	0.585	427.02	5124.24	15372.72
○	1 Yr All Upfront Reserved	5022.00	0.573	418.50	5022.00	15066.00
○	3 Yr Partial Upfront Reserved	5584.00	0.425	310.24	- - -	11168.32
○	3 Yr All Upfront Reserved	10499.00	0.399	291.64	- - -	10499.00
○	3 Yr No Upfront Convertible	0.00	0.528	385.44	- - -	13875.84
○	3 Yr Partial Upfront Convertible	6422.00	0.488	356.51	- - -	12834.32
○	3 Yr All Upfront Convertible	12588.00	0.479	349.67	- - -	12588.00

There are many other instance types. We suggest that you take a look at the other types and select the server that is best suited to your requirements.

In the next section, we will create a new model that can perform video action recognition with TensorFlow. We will also leverage the training performance using multiple GPUs.

Overview of the application

Human action recognition is a very interesting problem in computer vision and machine learning. There are two popular approaches to this problem, that is, **still image action recognition** and **video action recognition**. In still image action recognition, we can fine-tune a pre-trained model from ImageNet and perform a classification of the actions based on the static image. You can review the previous chapters for more information. In this chapter, we will create a model that can recognize human action from videos. At the end of the chapter, we will show you how to use multiple GPUs to speed up the training process.

Datasets

There are many available datasets that we can use in the training process, as follows:

- UCF101 (`http://crcv.ucf.edu/data/UCF101.php`) is an action recognition dataset of realistic action videos with 101 action categories. There are 13,320 videos in total for the 101 action categories, which makes this dataset a great choice for many research papers.
- ActivityNet (`http://activity-net.org/`) is a large-scale dataset for human activity understanding. There are 200 categories with over 648 hours of video. Each category has about 100 videos.
- Sports-1M (`http://cs.stanford.edu/people/karpathy/deepvideo/`) is another large-scale dataset for sports recognition. There are 1,133,158 videos in total, annotated with 487 sports labels.

In this chapter, we will use UCF101 to perform the training process. We also recommend that you try to apply the techniques discussed in this chapter to a large-scale dataset to take full advantage of multiple-GPU training.

Preparing the dataset and input pipeline

The UCF101 dataset contains 101 action categories, such as Basketball shooting, playing guitar, and Surfing. We can download the dataset from `http://crcv.ucf.edu/data/UCF101.php`.

On the website, you need to download the UCF101 dataset in the file named `UCF101.rar`, and the train/test splits for action recognition in the file named `UCF101TrainTestSplits-RecognitionTask.zip`. You need to extract the dataset before moving to the next section, where we will perform a pre-processing technique on videos before training.

Pre-processing the video for training

UCF101 contains 13,320 video clips with a fixed frame rate and resolution of 25 FPS and 320 x 240 respectively. All video clips are stored in AVI format, so it is not convenient to use them in TensorFlow. Therefore, in this section, we will extract video frames from all the videos into JPEG files. We will only extract video frames at the fixed frame rate of 4 FPS so that we can reduce the input size of the network.

Before we start implementing the code, we need to install the av library from `https://mikeboers.github.io/PyAV/installation.html`.

First, create a Python package named `scripts` in the `root` folder. Then, create a new Python file at `scripts/convert_ucf101.py`. In the newly created file, add the first code to import and define some parameters, as follows:

```python
import av
import os
import random
import tensorflow as tf
from tqdm import tqdm

FLAGS = tf.app.flags.FLAGS
tf.app.flags.DEFINE_string(
    'dataset_dir', '/mnt/DATA02/Dataset/UCF101',
    'The folder that contains the extracted content of UCF101.rar'
)

tf.app.flags.DEFINE_string(
    'train_test_list_dir',
'/mnt/DATA02/Dataset/UCF101/ucfTrainTestlist',
    'The folder that contains the extracted content of
UCF101TrainTestSplits-RecognitionTask.zip'
)

tf.app.flags.DEFINE_string(
    'target_dir', '/home/ubuntu/datasets/ucf101',
    'The location where all the images will be stored'
)

tf.app.flags.DEFINE_integer(
```

```
        'fps', 4,
        'Framerate to export'
)

def ensure_folder_exists(folder_path):
    if not os.path.exists(folder_path):
        os.mkdir(folder_path)

    return folder_path
```

In the preceding code, `dataset_dir` and `train_test_list_dir` are the locations of the folders containing the extracted content of `UCF101.rar` and `UCF101TrainTestSplits-RecognitionTask.zip` respectively. `target_dir` is the folder that all the training images will be stored in. `ensure_folder_exists` is a `utility` function that creates a folder if it doesn't exist.

Next, let's define the `main` function of the Python code:

```
def main(_):
    if not FLAGS.dataset_dir:
        raise ValueError("You must supply the dataset directory
with
 --dataset_dir")

    ensure_folder_exists(FLAGS.target_dir)
    convert_data(["trainlist01.txt", "trainlist02.txt",
 "trainlist03.txt"], training=True)
    convert_data(["testlist01.txt", "testlist02.txt",
 "testlist03.txt"], training=False)

if __name__ == "__main__":
    tf.app.run()
```

In the `main` function, we create the `target_dir` folder and call the `convert_data` function which we will create shortly. The `convert_data` function takes a list of train/test text files in the dataset and a Boolean called training that indicates whether the text files are for the training process.

Here are some lines from one of the text files:

```
ApplyEyeMakeup/v_ApplyEyeMakeup_g08_c01.avi 1
ApplyEyeMakeup/v_ApplyEyeMakeup_g08_c02.avi 1
ApplyEyeMakeup/v_ApplyEyeMakeup_g08_c03.avi 1
```

Each line of the text file contains the path to the `video` file and the correct label. In this case, we have three video paths from the `ApplyEyeMakeup` category, which is the first category in the dataset.

The main idea here is that we read each line of the text files, extract video frames in a JPEG format, and save the location of the extracted files with the corresponding label for further training. Here is the code for the `convert_data` function:

```
def convert_data(list_files, training=False):
    lines = []
    for txt in list_files:
        lines += [line.strip() for line in
open(os.path.join(FLAGS.train_test_list_dir, txt))]

    output_name = "train" if training else "test"

    random.shuffle(lines)

    target_dir =
ensure_folder_exists(os.path.join(FLAGS.target_dir,
output_name))
    class_index_file = os.path.join(FLAGS.train_test_list_dir,
"classInd.txt")
    class_index = {line.split(" ")[1].strip(): int(line.split(" ")
[0]) - 1 for line in open(class_index_file)}

    with open(os.path.join(FLAGS.target_dir, output_name + ".txt"),
"w") as f:
        for line in tqdm(lines):
            if training:
                filename, _ = line.strip().split(" ")
            else:
                filename = line.strip()
            class_folder, video_name = filename.split("/")

            label = class_index[class_folder]
            video_name = video_name.replace(".avi", "")
            target_class_folder =
ensure_folder_exists(os.path.join(target_dir, class_folder))
            target_folder =
ensure_folder_exists(os.path.join(target_class_folder,
video_name))

            container = av.open(os.path.join(FLAGS.dataset_dir,
filename))
            frame_to_skip = int(25.0 / FLAGS.fps)
            last_frame = -1
```

```
frame_index = 0
for frame in container.decode(video=0):
    if last_frame < 0 or frame.index > last_frame +
    frame_to_skip:
        last_frame = frame.index
        image = frame.to_image()
        target_file = os.path.join(target_folder,
        "%04d.jpg" % frame_index)
        image.save(target_file)
        frame_index += 1
    f.write("{} {} {}\n".format("%s/%s" % (class_folder,
    video_name), label, frame_index))

if training:
    with open(os.path.join(FLAGS.target_dir, "label.txt"), "w")
    as f:
        for class_name in sorted(class_index,
        key=class_index.get):
            f.write("%s\n" % class_name)
```

The preceding code is straightforward. We load the video path from the text files and use the av library to open the AVI files. Then, we use FLAGS.fps to control how many frames per second need to be extracted. You can run the scripts/convert_ucf101.py file using the following command:

```
python scripts/convert_ucf101.py
```

The total process needs about 30 minutes to convert all the video clips. At the end, the target_dir folder will contain the following files:

```
label.txt  test  test.txt  train  train.txt
```

In the train.txt file, the lines will look like this:

```
Punch/v_Punch_g25_c03 70 43
Haircut/v_Haircut_g20_c01 33 36
BrushingTeeth/v_BrushingTeeth_g25_c02 19 33
Nunchucks/v_Nunchucks_g03_c04 55 36
BoxingSpeedBag/v_BoxingSpeedBag_g16_c04 17 21
```

This format can be understood as follows:

```
<Folder location of the video> <Label> <Number of frames in the folder>
```

There is one thing that you must remember, which is that the labels in `train.txt` and `test.txt` go from 0 to 100. However, the labels in the UCF101 go from 1 to 101. This is because the `sparse_softmax_cross_entropy` function in TensorFlow needs class labels to start from 0.

Input pipeline with RandomShuffleQueue

If you have read Chapter 9, *Cruise Control - Automation*, you will know that we can use TextLineReader in TensorFlow to simply read the text files line by line and use the line to read the image directly in TensorFlow. However, things get more complex as the data only contains the folder location and the label. Moreover, we only want a subset of frames in one folder. For example, if the number of frames is 30 and we only want 10 frames to train, we will randomize from 0 to 20 and select 10 frames from that point. Therefore, in this chapter, we will use another mechanism to sample the video frames in pure Python and put the selected frame paths into `RandomShuffleQueue` for training. We also use `tf.train.batch_join` to leverage the training with multiple pre-processing threads.

First, create a new Python file named `utils.py` in the `root` folder and add the following code:

```
def lines_from_file(filename, repeat=False):
    with open(filename) as handle:
        while True:
            try:
                line = next(handle)
                yield line.strip()
            except StopIteration as e:
                if repeat:
                    handle.seek(0)
                else:
                    raise

if __name__ == "__main__":
    data_reader = lines_from_file("/home/ubuntu/datasets/ucf101/train.txt",
repeat=True)

    for i in range(15):
        print(next(data_reader))
```

In this code, we create a `generator` function named `lines_from_file` to read the text files line by line. We also add a `repeat` parameter so that the `generator` function can read the text from the beginning when it reaches the end of the file.

We have added a main section so you can try to run it to see how the `generator` works:

```
python utils.py
```

Now, create a new Python file named `datasets.py` in the `root` folder and add the following code:

```python
import tensorflow as tf
import cv2
import os
import random

from tensorflow.python.ops import data_flow_ops
from utils import lines_from_file

def sample_videos(data_reader, root_folder, num_samples,
num_frames):
    image_paths = list()
    labels = list()
    while True:
        if len(labels) >= num_samples:
            break
        line = next(data_reader)
        video_folder, label, max_frames = line.strip().split(" ")
        max_frames = int(max_frames)
        label = int(label)
        if max_frames > num_frames:
            start_index = random.randint(0, max_frames -
num_frames)
            frame_paths = list()
            for index in range(start_index, start_index +
num_frames):
                frame_path = os.path.join(root_folder,
video_folder,
 "%04d.jpg" % index)
                frame_paths.append(frame_path)
            image_paths.append(frame_paths)
            labels.append(label)
    return image_paths, labels

if __name__ == "__main__":
    num_frames = 5
    root_folder = "/home/ubuntu/datasets/ucf101/train/"
```

```
        data_reader =
lines_from_file("/home/ubuntu/datasets/ucf101/train.txt",
repeat=True)
image_paths, labels = sample_videos(data_reader,
root_folder=root_folder,
num_samples=3,
num_frames=num_frames)
    print("image_paths", image_paths)
    print("labels", labels)
```

The `sample_videos` function is easy to understand. It will receive the `generator` object from `lines_from_file` function and use the `next` function to get the required samples. You can see that we use a `random.randint` method to randomize the starting frame position.

You can run the main section to see how the `sample_videos` work with the following command:

python datasets.py

Up to this point, we have read the dataset text file into the `image_paths` and `labels` variables, which are Python lists. In the later training routine, we will use a built-in `RandomShuffleQueue` in TensorFlow to enqueue `image_paths` and `labels` into that queue.

Now, we need to create a method that will be used in the training routine to get data from `RandomShuffleQueue`, perform pre-processing in multiple threads, and send the data to the `batch_join` function to create a mini-batch for training.

In the `dataset.py` file, add the following code:

```
def input_pipeline(input_queue, batch_size=32, num_threads=8,
image_size=112):
    frames_and_labels = []
    for _ in range(num_threads):
        frame_paths, label = input_queue.dequeue()
        frames = []
        for filename in tf.unstack(frame_paths):
            file_contents = tf.read_file(filename)
            image = tf.image.decode_jpeg(file_contents)
            image = _aspect_preserving_resize(image, image_size)
            image = tf.image.resize_image_with_crop_or_pad(image,
            image_size, image_size)
            image = tf.image.per_image_standardization(image)
            image.set_shape((image_size, image_size, 3))
            frames.append(image)
```

```
            frames_and_labels.append([frames, label])

        frames_batch, labels_batch = tf.train.batch_join(
            frames_and_labels, batch_size=batch_size,
            capacity=4 * num_threads * batch_size,
        )
        return frames_batch, labels_batch
```

In this code, we prepare an array named `frames_and_labels` and use a for loop with a `num_threads` iteration. This is a very convenient way of adding multi-threading support to the pre-processing process. In each thread, we will call the method `dequeue` from the `input_queue` to get a `frame_paths` and `label`. From the `sample_video` function in the previous section, we know that `frame_paths` is a list of selected video frames. Therefore, we use another for loop to loop through each frame. In each frame, we read, resize, and perform image standardization. This part is similar to the code in Chapter 9, *Cruise Control - Automation*. At the end of the input pipeline, we add `frames_and_labels` with `batch_size` parameters. The returned `frames_batch` and `labels_batch` will be used for a later training routine.

Finally, you should add the following code, which contains the `_aspect_preserving_resize` function:

```
        def _smallest_size_at_least(height, width, smallest_side):
            smallest_side = tf.convert_to_tensor(smallest_side,
        dtype=tf.int32)

            height = tf.to_float(height)
            width = tf.to_float(width)
            smallest_side = tf.to_float(smallest_side)

            scale = tf.cond(tf.greater(height, width),
                        lambda: smallest_side / width,
                        lambda: smallest_side / height)
            new_height = tf.to_int32(height * scale)
            new_width = tf.to_int32(width * scale)
            return new_height, new_width


        def _aspect_preserving_resize(image, smallest_side):
            smallest_side = tf.convert_to_tensor(smallest_side,
        dtype=tf.int32)
            shape = tf.shape(image)
            height = shape[0]
            width = shape[1]
            new_height, new_width = _smallest_size_at_least(height, width,
        smallest_side)
```

```
        image = tf.expand_dims(image, 0)
        resized_image = tf.image.resize_bilinear(image, [new_height,
new_width], align_corners=False)
        resized_image = tf.squeeze(resized_image)
        resized_image.set_shape([None, None, 3])
        return resized_image
```

This code is the same as what you used in Chapter 9, *Cruise Control - Automation*.

In the next section, we will create the deep neural network architecture that we will use to perform video action recognitions with 101 categories.

Neural network architecture

In this chapter, we will create a neural network that will take an input of 10 video frames and output the probability over 101 action categories. We will create a neural network based on the conv3d operation in TensorFlow. This network is inspired on the work of D. Tran et al., Learning Spatiotemporal Features with 3D Convolutional Networks. However, we have simplified the model so it is easier to explain in a chapter. We have also used some techniques that are not mentioned by Tran et al., such as batch normalization and dropout.

Now, create a new Python file named nets.py and add the following code:

```
import tensorflow as tf
from utils import print_variables, print_layers
from tensorflow.contrib.layers.python.layers.layers import
batch_norm
def inference(input_data, is_training=False):
    conv1 = _conv3d(input_data, 3, 3, 3, 64, 1, 1, 1, "conv1")
    pool1 = _max_pool3d(conv1, 1, 2, 2, 1, 2, 2, "pool1")

    conv2 = _conv3d(pool1, 3, 3, 3, 128, 1, 1, 1, "conv2")
    pool2 = _max_pool3d(conv2, 2, 2, 2, 2, 2, 2, "pool2")
    conv3a = _conv3d(pool2, 3, 3, 3, 256, 1, 1, 1, "conv3a")
    conv3b = _conv3d(conv3a, 3, 3, 3, 256, 1, 1, 1, "conv3b")
    pool3 = _max_pool3d(conv3b, 2, 2, 2, 2, 2, 2, "pool3")
    conv4a = _conv3d(pool3, 3, 3, 3, 512, 1, 1, 1, "conv4a")
    conv4b = _conv3d(conv4a, 3, 3, 3, 512, 1, 1, 1, "conv4b")
    pool4 = _max_pool3d(conv4b, 2, 2, 2, 2, 2, 2, "pool4")
    conv5a = _conv3d(pool4, 3, 3, 3, 512, 1, 1, 1, "conv5a")
    conv5b = _conv3d(conv5a, 3, 3, 3, 512, 1, 1, 1, "conv5b")
    pool5 = _max_pool3d(conv5b, 2, 2, 2, 2, 2, 2, "pool5")

    fc6 = _fully_connected(pool5, 4096, name="fc6")
    fc7 = _fully_connected(fc6, 4096, name="fc7")
```

```
    if is_training:
        fc7 = tf.nn.dropout(fc7, keep_prob=0.5)
    fc8 = _fully_connected(fc7, 101, name='fc8', relu=False)
    endpoints = dict()
    endpoints["conv1"] = conv1
    endpoints["pool1"] = pool1
    endpoints["conv2"] = conv2
    endpoints["pool2"] = pool2
    endpoints["conv3a"] = conv3a
    endpoints["conv3b"] = conv3b
    endpoints["pool3"] = pool3
    endpoints["conv4a"] = conv4a
    endpoints["conv4b"] = conv4b
    endpoints["pool4"] = pool4
    endpoints["conv5a"] = conv5a
    endpoints["conv5b"] = conv5b
    endpoints["pool5"] = pool5
    endpoints["fc6"] = fc6
    endpoints["fc7"] = fc7
    endpoints["fc8"] = fc8
    return fc8, endpoints

if __name__ == "__main__":
    inputs = tf.placeholder(tf.float32, [None, 10, 112, 112, 3],
name="inputs")
    outputs, endpoints = inference(inputs)

    print_variables(tf.global_variables())
    print_variables([inputs, outputs])
    print_layers(endpoints)
```

In the `inference` function, we call `_conv3d`, `_max_pool3d`, and `_fully_connected` to create the network. It is not that different to the CNN network for images in previous chapters. At the end of the function, we also create a dictionary named `endpoints`, which will be used in the main section to visualize the network architecture.

Next, let's add the code of the `_conv3d` and `_max_pool3d` functions:

```
def _conv3d(input_data, k_d, k_h, k_w, c_o, s_d, s_h, s_w, name,
relu=True, padding="SAME"):
    c_i = input_data.get_shape()[-1].value
    convolve = lambda i, k: tf.nn.conv3d(i, k, [1, s_d, s_h, s_w,
1], padding=padding)
    with tf.variable_scope(name) as scope:
        weights = tf.get_variable(name="weights",
shape=[k_d, k_h, k_w, c_i, c_o],
regularizer = tf.contrib.layers.l2_regularizer(scale=0.0001),
initializer=tf.truncated_normal_initializer(stddev=1e-1,
```

```
dtype=tf.float32))
        conv = convolve(input_data, weights)
        biases = tf.get_variable(name="biases",
shape=[c_o], dtype=tf.float32,
initializer = tf.constant_initializer(value=0.0))
        output = tf.nn.bias_add(conv, biases)
        if relu:
            output = tf.nn.relu(output, name=scope.name)
        return batch_norm(output)


def _max_pool3d(input_data, k_d, k_h, k_w, s_d, s_h, s_w, name,
padding="SAME"):
    return tf.nn.max_pool3d(input_data,
ksize=[1, k_d, k_h, k_w, 1],
strides=[1, s_d, s_h, s_w, 1], padding=padding, name=name)
```

This code is similar to the previous chapters. However, we use the built-in `tf.nn.conv3d` and `tf.nn.max_pool3d` functions instead of `tf.nn.conv2d` and `tf.nn.max_pool3d` for images. Therefore, we need to add the `k_d` and `s_d` parameters to give information about the depth of the filters. Moreover, we will need to train this network from scratch without any pre-trained models. So, we need to use the `batch_norm` function to add the batch normalization to each layer.

Let's add the code for the fully connected layer:

```
def _fully_connected(input_data, num_output, name, relu=True):
    with tf.variable_scope(name) as scope:
        input_shape = input_data.get_shape()
        if input_shape.ndims == 5:
            dim = 1
            for d in input_shape[1:].as_list():
                dim *= d
            feed_in = tf.reshape(input_data, [-1, dim])
        else:
            feed_in, dim = (input_data, input_shape[-1].value)
        weights = tf.get_variable(name="weights",
shape=[dim, num_output],
regularizer = tf.contrib.layers.l2_regularizer(scale=0.0001),
initializer=tf.truncated_normal_initializer(stddev=1e-1,
dtype=tf.float32))
        biases = tf.get_variable(name="biases",
shape=[num_output], dtype=tf.float32,
initializer=tf.constant_initializer(value=0.0))
        op = tf.nn.relu_layer if relu else tf.nn.xw_plus_b
        output = op(feed_in, weights, biases, name=scope.name)
        return batch_norm(output)
```

This function is a bit different to what we used with images. First, we check that the `input_shape.ndims` is equal to 5 instead of 4. Secondly, we add the batch normalization to the output.

Finally, let's open the `utils.py` file and add the following `utility` functions:

```
from prettytable import PrettyTable
def print_variables(variables):
    table = PrettyTable(["Variable Name", "Shape"])
    for var in variables:
        table.add_row([var.name, var.get_shape()])
    print(table)
    print("")


def print_layers(layers):
    table = PrettyTable(["Layer Name", "Shape"])
    for var in layers.values():
        table.add_row([var.name, var.get_shape()])
    print(table)
    print("")
```

Now we can run `nets.py` to have a better understanding of the network's architecture:

```
python nets.py
```

In the first part of the console result, you will see a table like this:

Variable Name	Shape
conv1/weights:0	(3, 3, 3, 3, 64)
conv1/biases:0	(64,)
conv1/BatchNorm/beta:0	(64,)
conv1/BatchNorm/moving_mean:0	(64,)
conv1/BatchNorm/moving_variance:0	(64,)
...	...
fc8/weights:0	(4096, 101)
fc8/biases:0	(101,)
fc8/BatchNorm/beta:0	(101,)
fc8/BatchNorm/moving_mean:0	(101,)
fc8/BatchNorm/moving_variance:0	(101,)

These are the shapes of `variables` in the network. As you can see, three `variables` that have the text `BatchNorm` are added to each layer. These `variables` increase the total parameters that the network needs to learn. However, since we will train from scratch, it will be much for harder to train the network without batch normalization. Batch normalization also increases the ability of the network to regularize unseen data.

In the second table of the console, you will see the following table:

```
+-----------------------------------+--------------------------+
|           Variable Name           |          Shape           |
+-----------------------------------+--------------------------+
|              inputs:0             |  (?, 10, 112, 112, 3)    |
|  fc8/BatchNorm/batchnorm/add_1:0  |        (?, 101)          |
+-----------------------------------+--------------------------+
```

These are the shapes of the input and output of the network. As you can see, the input contains 10 video frames of size (112, 112, 3), and the output contains a vector of 101 elements.

In the last table, you will see how the shape of the output at each layer has changed through the network:

```
+-----------------------------------+--------------------------+
|            Layer Name             |          Shape           |
+-----------------------------------+--------------------------+
|  fc6/BatchNorm/batchnorm/add_1:0  |         (?, 4096)        |
|  fc7/BatchNorm/batchnorm/add_1:0  |         (?, 4096)        |
|  fc8/BatchNorm/batchnorm/add_1:0  |         (?, 101)         |
|              . . .                |          . . .           |
| conv1/BatchNorm/batchnorm/add_1:0 |  (?, 10, 112, 112, 64)   |
| conv2/BatchNorm/batchnorm/add_1:0 |   (?, 10, 56, 56, 128)   |
+-----------------------------------+--------------------------+
```

In the preceding table, we can see that the output of the `conv1` layer has the same size as the input, and the output of the `conv2` layer has changed due to the effect of max pooling.

Now, let's create a new Python file named `models.py` and add the following code:

```python
import tensorflow as tf

def compute_loss(logits, labels):
    labels = tf.squeeze(tf.cast(labels, tf.int32))

    cross_entropy =
tf.nn.sparse_softmax_cross_entropy_with_logits(logits=logits,
labels=labels)
    cross_entropy_loss= tf.reduce_mean(cross_entropy)
```

```
    reg_loss =
tf.reduce_mean(tf.get_collection(tf.GraphKeys.REGULARIZATION_LOSSES
))

    return cross_entropy_loss + reg_loss, cross_entropy_loss,
reg_loss


def compute_accuracy(logits, labels):
    labels = tf.squeeze(tf.cast(labels, tf.int32))
    batch_predictions = tf.cast(tf.argmax(logits, 1), tf.int32)
    predicted_correctly = tf.equal(batch_predictions, labels)
    accuracy = tf.reduce_mean(tf.cast(predicted_correctly,
    tf.float32))
    return accuracy


def get_learning_rate(global_step, initial_value, decay_steps,
decay_rate):
    learning_rate = tf.train.exponential_decay(initial_value,
    global_step, decay_steps, decay_rate, staircase=True)
    return learning_rate


def train(total_loss, learning_rate, global_step):
    optimizer = tf.train.AdamOptimizer(learning_rate)
    train_op = optimizer.minimize(total_loss, global_step)
    return train_op
```

These functions create the operation to calculate `loss`, `accuracy`, `learning rate`, and perform the train process. This is the same as the previous chapter, so we won't explain these functions.

Now, we have all the functions required to train the network to recognize video actions. In the next section, we will start the training routine on a single GPU and visualize the results on TensorBoard.

Training routine with single GPU

In the scripts package, create a new Python file named `train.py`. We will start by defining some parameters as follows:

```
import tensorflow as tf
import os
import sys
from datetime import datetime
```

```
from tensorflow.python.ops import data_flow_ops

import nets
import models
from utils import lines_from_file
from datasets import sample_videos, input_pipeline

# Dataset
num_frames = 16
train_folder = "/home/ubuntu/datasets/ucf101/train/"
train_txt = "/home/ubuntu/datasets/ucf101/train.txt"

# Learning rate
initial_learning_rate = 0.001
decay_steps = 1000
decay_rate = 0.7
# Training
image_size = 112
batch_size = 24
num_epochs = 20
epoch_size = 28747

train_enqueue_steps = 100
min_queue_size = 1000

save_steps = 200   # Number of steps to perform saving checkpoints
test_steps = 20   # Number of times to test for test accuracy
start_test_step = 50

max_checkpoints_to_keep = 2
save_dir = "/home/ubuntu/checkpoints/ucf101"
```

These parameters are self-explanatory. Now, we will define some operations for training:

```
train_data_reader = lines_from_file(train_txt, repeat=True)

image_paths_placeholder = tf.placeholder(tf.string, shape=(None,
num_frames), name='image_paths')
labels_placeholder = tf.placeholder(tf.int64, shape=(None,),
name='labels')

train_input_queue =
data_flow_ops.RandomShuffleQueue(capacity=10000,
min_after_dequeue=batch_size,
dtypes= [tf.string, tf.int64],
shapes= [(num_frames,), ()])

train_enqueue_op =
```

```
train_input_queue.enqueue_many([image_paths_placeholder,
labels_placeholder])

frames_batch, labels_batch = input_pipeline(train_input_queue,
batch_size=batch_size, image_size=image_size)

with tf.variable_scope("models") as scope:
    logits, _ = nets.inference(frames_batch, is_training=True)

total_loss, cross_entropy_loss, reg_loss =
models.compute_loss(logits, labels_batch)
train_accuracy = models.compute_accuracy(logits, labels_batch)

global_step = tf.Variable(0, trainable=False)
learning_rate = models.get_learning_rate(global_step,
initial_learning_rate, decay_steps, decay_rate)
train_op = models.train(total_loss, learning_rate, global_step)
```

In this code, we get a `generator` object from the text file. Then, we create two placeholders for `image_paths` and `labels`, which will be enqueued to `RandomShuffleQueue`. The `input_pipeline` function that we created in `datasets.py` will receive `RandomShuffleQueue` and return a batch of `frames` and labels. Finally, we create operations to compute loss, accuracy, and the training operation.

We also want to log the training process and visualize it in TensorBoard. So, we will create some summaries:

```
tf.summary.scalar("learning_rate", learning_rate)
tf.summary.scalar("train/accuracy", train_accuracy)
tf.summary.scalar("train/total_loss", total_loss)
tf.summary.scalar("train/cross_entropy_loss", cross_entropy_loss)
tf.summary.scalar("train/regularization_loss", reg_loss)

summary_op = tf.summary.merge_all()

saver = tf.train.Saver(max_to_keep=max_checkpoints_to_keep)
time_stamp = datetime.now().strftime("single_%Y-%m-%d_%H-%M-%S")
checkpoints_dir = os.path.join(save_dir, time_stamp)
summary_dir = os.path.join(checkpoints_dir, "summaries")
train_writer = tf.summary.FileWriter(summary_dir, flush_secs=10)

if not os.path.exists(save_dir):
    os.mkdir(save_dir)
if not os.path.exists(checkpoints_dir):
    os.mkdir(checkpoints_dir)
if not os.path.exists(summary_dir):
    os.mkdir(summary_dir)
```

saver and `train_writer` will be responsible for saving checkpoints and summaries respectively. Now, let's finish the training process by creating the `session` and performing the training loop:

```
config = tf.ConfigProto()
config.gpu_options.allow_growth = True

with tf.Session(config=config) as sess:
    coords = tf.train.Coordinator()
    threads = tf.train.start_queue_runners(sess=sess, coord=coords)

    sess.run(tf.global_variables_initializer())

    num_batches = int(epoch_size / batch_size)

    for i_epoch in range(num_epochs):
        for i_batch in range(num_batches):
            # Prefetch some data into queue
            if i_batch % train_enqueue_steps == 0:
                num_samples = batch_size * (train_enqueue_steps +
1)

                image_paths, labels =
sample_videos(train_data_reader, root_folder=train_folder,
num_samples=num_samples, num_frames=num_frames)
                print("\nEpoch {} Batch {} Enqueue {}
videos".format(i_epoch, i_batch, num_samples))

                sess.run(train_enqueue_op, feed_dict={
                    image_paths_placeholder: image_paths,
                    labels_placeholder: labels
                })

            if (i_batch + 1) >= start_test_step and (i_batch + 1) %
test_steps == 0:
                _, lr_val, loss_val, ce_loss_val, reg_loss_val,
summary_val, global_step_val, train_acc_val = sess.run([
                    train_op, learning_rate, total_loss,
cross_entropy_loss, reg_loss,
                    summary_op, global_step, train_accuracy
                ])
                train_writer.add_summary(summary_val,
global_step=global_step_val)
                print("\nEpochs {}, Batch {} Step {}: Learning Rate
{} Loss {} CE Loss {} Reg Loss {} Train Accuracy {}".format(
                    i_epoch, i_batch, global_step_val, lr_val,
loss_val, ce_loss_val, reg_loss_val, train_acc_val
                ))
```

```
                else:
                    _ = sess.run(train_op)
                    sys.stdout.write(".")
                    sys.stdout.flush()

                if (i_batch + 1) > 0 and (i_batch + 1) % save_steps ==
        0:
                        saved_file = saver.save(sess,
            os.path.join(checkpoints_dir, 'model.ckpt'),
                                            global_step=global_step)
                    print("Save steps: Save to file %s " % saved_file)

            coords.request_stop()
            coords.join(threads)
```

This code is very straightforward. We will use the sample_videos function to get a list of image paths and labels. Then, we will call the train_enqueue_op operation to add these image paths and labels to RandomShuffleQueue. After that, the training process can be run by using train_op without the feed_dict mechanism.

Now, we can run the training process by calling the following command in the root folder:

```
export PYTHONPATH=.
python scripts/train.py
```

You may see the OUT_OF_MEMORY error if your GPU memory isn't big enough for a batch size of 32. In the training process, we created a session with gpu_options.allow_growth so you can try to change the batch_size to use your GPU memory effectively.

The training process takes a few hours before it converges. We will take a look at the training process on TensorBoard.

In the directory that you have chosen to save the checkpoints, run the following command:

```
tensorboard --logdir .
```

Now, open your web browser and navigate to `http://localhost:6006`:

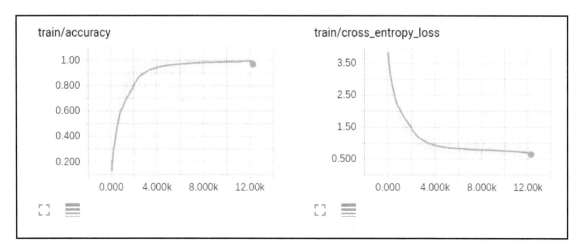

The regularization loss and total loss with one GPU are as follows:

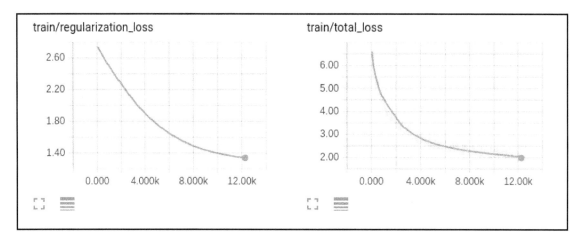

As you can see in these images, the training accuracy took about 10,000 steps to reach 100% accuracy on training data. These 10,000 steps took 6 hours on our machine. It may be different on your configuration.

The training loss is decreasing, and it may reduce if we train longer. However, the training accuracy is almost unchanged after 10,000 steps.

Now, let's move on to the most interesting part of this chapter. We will use multiple GPUs to train and see how that helps.

Training routine with multiple GPU

In our experiment, we will use our custom machine instead of Amazon EC2. However, you can achieve the same result on any server with GPUs. In this section, we will use two Titan X GPUs with a batch size of 32 on each GPU. That way, we can compute up to 64 videos in one step, instead of 32 videos in a single GPU configuration.

Now, let's create a new Python file named `train_multi.py` in the `scripts` package. In this file, add the following code to define some parameters:

```python
import tensorflow as tf
import os
import sys
from datetime import datetime
from tensorflow.python.ops import data_flow_ops

import nets
import models
from utils import lines_from_file
from datasets import sample_videos, input_pipeline

# Dataset
num_frames = 10
train_folder = "/home/aiteam/quan/datasets/ucf101/train/"
train_txt = "/home/aiteam/quan/datasets/ucf101/train.txt"

# Learning rate
initial_learning_rate = 0.001
decay_steps = 1000
decay_rate = 0.7

# Training
num_gpu = 2

image_size = 112
batch_size = 32 * num_gpu
num_epochs = 20
epoch_size = 28747

train_enqueue_steps = 50

save_steps = 200  # Number of steps to perform saving checkpoints
test_steps = 20   # Number of times to test for test accuracy
start_test_step = 50

max_checkpoints_to_keep = 2
save_dir = "/home/aiteam/quan/checkpoints/ucf101"
```

These parameters are the same as in the previous `train.py` file, except `batch_size`. In this experiment, we will use the data parallelism strategy to train with multiple GPUs. Therefore, instead of using 32 for the batch size, we will use a batch size of 64. Then, we will split the batch into two parts; each will be processed by a GPU. After that, we will combine the gradients from the two GPUs to update the weights and biases of the network.

Next, we will use the same operations as before, as follows:

```
train_data_reader = lines_from_file(train_txt, repeat=True)

image_paths_placeholder = tf.placeholder(tf.string, shape=(None,
num_frames), name='image_paths')
labels_placeholder = tf.placeholder(tf.int64, shape=(None,),
name='labels')

train_input_queue =
data_flow_ops.RandomShuffleQueue(capacity=10000,
min_after_dequeue=batch_size,
dtypes= [tf.string, tf.int64],
shapes= [(num_frames,), ()])

train_enqueue_op =
train_input_queue.enqueue_many([image_paths_placeholder,
labels_placeholder])

frames_batch, labels_batch = input_pipeline(train_input_queue,
batch_size=batch_size, image_size=image_size)

global_step = tf.Variable(0, trainable=False)
learning_rate = models.get_learning_rate(global_step,
initial_learning_rate, decay_steps, decay_rate)
```

Now, instead of creating a training operation with `models.train`, we will create a optimizer and compute gradients in each GPU.

```
optimizer = tf.train.AdamOptimizer(learning_rate=learning_rate)

total_gradients = []

frames_batch_split = tf.split(frames_batch, num_gpu)
labels_batch_split = tf.split(labels_batch, num_gpu)
for i in range(num_gpu):
    with tf.device('/gpu:%d' % i):
        with tf.variable_scope(tf.get_variable_scope(), reuse=(i >
0)):
            logits_split, _ = nets.inference(frames_batch_split[i],
is_training=True)
```

```
                    labels_split = labels_batch_split[i]
                    total_loss, cross_entropy_loss, reg_loss =
            models.compute_loss(logits_split, labels_split)
                    grads = optimizer.compute_gradients(total_loss)
                    total_gradients.append(grads)
                    tf.get_variable_scope().reuse_variables()

            with tf.device('/cpu:0'):
                gradients = models.average_gradients(total_gradients)
                train_op = optimizer.apply_gradients(gradients, global_step)

                train_accuracy = models.compute_accuracy(logits_split,
            labels_split)
```

The gradients will be computed on each GPU and added to a list named
`total_gradients`. The final gradients will be computed on the CPU using
`average_gradients`, which we will create shortly. Then, the training operation will be
created by calling `apply_gradients` on the optimizer.

Now, let's add the following function to the `models.py` file in the `root` folder to compute
the `average_gradient`:

```
            def average_gradients(gradients):
                average_grads = []
                for grad_and_vars in zip(*gradients):
                    grads = []
                    for g, _ in grad_and_vars:
                        grads.append(tf.expand_dims(g, 0))

                    grad = tf.concat(grads, 0)
                    grad = tf.reduce_mean(grad, 0)

                    v = grad_and_vars[0][1]
                    grad_and_var = (grad, v)
                    average_grads.append(grad_and_var)
                return average_grads
```

Now, back in the `train_multi.py` file, we will create the `saver` and `summaries` operation
to save the `checkpoints` and `summaries`, like before:

```
            tf.summary.scalar("learning_rate", learning_rate)
            tf.summary.scalar("train/accuracy", train_accuracy)
            tf.summary.scalar("train/total_loss", total_loss)
            tf.summary.scalar("train/cross_entropy_loss", cross_entropy_loss)
            tf.summary.scalar("train/regularization_loss", reg_loss)
            summary_op = tf.summary.merge_all()
```

```
saver = tf.train.Saver(max_to_keep=max_checkpoints_to_keep)
time_stamp = datetime.now().strftime("multi_%Y-%m-%d_%H-%M-%S")
checkpoints_dir = os.path.join(save_dir, time_stamp)
summary_dir = os.path.join(checkpoints_dir, "summaries")

train_writer = tf.summary.FileWriter(summary_dir, flush_secs=10)

if not os.path.exists(save_dir):
    os.mkdir(save_dir)
if not os.path.exists(checkpoints_dir):
    os.mkdir(checkpoints_dir)
if not os.path.exists(summary_dir):
    os.mkdir(summary_dir)
```

Finally, let's add the training loop to train the network:

```
config = tf.ConfigProto(allow_soft_placement=True)
config.gpu_options.allow_growth = True

sess = tf.Session(config=config)
coords = tf.train.Coordinator()
threads = tf.train.start_queue_runners(sess=sess, coord=coords)
sess.run(tf.global_variables_initializer())

num_batches = int(epoch_size / batch_size)

for i_epoch in range(num_epochs):
    for i_batch in range(num_batches):
        # Prefetch some data into queue
        if i_batch % train_enqueue_steps == 0:
            num_samples = batch_size * (train_enqueue_steps + 1)
            image_paths, labels = sample_videos(train_data_reader,
root_folder=train_folder,
num_samples=num_samples, num_frames=num_frames)
            print("\nEpoch {} Batch {} Enqueue {}
videos".format(i_epoch, i_batch, num_samples))

            sess.run(train_enqueue_op, feed_dict={
                image_paths_placeholder: image_paths,
                labels_placeholder: labels
            })

        if (i_batch + 1) >= start_test_step and (i_batch + 1) %
test_steps == 0:
            _, lr_val, loss_val, ce_loss_val, reg_loss_val,
summary_val, global_step_val, train_acc_val = sess.run([
                train_op, learning_rate, total_loss,
cross_entropy_loss, reg_loss,
```

```
                summary_op, global_step, train_accuracy
            ])
            train_writer.add_summary(summary_val,
    global_step=global_step_val)

            print("\nEpochs {}, Batch {} Step {}: Learning Rate {}
    Loss {} CE Loss {} Reg Loss {} Train Accuracy {}".format(
                i_epoch, i_batch, global_step_val, lr_val,
    loss_val,
    ce_loss_val, reg_loss_val, train_acc_val
            ))
        else:
            _ = sess.run([train_op])
            sys.stdout.write(".")
            sys.stdout.flush()

        if (i_batch + 1) > 0 and (i_batch + 1) % save_steps == 0:
            saved_file = saver.save(sess,
                                    os.path.join(checkpoints_dir,
    'model.ckpt'),
                                    global_step=global_step)
            print("Save steps: Save to file %s " % saved_file)

    coords.request_stop()
    coords.join(threads)
```

The training loop is similar to the previous, except that we have added the `allow_soft_placement=True` option to the session configuration. This option will allow TensorFlow to change the placement of `variables`, if necessary.

Now we can run the training scripts like before:

```
python scripts/train_multi.py
```

After a few hours of training, we can look at the TensorBoard to compare the results:

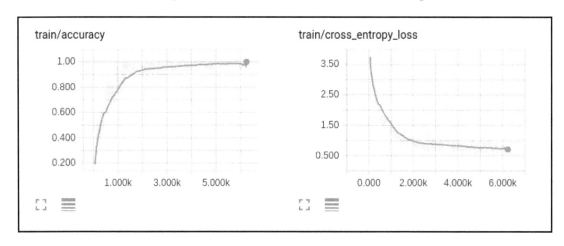

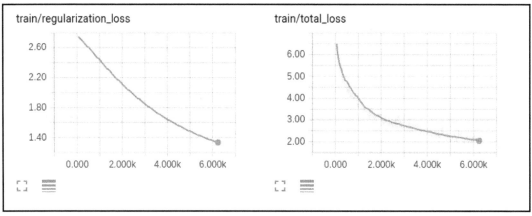

Figure 04—Plot on Tensorboard of multiple GPUs training process

As you can see, the training on multiple GPUs achieves 100% accuracy after about 6,000 steps in about four hours on our computer. This almost reduces the training time by half.

Now, let's see how the two training strategies compare:

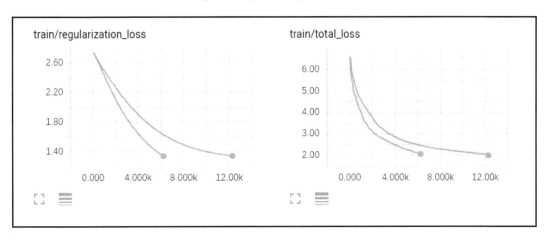

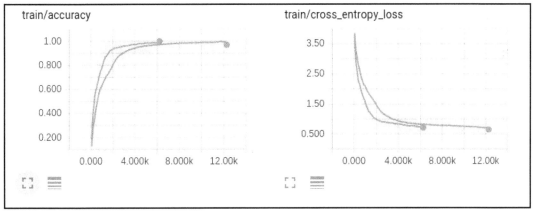

Figure 05—Plot on TensorBoard with single and multiple GPUs compared side by side

The orange line is the multiple GPUs result and the blue line is the single GPU result. We can see that the multiple GPUs setup can achieve better results sooner than the single GPU. The different is not very large. However, we can achieve faster training with more and more GPUs. On the P1 instance on Amazon EC2, there are even eight and 16 GPUs. However, the benefit of training on multiple GPUs will be better if we train on large-scale datasets such as ActivityNet or Sports 1M, as the single GPU will take a very long time to converge.

In the next section, we will take a quick look at another Amazon Service, Mechanical Turk.

Overview of Mechanical Turk

Mechanical Turk is a service that allows us to create and manage online human intelligence tasks that will be completed by human workers. There are lots of tasks that humans can do better than computers. Therefore, we can take advantage of this service to support our machine learning system.

You can view this system at `https://www.mturk.com`. Here is the website of the service:

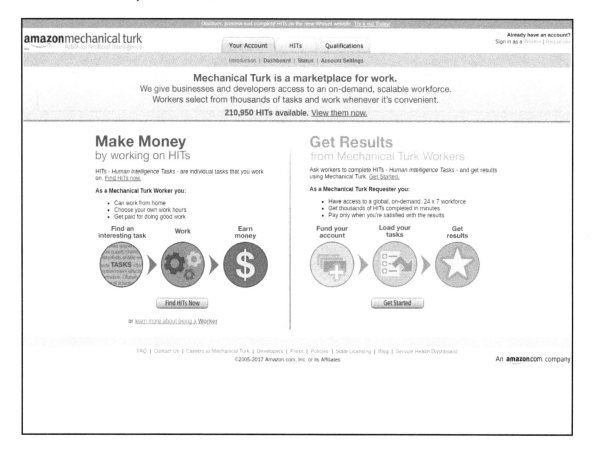

Here are a couple of examples of tasks that you can use to support your machine learning system:

- **Dataset labeling**: You usually have a lot of unlabeled data, and you can use Mechanical Turk to help you build a consistent ground truth for your machine learning workflow.
- **Generate dataset**: You can ask the workers to build a large amount of training data. For example, we can ask workers to create text translations or chat sentences for a natural language system. You can ask them to annotate the sentiments of the comments.

Beyond labeling, Mechanical Turk can also clean up your messy datasets ready for training, data categorization, and metadata tagging. You can even use this service to have them judge your system output.

Summary

We have taken a look at the Amazon EC2 services to see how many server types we can use. Then, we created a neural network to perform human video action recognition on a single GPU. After that, we applied the data parallelism strategy to speed up the training process. Finally, we had a quick look at the Mechanical Turk service. We hope that you can take advantage of these services to bring your machine learning system to a higher level.

11
Going Further - 21 Problems

In this chapter, we are going to introduce 21 real life problems that you can use deep learning and TensorFlow to tackle. We will start by talking about some public large-scale datasets and competitions. Then, we will show some awesome TensorFlow projects on Github. We will also introduce some interesting projects that have been done in other deep learning frameworks so that you can get inspired and implement your own TensorFlow solution. Finally, we will work through a simple technique to convert a Caffe model to a TensorFlow model and introduce using a high-level TensorFlow library, TensorFlow-Slim.

In this chapter, we will look into the following topics:

- Large-scale, public datasets and competitions
- Awesome TensorFlow projects
- Some inspired deep learning projects from other frameworks
- Converting a Caffe model to TensorFlow
- Introducing TensorFlow-Slim

Dataset and challenges

In this section, we will show you some popular datasets and competitions.

Problem 1 - ImageNet dataset

Project link: `http://image-net.org/`

ImageNet is a large scale visual recognition challenge that has runs annually since 2010. The dataset is organized according to the WorkNet hierarchy. There are over ten million URLs of images with hand-annotated labels to indicate what objects are in the picture. There are at least one million images that have bounding boxes included.

The ImageNet challenge is held every year to evaluate algorithms for the following three problems:

- Object localization for 1,000 categories.
- Object detection for 200 fully-labeled categories.
- Object detection from video for 30 fully labeled categories. In July 17, 2017, the results of the 2017 challenge were announced with many advanced and interesting algorithms.

Problem 2 - COCO dataset

Project link: `http://mscoco.org/`

COCO is a dataset for image recognition, segmentation, and captioning sponsored by Microsoft. There are 80 object categories in this dataset with more than 300,000 images and two million instances. There are also challenges for detections, captions, and key-points every year.

Problem 3 - Open Images dataset

Project link: `https://github.com/openimages/dataset`

Open Images is a new dataset from Google, with over nine million URLs spanning over 6000 categories. Each image is processed by Google's vision model and verified by a human. As of July 20, 2017, there are also over two million bounding box annotations spanning over 600 objects.

The difference is that Open Images covers more real-life objects than others, which can be very useful when developing real-life applications.

Problem 4 - YouTube-8M dataset

Project link: https://research.google.com/youtube8m/

YouTube-8M is a large-scale video dataset from Google with 7 million video URLs over 4,716 classes and 450,000 hours of video. Google also provides pre-computed, state-of-the-art audio-visual features, so that one can build their model based on these features with ease. Training from raw videos may take weeks, which is not reasonable in normal situations. This dataset's goal is to achieve video understanding, representation learning, noisy data modeling, transfer learning, and domain adaptation for videos.

Problem 5 - AudioSet dataset

Project link: https://research.google.com/audioset/

AudioSet is a large-scale audio events dataset from Google with 632 audio event classes and a collection of over 2.1 million manually annotated sound clips. Audio classes span from human and animal sounds to musical instruments and common, everyday environmental sounds. Using this dataset, you can create a system to recognize audio events for audio understanding, security applications, and much more.

Problem 6 - LSUN challenge

Project link: http://lsun.cs.princeton.edu/2017/

LSUN challenge provides a large scale scene understanding dataset covering three major problems:

- Scene classification
- Segmentation task on street images
- Saliency prediction

In scene classification problems, the expected output of the algorithm is the top most likely scene category in the image. At the time of writing, there are 10 different classes such as bedroom, classroom, and restaurant. In the segmentation problem, you can try to solve the pixel-level segmentation and instance-specific segmentation. In saliency prediction problems, the goal is to predict where a human looks in a scene image.

Problem 7 - MegaFace dataset

Project link: `http://megaface.cs.washington.edu/`

MegaFace provides a large scale dataset for face recognition. The MegaFace dataset is divided into three parts:

- Training set
- Test set
- Distractors

The **Training set** contains 4.7 million photos of over 672,057 unique identities. The **test set** contains the images from the FaceScrub and FGNet dataset. The **distractors** contain one million photos of 690,572 unique users. Currently, there are two challenges in the MegaFace website. In challenge 1, you can train using any dataset and test your method with the one million distractors. Your method needs to discriminate between a set of known people while classifying the distractors as unknown people. In challenge 2, you will train using the training set with 672K unique identities and test with 1 million distractors. MegaFace is currently the largest dataset for face recognition at the time of writing.

Problem 8 - Data Science Bowl 2017 challenge

Project link: `https://www.kaggle.com/c/data-science-bowl-2017`

Data Science Bowl 2017 is a one million dollar challenge focused on lung cancer detection. In the dataset, you will be given over a thousand CT images of high-risk patients. The goal of this challenge is to create an automatic system that can determine whether a patient will be diagnosed with lung cancer within one year. This is a very interesting and important project to work on that will save thousands of people in the near future.

Problem 9 - StarCraft Game dataset

Project link: `https://github.com/TorchCraft/StarData`

This is the largest StarCraft--Brood War replay dataset at the time of writing this book. This dataset contains more than 60,000 games in 365GB, 1535 million frames, and 496 million player actions. This dataset is best suit for those who want to research about AI game playing.

TensorFlow-based Projects

In this section, we will introduce you to several problems that are implemented in TensorFlow and open-source on Github. We suggest that you take a look at these projects and learn how to improve your TensorFlow skills.

Problem 10 - Human Pose Estimation

Project Link: `https://github.com/eldar/pose-tensorflow`

This project is the open-source implementation of Deep Cut and ArtTrack in human body pose estimation. The goal of this project is to jointly solve the tasks of detection and pose estimation. We can use this method for various applications such as person detection in security or human action understanding. This project also provides great starting points for a lot of further research on human shape estimation with applications for virtual-try-on or garment recommendation.

Problem 11 - Object Detection - YOLO

Project link: `https://github.com/thtrieu/darkflow`

Object detection is an interesting problem in Computer Vision. There are lots of methods to solve this problem. YOLO, by Joseph Redmon and others, is one of the state-of-the-art techniques. YOLO provides real-time object detection using deep neural networks. Version 2 of YOLO can recognize up to 9,000 different objects with high accuracy in real time. The original YOLO project is programmed in the darknet framework.

In TensorFlow, there is a great implementation of YOLO, called **darkflow**. The darkflow repository even has the utility that can allow you to export the model and serve on mobile devices.

Problem 12 - Object Detection - Faster RCNN

Project link: `https://github.com/smallcorgi/Faster-RCNN_TF`

Faster RCNN is another state-of-the-art method for Object Detection. This method offers high precision on the result and also inspires lots of methods for many other problems. The inference speed of Faster RCNN is not as fast as YOLO. However, if you need high precision on the detection results, you may want to consider Faster RCNN.

Problem 13 - Person Detection - tensorbox

Project link: `https://github.com/Russell91/TensorBox`

Tensorbox is a TensorFlow implementation of the method by Russell Stewart and Mykhaylo Andriluka. The goal of this method is a bit different from the preceding methods. Tensorbox focuses on solving the problem of crowd person detection. They use a recurrent LSTM layer for sequence generation of the bounding boxes and define a new loss function that operates of the set of detection results.

Problem 14 - Magenta

Project link: `https://github.com/tensorflow/magenta`

Magenta is a project from the Google Brain team that focuses on Music and Art Generation using Deep Learning. This is a very active repository with many implementations of interesting problems such as image stylization, melody generation, or generating sketches. You can visit the following link to have access to Magenta's models:

`https://github.com/tensorflow/magenta/tree/master/magenta/models`

Problem 15 - Wavenet

Project link: `https://github.com/ibab/tensorflow-wavenet`

WaveNet is a neural network architecture for audio generation from Google Deep Mind. WaveNet is trained to generate raw audio waveform and has shown good results for text-to-speech and audio generation. According to Deep Mind, WaveNet reduced the gap between the previous methods and human-level performance by over 50% in text-to-speech problems for both US English and Mandarin Chinese.

Problem 16 - Deep Speech

Project link: `https://github.com/mozilla/DeepSpeech`

Deep Speech is an open source speech-to-text engine, based on a research paper from Baidu. Speech-to-text is a very interesting problem and Deep Speech is one of the state-of-the-art methods for solving it. With the TensorFlow implementation of Mozilla, you can even learn how to use TensorFlow across more than one machine. However, there is still a problem that personal researchers can't access the same large scale speech-to-text datasets as a large company. So, even though we can use Deep Speech or implement it ourselves, it is still hard to have a good model for production.

Interesting Projects

In this section, we will show you some interesting projects that are implemented in other deep learning frameworks. These projects give significant results over very difficult problems. You may want to challenge yourself to implement these methods in TensorFlow.

Problem 17 - Interactive Deep Colorization - iDeepColor

Project link: `https://richzhang.github.io/ideepcolor/`

Interactive Deep Colorization is research being carried out by Richard Zhang and Jun-Yan Zun, and others, for user-guided image colorization. In this system, users can give the network a few hints of colors for some points in the image and the network will propagate user inputs along with semantic information learned from large scale data. The colorization can be performed in real time with one single forward pass.

Problem 18 - Tiny face detector

Project link: `https://github.com/peiyunh/tiny`

This project is a face detector that focuses on finding the small faces in the image by Peiyun Hu and Deva Ramanan. While most face detectors only focus on large objects in the image, this tiny face detector method can work with very small faces, but still, reduce the error by a factor of two compared with prior methods on the WIDER FACE dataset.

Problem 19 - People search

Project link: `https://github.com/ShuangLI59/person_search`

This project is the implementation of the paper by Tong Xiao, and others that focuses on the problem of person detection and re-identification. This project can be used in video surveillance. The existing person re-identification methods mainly assume that the person is cropped and aligned. However, in real-world scenarios, the person detection algorithm may fail to extract the perfect crop region of the person and lower the identification accuracy. In this project, the authors solve detection and identification jointly in a novel architecture inspired by Faster RCNN. The current project is implemented in the Caffe Deep Learning Framework.

Problem 20 - Face Recognition - MobileID

Project link: `https://github.com/liuziwei7/mobile-id`

This project provides an extremely fast face recognition system that can run in 250 FPS with high accuracy. The model is learned by using the output of the state-of-the-art face recognition DeepID. However, the mobile ID model can perform so fast that it can be used in situations where processing and memory are limited.

Problem 21 - Question answering - DrQA

Project link: `https://github.com/facebookresearch/DrQA`

DrQA is a system for open-domain question answering from Facebook. DrQA focuses on solving the task of *machine reading* where the model will try to understand the Wikipedia documents and give the answer for any question from users. The current project is implemented in PyTorch. You may find it interesting to implement our own solution in TensorFlow.

Caffe to TensorFlow

In this section, we will show you how to take advantage of many pre-trained models from Caffe Model Zoo (`https://github.com/BVLC/caffe/wiki/Model-Zoo`). There are lots of Caffe models for different tasks with all kinds of architectures. After converting these models to TensorFlow, you can use it as a part of your architectures or you can fine-tune our model for different tasks. Using these pre-trained models as initial weights is an effective approach for training instead of training from scratch. We will show you how to use a `caffe-to-tensorflow` approach from Saumitro Dasgupta at `https://github.com/ethereon/caffe-tensorflow`.

However, there are lots of differences between Caffe and TensorFlow. This technique only supports a subset of layer types from Caffe. Even though there are some Caffe architectures that are verified by the author of this project such as ResNet, VGG, and GoogLeNet.

First, we need to clone the `caffe-tensorflow` repository using the `git clone` command:

```
ubuntu@ubuntu-PC:~/github$ git clone
https://github.com/ethereon/caffe-tensorflow
Cloning into 'caffe-tensorflow'...
remote: Counting objects: 479, done.
remote: Total 479 (delta 0), reused 0 (delta 0), pack-reused 479
Receiving objects: 100% (510/510), 1.71 MiB | 380.00 KiB/s, done.
Resolving deltas: 100% (275/275), done.
Checking connectivity... done.
```

Then, we need to change the directory to the `caffe-to-tensorflow` directory and run the convert python script to see some help messages:

```
cd caffe-tensorflow
python convert.py -h
The resulting console will look like this:
usage: convert.py [-h] [--caffemodel CAFFEMODEL]
                  [--data-output-path DATA_OUTPUT_PATH]
                  [--code-output-path CODE_OUTPUT_PATH] [-p PHASE]
                  def_path
positional arguments:
def_path                Model definition (.prototxt) path
optional arguments:
  -h, --help            show this help message and exit
  --caffemodel CAFFEMODEL
                        Model data (.caffemodel) path
  --data-output-path DATA_OUTPUT_PATH
                        Converted data output path
  --code-output-path CODE_OUTPUT_PATH
                        Save generated source to this path
```

```
    -p PHASE, --phase PHASE
                        The phase to convert: test (default) or train
```

According to this help message, we can know the parameters of the convert.py script. In summary, we will use this convert.py to create the network architecture in TensorFlow with the flag code-output-path and convert the pre-trained weights with the flag data-output-path.

Before we start converting the models, we need to get some pull requests from contributors of this project. There are some issues with the current master branch that we can't use the latest TensorFlow (version 1.3 at the time of writing) and python-protobuf (version 3.4.0 at the time of writing). Therefore, we will get the code using the following pull requests:

https://github.com/ethereon/caffe-tensorflow/pull/105

https://github.com/ethereon/caffe-tensorflow/pull/133

You need to open the preceding links to see if the pull requests are merged or not. If it is still in open status, you will need to follow the next part. Otherwise, you can skip the merged pull requests.

First, we will get the code from pull request 105:

```
ubuntu@ubuntu-PC:~/github$ git pull origin pull/105/head
remote: Counting objects: 33, done.
remote: Total 33 (delta 8), reused 8 (delta 8), pack-reused 25
Unpacking objects: 100% (33/33), done.
From https://github.com/ethereon/caffe-tensorflow
 * branch              refs/pull/105/head -> FETCH_HEAD
Updating d870c51..ccd1a52
Fast-forward
 .gitignore                               |  5 +++++
 convert.py                               |  8 ++++++++
 examples/save_model/.gitignore           | 11 ++++++++++
 examples/save_model/READMD.md            | 17 +++++++++++++++++
 examples/save_model/__init__.py          |  0
 examples/save_model/save_model.py        | 51
++++++++++++++++++++++++++++++++++++++++++
 kaffe/caffe/{caffepb.py => caffe_pb2.py} |  0
 kaffe/caffe/resolver.py                  |  4 ++--
 kaffe/tensorflow/network.py              |  8 ++++----
 9 files changed, 98 insertions(+), 6 deletions(-)
 create mode 100644 examples/save_model/.gitignore
 create mode 100644 examples/save_model/READMD.md
 create mode 100644 examples/save_model/__init__.py
 create mode 100755 examples/save_model/save_model.py
 rename kaffe/caffe/{caffepb.py => caffe_pb2.py} (100%)
```

Then, from pull request `133`:

```
- git pull origin pull/133/head
remote: Counting objects: 31, done.
remote: Total 31 (delta 20), reused 20 (delta 20), pack-reused 11
Unpacking objects: 100% (31/31), done.
From https://github.com/ethereon/caffe-tensorflow
* branch              refs/pull/133/head -> FETCH_HEAD
Auto-merging kaffe/tensorflow/network.py
CONFLICT (content): Merge conflict in kaffe/tensorflow/network.py
Auto-merging .gitignore
CONFLICT (content): Merge conflict in .gitignore
Automatic merge failed; fix conflicts and then commit the result.
```

As you can see, there are some conflicts in the `kaffe/tensorflow/network.py` file. We will show you how to resolve these `conflicts`, as follows.

First, we will solve the conflict at line **137**:

```
136                    # Concatenate the groups
137  <<<<<<< HEAD
138                    output = tf.concat(output_groups, 3)
139                    # Add the biases
140  =======
141                    output = tf.concat(3, output_groups)
142                    # Add the bias
143  >>>>>>> 1324afea14711a09ea9d689ce06ea0b0cdf84a17
```

We remove the HEAD part from line **137** to line **140**. The final result will look like this:

```
136                    # Concatenate the groups
137
138                    output = tf.concat(3, output_groups)
139                    # Add the bias
140  |
141                    if biased:
```

Next, we will solve the conflict at line **185**:

```
183        @layer
184        def concat(self, inputs, axis, name):
185    <<<<<<< HEAD
186            return tf.concat(values=inputs, axis=axis,  name=name)
187    =======
188            return tf.concat(axis=axis, values=inputs, name=name)
189    >>>>>>> 1324afea14711a09ea9d689ce06ea0b0cdf84a17
190
```

We also remove the HEAD part from line **185** to line **187**. The final result will look like this:

```
179
180        @layer
181        def concat(self, inputs, axis, name):|
182            return tf.concat(axis=axis, values=inputs, name=name)
183
```

In the `caffe-to-tensorflow` directory, there is a directory named examples that contains the code and data for the MNIST and ImageNet challenge. We will show you how to work with the MNIST model. The ImageNet challenge is not much different.

First, we will convert the MNIST architecture from Caffe to TensorFlow using the following command:

```
    ubuntu@ubuntu-PC:~/github$ python ./convert.py
examples/mnist/lenet.prototxt --code-output-path=./mynet.py
    The result will look like this:
    ----------------------------------------------------------------
        WARNING: PyCaffe not found!
        Falling back to a pure protocol buffer implementation.
        * Conversions will be drastically slower.
        * This backend is UNTESTED!
    ----------------------------------------------------------------
    Type                    Name
Param           Output
    ----------------------------------------------------------------

------------------------
    Input                   data                                    -
    -     (64, 1, 28, 28)
    Convolution             conv1                                   -
    -     (64, 20, 24, 24)
    Pooling                 pool1                                   -
    -     (64, 20, 12, 12)
    Convolution             conv2                                   -
    -       (64, 50, 8, 8)
```

```
    Pooling           pool2
-       (64, 50, 4, 4)
    InnerProduct      ip1
-       (64, 500, 1, 1)
    InnerProduct      ip2
-       (64, 10, 1, 1)
    Softmax           prob
-       (64, 10, 1, 1)
    Converting data...
    Saving source...
    Done.
```

Then, we will convert the MNIST pre-trained Caffe model at
`examples/mnist/lenet_iter_10000.caffemodel` using the following command:

```
ubuntu@ubuntu-PC:~/github$ python ./convert.py
examples/mnist/lenet.prototxt --caffemodel
examples/mnist/lenet_iter_10000.caffemodel --data-output-
path=./mynet.npy
```

The result will look like this:

```
    ----------------------------------------------------------------
    WARNING: PyCaffe not found!
    Falling back to a pure protocol buffer implementation.
    * Conversions will be drastically slower.
    * This backend is UNTESTED!
    ----------------------------------------------------------------
    Type                  Name
Param                     Output
    ----------------------------------------------------------------
------------------------
    Input                 data
-       (64, 1, 28, 28)
    Convolution           conv1
(20, 1, 5, 5)     (64, 20, 24, 24)
    Pooling               pool1
-       (64, 20, 12, 12)
    Convolution           conv2
(50, 20, 5, 5)        (64, 50, 8, 8)
    Pooling               pool2
-       (64, 50, 4, 4)
    InnerProduct          ip1
  (500, 800)      (64, 500, 1, 1)
    InnerProduct          ip2
(10, 500)         (64, 10, 1, 1)
    Softmax               prob
-       (64, 10, 1, 1)
```

```
Converting data...
Saving data...
Done.
```

As you can see, these commands will create a python file named mynet.py and a numpy file named mynet.npy in the current directory. We also need to add the current directory to the PYTHONPATH to allow the further code to import mynet.py:

```
ubuntu@ubuntu-PC:~/github$ export PYTHONPATH=$PYTHONPATH:.
ubuntu@ubuntu-PC:~/github$ python examples/mnist/finetune_mnist.py
....
('Iteration: ', 900, 0.0087626642, 1.0)
('Iteration: ', 910, 0.018495116, 1.0)
('Iteration: ', 920, 0.0029206357, 1.0)
('Iteration: ', 930, 0.0010091728, 1.0)
('Iteration: ', 940, 0.071255416, 1.0)
('Iteration: ', 950, 0.045163739, 1.0)
('Iteration: ', 960, 0.005758767, 1.0)
('Iteration: ', 970, 0.012100354, 1.0)
('Iteration: ', 980, 0.12018739, 1.0)
('Iteration: ', 990, 0.079262167, 1.0)
```

The last two numbers in each line is the loss and accuracy of the fine-tune process. You can see that the fine-tune process can easily achieve 100% accuracy with the pre-trained weights from the Caffe model.

Now, we will take a look at the finetune_mnist.py file to see how the pre-trained weights are used.

First, they import the mynet python with the following code:

```
from mynet import LeNet as MyNet
```

Then, they create some placeholders for images and labels and compute the loss using the layers ip2 as follows:

```
images = tf.placeholder(tf.float32, [None, 28, 28, 1])
labels = tf.placeholder(tf.float32, [None, 10])
net = MyNet({'data': images})

ip2 = net.layers['ip2']
pred = net.layers['prob']

loss =
tf.reduce_mean(tf.nn.softmax_cross_entropy_with_logits(logits=ip2,
labels=labels), 0)
Finally, they load the numpy file into the graph, using the load
```

```
method in the network class.
with tf.Session() as sess:
    # Load the data
    sess.run(tf.global_variables_initializer())
    net.load('mynet.npy', sess)
```

After that, the fine-tune process is independent from the Caffe framework.

TensorFlow-Slim

TensorFlow-Slim is a light-weight library for defining, training, and evaluating complex models in TensorFlow. With the TensorFlow-Slim library, we can build, train, and evaluate the model easier by providing lots of high-level layers, variables, and regularizers. We recommend that you take a look at the TensorFlow-Slim library at the following link:
`https://github.com/tensorflow/tensorflow/tree/master/tensorflow/contrib/slim`

There are also lots of pre-trained models that are provided using TensorFlow-Slim. You can take advantage of high-level TensorFlow layers and models at the following link:

`https://github.com/tensorflow/tensorflow/tree/master/tensorflow/contrib/slim`

Summary

In this chapter, we have provided lots of interesting challenges and problems that you can try to solve and learn from to improve your TensorFlow skills. At the end of this chapter, we also guided you to convert the Caffe model to TensorFlow and introduced you to the high-level TensorFlow library, TensorFlow-Slim.

Advanced Installation

Deep learning involves a huge amount of matrix multiplications, and **Graphic Processing Units** (**GPUs**) are a very important aspect when one begins to learn deep learning. Without a GPU, the experiment process may take a day or more. With a good GPU, we can quickly iterate over deep learning networks and large training datasets, and run multiple experiments in a short amount of time. With TensorFlow, we can work on a single GPU or even multiple GPUs with ease. However, most machine learning platform installations are very complicated once GPUs get involved.

In this chapter, we are going to discuss GPUs and focus on a step-by-step CUDA setup and a GPU-based TensorFlow installation. We will start by installing Nvidia drivers, the CUDA Toolkit, and the cuDNN library. Then, we will install GPU-enabled TensorFlow with `pip`. Finally, we show how to use Anaconda to simplify the installation process even further.

Installation

In this chapter, we will work on an Ubuntu 16.06 computer with a Nvidia Titan X GPU.

We suggest that you use Ubuntu 14.04 or 16.06 to avoid further issues.

The choice of GPU is beyond the scope of this chapter. However, you must choose a Nvidia device with a high memory capacity in order to take full advantage of the GPU when compared to a CPU. Currently, AMD GPUs are not officially supported by TensorFlow and most other deep learning frameworks. At the time of writing, Windows can use Tensorflow with GPU on Python 3.5 or Python 3.6. However, Tensorflow dropped the support for GPU on macOS from Tensorflow 1.2. If you are using Windows, we suggest that you follow the official tutorial for Windows at the following link:
https://www.tensorflow.org/install/install_windows.

Installing Nvidia driver

There are many ways to install Nvidia drivers in Ubuntu. In this section, we will show you the easiest approach by using Proprietary GPU Drivers PPA, which offers stable proprietary Nvidia graphics driver updates.

First, open your terminal and run the following commands to add the PPA to Ubuntu:

```
sudo add-apt-repository ppa:graphics-drivers/ppa
sudo apt update
```

Now, we need to choose a version of Nvidia driver to install. Run the following command to see the latest version of your machine:

```
sudo apt-cache search nvidia
```

The result of the preceding command may look like this:

```
libcuda1-375 - NVIDIA CUDA runtime library
nvidia-304 - NVIDIA legacy binary driver - version 304.135
nvidia-304-updates - Transitional package for nvidia-304
nvidia-304-updates-dev - Transitional package for nvidia-304-dev
nvidia-340 - NVIDIA binary driver - version 340.102
nvidia-361 - Transitional package for nvidia-367
nvidia-361-dev - Transitional package for nvidia-367-dev
nvidia-367 - Transitional package for nvidia-375
nvidia-367-dev - Transitional package for nvidia-375-dev
nvidia-375 - NVIDIA binary driver - version 375.66
nvidia-375-dev - NVIDIA binary Xorg driver development files
nvidia-libopencl1-367 - Transitional package for nvidia-libopencl1-375
nvidia-libopencl1-375 - NVIDIA OpenCL Driver and ICD Loader library
nvidia-opencl-icd-304-updates - Transitional package for nvidia-opencl-icd-304
nvidia-opencl-icd-361 - Transitional package for nvidia-opencl-icd-367
nvidia-opencl-icd-367 - Transitional package for nvidia-opencl-icd-375
nvidia-opencl-icd-375 - NVIDIA OpenCL ICD
nvidia-libopencl1-304-updates - Transitional package for nvidia-libopencl1-304
nvidia-libopencl1-361 - Transitional package for nvidia-libopencl1-367
nvidia-352 - Transitional package for nvidia-375
cuda-visual-tools-8-0 - CUDA visual tools
nvidia-361-updates - Transitional package for nvidia-375
cuda-drivers - CUDA Driver meta-package
nvidia-opencl-icd-352-updates - Transitional package for nvidia-opencl-icd-375
nvidia-libopencl1-361-updates - Transitional package for nvidia-libopencl1-375
nvidia-libopencl1-352 - Transitional package for nvidia-libopencl1-375
nvidia-opencl-icd-361-updates - Transitional package for nvidia-opencl-icd-375
nvidia-modprobe - Load the NVIDIA kernel driver and create device files
nvidia-libopencl1-352-updates - Transitional package for nvidia-libopencl1-375
nvidia-352-updates-dev - Transitional package for nvidia-375-dev
nvidia-352-dev - Transitional package for nvidia-375-dev
nvidia-361-updates-dev - Transitional package for nvidia-375-dev
nvidia-352-updates - Transitional package for nvidia-375
nvidia-opencl-icd-352 - Transitional package for nvidia-opencl-icd-375
ubuntu@ubuntu-TITAN:~/Downloads$
```

As you can see, the latest driver is 375.66 on my machine, which is on the line with the text NVIDIA binary driver. Now, we can install Nvidia driver version 375.66 with the following command:

```
sudo apt-get install nvidia-375
```

The result of the preceding command may look like this:

```
ubuntu@ubuntu-TITAN:~/Downloads$ sudo apt-get install nvidia-375
Reading package lists... Done
Building dependency tree
Reading state information... Done
The following packages were automatically installed and are no longer required:
  cuda-command-line-tools-8-0 cuda-core-8-0 cuda-cublas-8-0
  cuda-cublas-dev-8-0 cuda-cudart-8-0 cuda-cudart-dev-8-0 cuda-cufft-8-0
  cuda-cufft-dev-8-0 cuda-curand-8-0 cuda-curand-dev-8-0 cuda-cusolver-8-0
  cuda-cusolver-dev-8-0 cuda-cusparse-8-0 cuda-cusparse-dev-8-0
  cuda-documentation-8-0 cuda-driver-dev-8-0 cuda-license-8-0
  cuda-misc-headers-8-0 cuda-npp-8-0 cuda-npp-dev-8-0 cuda-nvgraph-8-0
  cuda-nvgraph-dev-8-0 cuda-nvml-dev-8-0 cuda-nvrtc-8-0 cuda-nvrtc-dev-8-0
  cuda-samples-8-0 cuda-toolkit-8-0 cuda-visual-tools-8-0 libgles1-mesa
  libxmu-dev libxmu-headers linux-headers-4.8.0-52
  linux-headers-4.8.0-52-generic linux-headers-4.8.0-54
  linux-headers-4.8.0-54-generic linux-image-4.8.0-52-generic
  linux-image-4.8.0-54-generic linux-image-extra-4.8.0-52-generic
  linux-image-extra-4.8.0-54-generic linux-signed-image-4.8.0-52-generic
  linux-signed-image-4.8.0-54-generic nvidia-modprobe screen snap-confine
Use 'sudo apt autoremove' to remove them.
The following additional packages will be installed:
  libcuda1-375 nvidia-opencl-icd-375
The following NEW packages will be installed:
  libcuda1-375 nvidia-375 nvidia-opencl-icd-375
0 upgraded, 3 newly installed, 0 to remove and 65 not upgraded.
Need to get 75,2 MB of archives.
After this operation, 333 MB of additional disk space will be used.
Do you want to continue? [Y/n] 
```

When the installation is finished, you should see the following screen:

```
- Installation
  - Installing to /lib/modules/4.8.0-58-generic/updates/dkms/

nvidia_375_drm.ko:
Running module version sanity check.
  - Original module
    - No original module exists within this kernel
  - Installation
    - Installing to /lib/modules/4.8.0-58-generic/updates/dkms/

nvidia_375_uvm.ko:
Running module version sanity check.
  - Original module
    - No original module exists within this kernel
  - Installation
    - Installing to /lib/modules/4.8.0-58-generic/updates/dkms/

depmod....

DKMS: install completed.
Setting up libcuda1-375 (375.66-0ubuntu0.16.04.1) ...
Setting up nvidia-opencl-icd-375 (375.66-0ubuntu0.16.04.1) ...
Processing triggers for libc-bin (2.23-0ubuntu9) ...
/sbin/ldconfig.real: /usr/local/lib/libpocketsphinx.so.3 is not a symbolic link

/sbin/ldconfig.real: /usr/lib/nvidia-375/libEGL.so.1 is not a symbolic link

/sbin/ldconfig.real: /usr/lib32/nvidia-375/libEGL.so.1 is not a symbolic link

Processing triggers for initramfs-tools (0.122ubuntu8.8) ...
update-initramfs: Generating /boot/initrd.img-4.8.0-58-generic
Processing triggers for shim-signed (1.28~16.04.1+0.9+1474479173.6c180c6-1ubuntu
1) ...
Secure Boot not enabled on this system.
ubuntu@ubuntu-TITAN:~/Downloads$
```

Now, we will install the CUDA toolkit from Nvidia.

Installing the CUDA toolkit

First, we will need to open the Nvidia website to download the **CUDA toolkit**. Navigate to `https://developer.nvidia.com/cuda-downloads`. You will see the following screen:

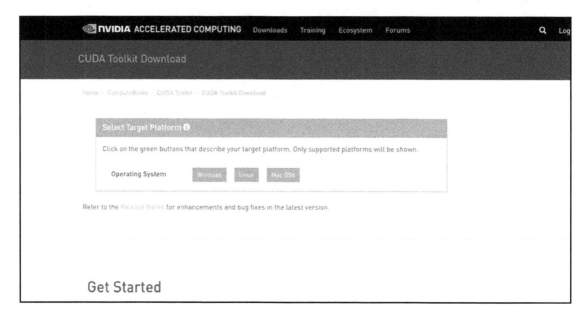

Then, select **Linux** | **x86_64** | **Ubuntu** | **16.04** | **runfile(local)**, as shown in the following screenshot:

Next, click on the **Download (1.4 GB)** button to download the installer. The installer size is 1.4 GB and it will take a while to finish downloading. After that, open your terminal, change the directory to the folder that contains the installer, and run the following command:

```
sudo sh cuda_8.0.61_375.26_linux.run
```

In the command-line prompts, you will see the **End User License Agreement**:

```
End User License Agreement
--------------------------


Preface
-------

The following contains specific license terms and conditions
for four separate NVIDIA products. By accepting this
agreement, you agree to comply with all the terms and
conditions applicable to the specific product(s) included
herein.


NVIDIA CUDA Toolkit


Description

The NVIDIA CUDA Toolkit provides command-line and graphical
tools for building, debugging and optimizing the performance
of applications accelerated by NVIDIA GPUs, runtime and math
libraries, and documentation including programming guides,
--More--(0%)
```

You can use your arrow keys to navigate through the agreement. Otherwise, you can press
: q and see the following screen:

```
- - - - - - - - - - - - - - - - - - - - - - - -


Preface
- - - - - - -

The following contains specific license terms and conditions
for four separate NVIDIA products. By accepting this
agreement, you agree to comply with all the terms and
conditions applicable to the specific product(s) included
herein.


NVIDIA CUDA Toolkit


Description

The NVIDIA CUDA Toolkit provides command-line and graphical
tools for building, debugging and optimizing the performance
of applications accelerated by NVIDIA GPUs, runtime and math
libraries, and documentation including programming guides,
Do you accept the previously read EULA?
accept/decline/quit:
```

Now, you can type accept to accept the agreement. After that, you will need to answer some questions, as shown on the following screen:

```
Default Install Location of CUDA Toolkit

Windows platform:

Do you accept the previously read EULA?
accept/decline/quit: accept

Install NVIDIA Accelerated Graphics Driver for Linux-x86_64 375.26?
(y)es/(n)o/(q)uit: n

Install the CUDA 8.0 Toolkit?
(y)es/(n)o/(q)uit: y

Enter Toolkit Location
 [ default is /usr/local/cuda-8.0 ]:

Do you want to install a symbolic link at /usr/local/cuda?
(y)es/(n)o/(q)uit: y

Install the CUDA 8.0 Samples?
(y)es/(n)o/(q)uit: y

Enter CUDA Samples Location
 [ default is /home/ubuntu ]:

Installing the CUDA Toolkit in /usr/local/cuda-8.0 ...
```

You may notice that we will not install Nvidia drivers in this prompt since we already installed the latest driver in the previous section. When the installation completes, you will see a screen like this:

```
============
= Summary =
============

Driver:   Not Selected
Toolkit:  Installed in /usr/local/cuda-8.0
Samples:  Installed in /home/ubuntu

Please make sure that
 -    PATH includes /usr/local/cuda-8.0/bin
 -    LD_LIBRARY_PATH includes /usr/local/cuda-8.0/lib64, or, add /usr/local/cuda
-8.0/lib64 to /etc/ld.so.conf and run ldconfig as root

To uninstall the CUDA Toolkit, run the uninstall script in /usr/local/cuda-8.0/b
in

Please see CUDA_Installation_Guide_Linux.pdf in /usr/local/cuda-8.0/doc/pdf for
detailed information on setting up CUDA.

***WARNING: Incomplete installation! This installation did not install the CUDA
Driver. A driver of version at least 361.00 is required for CUDA 8.0 functionali
ty to work.
To install the driver using this installer, run the following command, replacing
 <CudaInstaller> with the name of this run file:
      sudo <CudaInstaller>.run -silent -driver

Logfile is /tmp/cuda_install_10612.log
ubuntu@ubuntu-TITAN:~/Downloads$
```

Now, open your `~/.bashrc` file and add the following line at the end of the file:

```
export LD_LIBRARY_PATH=$LD_LIBRARY_PATH:/usr/local/cuda/lib64/
```

We have successfully installed the CUDA toolkit into the machine. You can try the following command to see your graphic card information:

```
nvidia-smi
```

The result on our machine looks like this:

```
ubuntu@ubuntu-TITAN:~/Downloads$ nvidia-smi
Mon Jul 17 23:52:48 2017
+-----------------------------------------------------------------------------+
| NVIDIA-SMI 375.66                 Driver Version: 375.66                     |
|-------------------------------+----------------------+----------------------+
| GPU  Name        Persistence-M| Bus-Id        Disp.A | Volatile Uncorr. ECC |
| Fan  Temp  Perf  Pwr:Usage/Cap|         Memory-Usage | GPU-Util  Compute M. |
|===============================+======================+======================|
|   0  GeForce GTX TIT...  Off  | 0000:01:00.0     On  |                  N/A |
| 22%   42C    P8    18W / 250W  |    446MiB / 12204MiB |      0%      Default |
+-------------------------------+----------------------+----------------------+

+-----------------------------------------------------------------------------+
| Processes:                                                       GPU Memory |
|  GPU       PID   Type   Process name                             Usage      |
|=============================================================================|
|    0      1076    G   /usr/lib/xorg/Xorg                           175MiB   |
|    0      2550    G   /usr/bin/gnome-shell                          95MiB   |
|    0      3664    G   ...el-token=27266A619B706F41F299C68AACC2AAFF   95MiB  |
|    0     25087    G   ...s-passed-by-fd --v8-snapshot-passed-by-fd   78MiB  |
+-----------------------------------------------------------------------------+
ubuntu@ubuntu-TITAN:~/Downloads$ 
```

Installing cuDNN

In order to use TensorFlow with GPU support, you need to install another library from Nvidia named cuDNN. First, you need to navigate the Nvidia website and download the cuDNN library from https://developer.nvidia.com/cudnn.

You may need to register a new Nvidia account. After you have logged in to the Nvidia website and opened the cuDNN link, you will see the following screen:

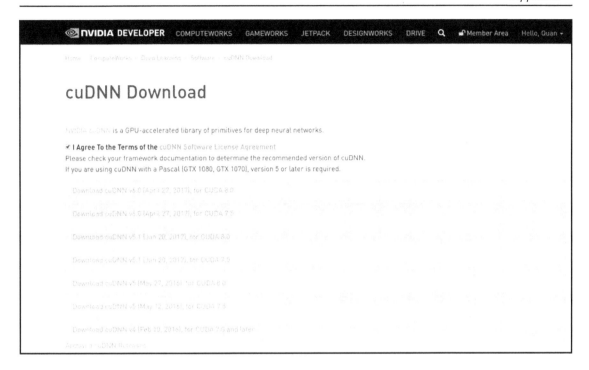

As you can see, cuDNN has several versions, and we will use the **cuDNN v5.1 for CUDA 8.0**, which is the cuDNN version required by TensorFlow. Now, you can download the library by clicking the **cuDNN v5.1 Library for Linux** link:

You can continue with your terminal and use the following commands to install cuDNN on your machine:

```
tar -xf cudnn-8.0-linux-x64-v5.1.tgz
cd cuda
sudo cp -P include/cudnn.h /usr/include/
sudo cp -P lib64/libcudnn* /usr/lib/x86_64-linux-gnu/
sudo chmod a+r /usr/lib/x86_64-linux-gnu/libcudnn*
```

```
ubuntu@ubuntu-TITAN:~/Downloads$ tar -xf cudnn-8.0-linux-x64-v5.1.tgz
ubuntu@ubuntu-TITAN:~/Downloads$ cd cuda
ubuntu@ubuntu-TITAN:~/Downloads/cuda$ sudo cp -P include/cudnn.h /usr/include/
ubuntu@ubuntu-TITAN:~/Downloads/cuda$ sudo cp -P lib64/libcudnn* /usr/lib/x86_64-linux-gnu/
ubuntu@ubuntu-TITAN:~/Downloads/cuda$ sudo chmod a+r /usr/lib/x86_64-linux-gnu/libcudnn*
ubuntu@ubuntu-TITAN:~/Downloads/cuda$
```

Installing TensorFlow

With everything set up, we can easily install TensorFlow with GPU support with the `pip` tool, as follows:

```
sudo pip install tensorflow-gpu
```

The result of the command should look like this:

```
Installing collected packages: html5lib, bleach, markdown, backports.weakref, te
nsorflow-gpu
  Running setup.py install for html5lib ... done
  Running setup.py install for markdown ... done
Successfully installed backports.weakref-1.0rc1 bleach-1.5.0 html5lib-0.9999999
markdown-2.6.8 tensorflow-gpu-1.2.1
ubuntu@ubuntu-TITAN:~/Downloads$
```

Verifying TensorFlow with GPU support

Now, you can type `python` on your command line and type the following Python command to see if TensorFlow can see your GPU:

```
import tensorflow as tf
tf.Session()
```

The result should look like the following image:

Congratulations! TensorFlow can work with your GPU now. Our GPU is recognized as GeForce GTX TITAN X with 11.92 GB of memory. In the next section, we will show you the recommended approach to working with multiple versions of TensorFlow and libraries such as OpenCV.

Using TensorFlow with Anaconda

During your work, you will encounter situations where you need multiple versions of TensorFlow on the same machine, such as TensorFlow 1.0 or TensorFlow 1.2. We may need to use TensorFlow with Python 2.7 or 3.0. With the previous installation, we have already successfully installed TensorFlow in the system Python. Now, we will show you how to use Anaconda to have multiple working environments on the same machine. With Anaconda, we can even use different versions of other popular libraries, such as OpenCV, NumPy, and scikit-learn.

First, we need to download and install miniconda from `https://conda.io/miniconda.html`. In our case, we select Python 2.7 64-bit bash installer, as we want to use Python 2.7 as the default Python. Nevertheless, we can create environments with either Python 2.7 or Python 3 later. We need to run the following command to run the installer:

```
bash Miniconda3-latest-Linux-x86_64.sh
```

We need to accept the **End User License Agreement**:

```
Do you approve the license terms? [yes|no]
>>> yes

Miniconda2 will now be installed into this location:
/home/ubuntu/miniconda2

  - Press ENTER to confirm the location
  - Press CTRL-C to abort the installation
  - Or specify a different location below
```

After that, we can continue the installation. The result should look like this:

```
installing: yaml-0.1.6-0 ...
installing: zlib-1.2.8-3 ...
installing: conda-4.3.21-py27_0 ...
installing: pip-9.0.1-py27_1 ...
installing: wheel-0.29.0-py27_0 ...
Python 2.7.13 :: Continuum Analytics, Inc.
creating default environment...
installation finished.
Do you wish the installer to prepend the Miniconda2 install location
to PATH in your /home/ubuntu/.bashrc ? [yes|no]
[no] >>> yes

Prepending PATH=/home/ubuntu/miniconda2/bin to PATH in /home/ubuntu/.bashrc
A backup will be made to: /home/ubuntu/.bashrc-miniconda2.bak

For this change to become active, you have to open a new terminal.

Thank you for installing Miniconda2!

Share your notebooks and packages on Anaconda Cloud!
Sign up for free: https://anaconda.org

ubuntu@ubuntu-TITAN:~/github/chapter11$
```

Finally, we need to source the `.bashrc` file to get Anaconda up and running:

```
source ~/.bashrc
```

In the source code of this chapter, we have already provided some environment configurations that you can use to create your desired environment.

Here is an environment that uses Python 2.7, OpenCV 3, and TensorFlow 1.2.1 with GPU support. The configuration is named `env2.yml`:

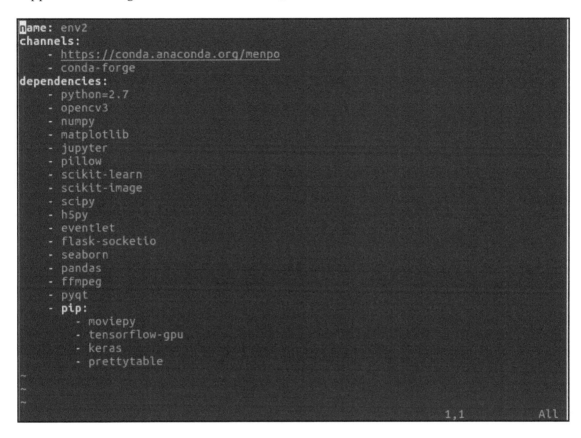

You can easily change `python=2.7` to `python=3` and `opencv3` to `opencv` to have Python 3 and OpenCV 2.4 respectively.

Now, let's run the following command to create the environment:

```
conda env create -f env2.yml
```

The result should look like following:

```
Successfully installed backports.weakref-1.0rc1 funcsigs-1.0.2 imageio-2.1.2 keras-2.0.6 markdown-
2.6.8 mock-2.0.0 moviepy-0.2.3.2 pbr-3.1.1 prettytable-0.7.2 protobuf-3.3.0 tensorflow-gpu-1.2.1 t
heano-0.9.0 tqdm-4.11.2
#
# To activate this environment, use:
# > source activate env2
#
# To deactivate this environment, use:
# > source deactivate env2
#
ubuntu@ubuntu-TITAN:~/github/chapter11$
```

Next, you can type `source activate env2` to activate the environment.

Finally, we will need to verify TensorFlow, as before:

```
(env2) ubuntu@ubuntu-TITAN:~/github/chapter11$ python
Python 2.7.13 | packaged by conda-forge | (default, May  2 2017, 12:48:11)
[GCC 4.8.2 20140120 (Red Hat 4.8.2-15)] on linux2
Type "help", "copyright", "credits" or "license" for more information.
>>> import tensorflow as tf
>>> tf.Session()
2017-07-18 00:35:14.578038: W tensorflow/core/platform/cpu_feature_guard.cc:45] The TensorFlow lib
rary wasn't compiled to use SSE4.1 instructions, but these are available on your machine and could
 speed up CPU computations.
2017-07-18 00:35:14.578051: W tensorflow/core/platform/cpu_feature_guard.cc:45] The TensorFlow lib
rary wasn't compiled to use SSE4.2 instructions, but these are available on your machine and could
 speed up CPU computations.
2017-07-18 00:35:14.578055: W tensorflow/core/platform/cpu_feature_guard.cc:45] The TensorFlow lib
rary wasn't compiled to use AVX instructions, but these are available on your machine and could sp
eed up CPU computations.
2017-07-18 00:35:14.578058: W tensorflow/core/platform/cpu_feature_guard.cc:45] The TensorFlow lib
rary wasn't compiled to use AVX2 instructions, but these are available on your machine and could s
peed up CPU computations.
2017-07-18 00:35:14.578061: W tensorflow/core/platform/cpu_feature_guard.cc:45] The TensorFlow lib
rary wasn't compiled to use FMA instructions, but these are available on your machine and could sp
eed up CPU computations.
2017-07-18 00:35:14.710152: I tensorflow/stream_executor/cuda/cuda_gpu_executor.cc:893] successful
 NUMA node read from SysFS had negative value (-1), but there must be at least one NUMA node, so r
eturning NUMA node zero
2017-07-18 00:35:14.710550: I tensorflow/core/common_runtime/gpu/gpu_device.cc:940] Found device 0
with properties:
name: GeForce GTX TITAN X
major: 5 minor: 2 memoryClockRate (GHz) 1.076
pciBusID 0000:01:00.0
Total memory: 11.92GiB
Free memory: 11.27GiB
2017-07-18 00:35:14.710563: I tensorflow/core/common_runtime/gpu/gpu_device.cc:961] DMA: 0
2017-07-18 00:35:14.710567: I tensorflow/core/common_runtime/gpu/gpu_device.cc:971] 0:   Y
2017-07-18 00:35:14.710586: I tensorflow/core/common_runtime/gpu/gpu_device.cc:1030] Creating Tens
orFlow device (/gpu:0) -> (device: 0, name: GeForce GTX TITAN X, pci bus id: 0000:01:00.0)
<tensorflow.python.client.session.Session object at 0x7fd15b3e4110>
>>>
```

You may notice the **(env2)** in the top-left of the preceding image. That shows the name of the current environment. The Python version on the second line is 2.7.13 and is packaged by conda-forge.

Now, you can create several different environments to use in your workflow. Here is an example of an environment named **env3** with Python 3 and OpenCV 2.4:

```
name: env3
channels:
    - https://conda.anaconda.org/menpo
    - conda-forge
dependencies:
    - python=3
    - opencv
    - numpy
    - matplotlib
    - jupyter
    - pillow
    - scikit-learn
    - scikit-image
    - scipy
    - h5py
    - eventlet
    - flask-socketio
    - seaborn
    - pandas
    - ffmpeg
    - pyqt
    - pip:
        - moviepy
        - tensorflow-gpu
        - keras
        - prettytable
~
~
~
"env3.yml" 26L, 416C                          4,1            All
```

Summary

In this chapter, we discussed the advantages of using GPUs in a machine learning workflow, especially in deep learning. Then, we showed the step-by-step installation of a Nvidia driver, the CUDA Toolkit, cuDNN, and TensorFlow with GPU support. We also introduced our recommended workflow for using multiple versions of TensorFlow and other libraries.

Index

CPSIA information can be obtained
at www.ICGtesting.com
Printed in the USA
LVHW02s0016260118
564091LV00003B/66/P

9 781786 462961